Greenhill Books

UP CLOSE
AND
PERSONAL

UP CLOSE AND PERSONAL

The Reality of Close-Quarter
Fighting in World War II

David Lee

Greenhill Books, London
Naval Institute Press, Annapolis, Maryland

Up Close and Personal

First published in 2006 by Greenhill Books, Lionel Leventhal Limited,
Park House, 1 Russell Gardens, London NW11 9NN
www.greenhillbooks.com

Published and distributed in the United States of America and Canada by the Naval
Institute Press, Beach Hall, 291 Wood Road, Annapolis, Maryland 21402-5034

British Library Cataloguing-in Publication Data
Lee, David
Up close and personal : the reality of close-quarter fighting in World War II
World War, 1939–1945 – Campaigns
Infantry drill and tactics
Combat – Psychological aspects
I. Title
940.5'41

Greenhill edition
ISBN-13: 978-1-85367-668-0
ISBN-10: 1-85367-668-3

NIP edition
ISBN 1-59114-907-X

Library of Congress Catalog Card No. 2006922376

For more information on our other books, and to enter our 2006 draw to win
military books worth £1,000, please visit www.greenhillbooks.com. You can also email
sales@greenhillbooks.com, telephone us within the UK on 020 8458 6314 or write to
us at the above London address.

Printed and bound in Great Britain by
Creative Print and Design (Wales), Ebbw Vale

For those who fought

Contents

Illustrations

Maps

Foreword

The M25, London's orbital motorway, is a bad place in the rush hour. I had figured on two hours to drive forty miles but the section past Heathrow Airport caught me out and I was twenty minutes late arriving at Joe Swann's house. He was standing outside waiting for me and, knowing he had been a very good regimental sergeant-major, I hoped my late arrival would not create a bad impression.

He looked me up and down, shook my hand with a strength which made me wonder if he wasn't approaching ninety, and then said, 'I'm Joe.' His house was a haven of peace after the madness of the M25 and he poured me a huge mug of very sweet tea and told me his story.

Joe Swann's act of incredible bravery is described later in this book but he saved a crucial position (Snipe) at a crucial point in a crucial battle (El Alamein). After he had told me his story we both fell silent for a bit. Then I ventured my opinion that he should have been awarded the Victoria Cross rather than the Distinguished Conduct Medal. A gleam came into his eye, 'Have you ever seen a Distinguished Conduct Medal?' he asked.

I had to confess I had not.

After a couple of hours I took my leave, packed up my tape recorder and notebook and said goodbye to him. He came out of his house and waved me off – and the picture I have in my mind is of him standing there, still every inch the sergeant-major, waving me off.

I had just written the chapter on Snipe when I found out he had died.

My grateful thanks go to Joe Swann and to all the veterans who helped me with this book. Many of their personal accounts appear in this book as written or told to me. Other accounts have come from the Imperial War Museum whose staff work wonders in dealing with persistent requests from people like me not only to provide copies of documents and tapes but also in tracking down copyright holders.

Two veterans, Henry Hall and James Dunning, deserve a special mention and their help and insights have been invaluable. I am also grateful to the following for their help and assistance: Kate Thaxton, who looks after the Royal Norfolks' Museum in Norwich; Emyr Jones for his help with Dieppe and No. 4 Commando; Geoff Pain, the secretary of the Rifle Brigade Association; and Alex Bowlby (who has also sadly since died), Nick O' Connor and Peter White. Unfortunately many veterans whose accounts appear in this book are no longer with us. In those cases I am very grateful to their families for letting me use their accounts. During the writing of this book every effort was made to track down copyright holders or their representatives; in the event of any inadvertent omissions any further information would be welcome.

As we leave the twentieth century further behind, more and more veterans of World War II, like Joe Swann, are leaving us. I am privileged to have known some of them and I hope that this book will, if nothing else, show something of what they were up against.

David Lee

On Danger in War

by General Carl von Clausewitz

Let us accompany the novice soldier on to the battlefield. As we come closer the thunder of the guns becomes more clearly defined and finally transforms into the shrieking of cannon fire, and this draws the attention of the inexperienced. Cannon balls begin to fall to the front and rear of us. We hurry to the hill where the general and his numerous staff officers are positioned. Here the frequency of the cannon balls landing close by and of shells exploding is such that the serious side of life forces its way into our youthful imagination. Suddenly someone we know is down. A shell hits the crowd and forces it to shift. One starts to feel that one is no longer completely calm and collected and even the bravest is at least a little distracted. Now to step into the battle which is raging before our eyes like a play in a theatre, so as to get as far as the nearest general of a division. Here the cannon balls are chasing each other and the noise from our own guns increases the confusion. From the divisional general we proceed to the brigadier general. He is a man whose bravery is already well respected and he keeps prudently behind a hill, a house or trees, a sure sign that it is becoming more dangerous. Grape shot clatters on roofs and fields, cannon balls roar in all directions at us, over us, and away. At the same time musket balls have begun to whistle. Now to step further along, to the infantry soldiers who have held out for hours in the battle with commendable steadfastness. Here the cannon balls whizz through the air and announce their arrival with a sharp crack as they fly past, only a hair's breadth from one's ear, head or chest. On top of all this one's heart is touched by pity at the sight of the wounded and fallen.

The novice soldier will not go through these various levels of danger without feeling that rational thought works in a different way in this environment, in a way which is contrary to simple thought processes.

Indeed it must be an extraordinary person who does not lose the ability to make instant decisions when faced with this environment for the first time. Of course familiarity quickly deadens the impact of these first impressions and after half an hour we begin to be indifferent to everything around us, some of us more so and others less so, although a normal person will never be completely at ease nor have full control of his thought processes.

Carl von Clausewitz, *Vom Kriege* (*On War*), Book 1, Chapter 4, translation by the author

CHAPTER 1

The World War II Battlefield

In May 1939 Adolf Hitler attended a demonstration of Waffen SS battle tactics. The Führer was keen to see how the Waffen SS was using assault groups of infantry together with field artillery and how effective this was in a battlefield scenario.

For the demonstration the Waffen SS Regiment *Deutschland* was to attack an enemy outpost and drive the defenders back to their main defensive positions. Once this happened the supporting field artillery was to open up on the enemy positions, at which point the assault troops would break through the barbed wire defences with bangalore torpedoes to capture their objective.

Twenty minutes after the exercise was due to start Hitler asked when it was going to begin. He was told that it had in fact been under way for the previous twenty minutes. Hitler then became aware that he could see brief glimpses of Waffen SS soldiers moving quickly from cover to cover. Needless to say the exercise with the field guns went exactly according to plan and was a complete success. As a result Hitler ordered artillery to be added to the Waffen SS formations.[1]

Eight months later, in January 1940, Winston Churchill visited the 2nd Battalion, The Royal Norfolk Regiment, in its positions on the Belgian frontier. Although not yet Prime Minister he was at that point First Lord of the Admiralty and already heavily involved in developing wartime strategy. The Royal Norfolks had been spending much of their time digging trenches, an activity which would have been familiar to any old soldier from World War I, as part of a defensive line called the Gort Line, after General Lord Gort who commanded the British Expeditionary Force.

When Churchill arrived he was accompanied by three senior generals and a clutch of staff officers. He was shown round A Company's positions by Captain Peter Barclay, the company commander. Barclay had acquired a small dog which had come across from the other side of the Belgian border and which he used to hunt rats and rabbits. As they were walking along inspecting the positions the party came to a pile of wooden bundles. The dog immediately started barking, having sensed a rabbit, and Churchill was interested. He asked Barclay if they might have a little sport. Barclay replied that that he would need three officers on top of the pile of wooden bundles to jump up and down to get the rabbit out. Churchill promptly ordered the three generals on to the pile where he directed their jumps to make sure they were all jumping at the same time to get the rabbit to bolt. There was some embarrassment as the generals bounced up and down while their aides-de-camp looked on. But they were all delighted when the rabbit shot out and was chased by the dog, which duly caught it.[2]

The difference in approach between the German and British Armies had started at the end of World War I. And what was interesting was the way in which the German Army used its defeat to its advantage whereas the British Army learned very little from its victory.

The victory of the Allied armies over the old German Army in 1918 was more than just a simple defeat for Germany because the German people had believed sincerely that victory would be theirs. Because of their implicit faith in their army it was all the more traumatic for them that it was their army which had failed them. The Armistice had dealt another blow as the Treaty of Versailles restricted the post-war German Army to 100,000 men, including no more than 4,000 officers.

For General Hans von Seeckt, appointed Chief of the German Army Command in 1921, the situation must have appeared a gloomy one. But, crucially for the German Army, he was not infected with the trench warfare mentality which afflicted the British Army for so long. Seeckt had served on the Eastern Front in World War I and refused to believe that *Der Stellungskrieg*, trench warfare, was the future. His experiences had taught him that the use of fire and movement under the control of good leadership, was the way forward.[3] For Seeckt mobility meant machines, armour, artillery, infantry, all mechanised and mobile and working together. In 1921, while the British Army was fighting an uprising in Ireland, the German Army was conducting its first exercises with motorised units.

Between the wars the German Army devoted much time to exercises in the field. All units took part and used blank ammunition to fire their weapons at the enemy.[4] This is an important point because already the German soldier was being conditioned for service on the battlefield in World War II where, as we shall see, the type of training was to have a profound effect on the course of battle.

With constant training and refinement the German Army was ready in principle, if not in men and machines, for the Blitzkrieg by the time Hitler came to power in 1933. And it was Hitler's enthusiasm for the Panzer and for the concept of *Bewegungskrieg* or mobile war which led to the creation of the first Panzer divisions in 1935.[5]

Of course the British Army had not been idle during the interwar period. But the British themselves were sick of war and by the 1930s the general feeling was that another war was best avoided at all costs. And there were other priorities. There were the colonies to police. There were social obligations too – while the Germans were practising endlessly on exercise with armour and infantry, British cavalry officers were busy on the polo field. The notion that they should give this up in favour of more soldiering in tanks and other armoured vehicles was, of course, quite out of the question.[6]

Despite these limitations the British Army did make progress. In 1926 and 1927, Lord Milne, the Chief of the Imperial General Staff, allowed the Army to experiment with armour.[7] And some regiments did make the changeover in the inter-war period. One example of this was the Rifle Brigade. This was a regiment which had started out as sharpshooters in the early 1800s but whose riflemen had served in the trenches as ordinary infantry in World War I and which moved to being a motorised regiment in the late 1930s.[8] It was to use Bren carriers with anti-tank guns in the desert to great effect.

All of this gives us clues as to why the Germans were better prepared for World War II than the British. And it is the Allied generals who take the blame for the early success of the German Army. Most historians will point to bad leadership by the British and French generals and their staffs as the reason why 1940 was such a disaster for the Allies. After all General Erich von Manstein's master strategy for the Blitzkrieg went exactly according to plan and the French, British, Belgian and Dutch Armies were crushed by a numerically inferior German force.

But there was something else which contributed to the downfall of the British Expeditionary Force. And that something else has been overlooked by modern historians just as it was by the British Army itself before the war. Yet it was a key factor in the way the whole of World War II was fought and it tells us why some British units were far more effective than others.

The simple fact was that British soldiers were not very good at killing.

In 1947 a United States Army general called S. L. A. 'Slam' Marshall surprised the military world by writing his classic book *Men Against Fire*.[9] The book detailed Marshall's observations on the battles of World War II which he had studied in his role as a US Army military historian — a task which he had undertaken by travelling all over the battlefields of Europe and the Far East where he talked to soldiers in the immediate aftermath of battle.

Marshall's central theory was simple, 'We found that on an average not more than 15 per cent of the men had actually fired at the enemy positions or personnel with rifles, carbines, grenades, bazookas, BARs, or machine guns during the course of an entire engagement. Even allowing for the dead and wounded and assuming that in their numbers there would be the same proportion of active firers as among the living the figure did not rise above 20 to 25 per cent of the total for any action.'[10]

The idea that in battle only a quarter of soldiers were actually prepared to kill was a surprising one. However, Marshall was not alone. During the Sicily campaign in 1943 Lieutenant-Colonel Lionel Wigram of the British School of Infantry had observed that only a quarter of the men in a typical British platoon could be relied upon in battle.[11]

Therefore Marshall's conclusions would seem to be solidly based. But the new edition of Marshall's book contains an introduction by Russell Glenn in which he outlines problems with Marshall's methodology.[12] In the late 1980s Dr Roger Spiller of the US Army Command and the General Staff Command started to investigate Marshall's work. He reviewed Marshall's notes and his letters and he talked to one of Marshall's fellow combat historians, John Westover, who could not remember Marshall asking soldiers if they had fired or not. Spiller therefore came to the conclusion that Marshall's theory about the numbers of soldiers firing at the enemy was not based upon solid evidence.[13]

Marshall's legacy received another blow from Marshall's grandson who quoted one of Marshall's friends as saying that Marshall had invented the 15–25 per cent proportion on the basis that these were what he believed, rather than knew, were the accurate figures.[14]

After this the academics weighed in with their own debunking of the 'Marshall myth'. In 1999 the Professor of History at Birkbeck College, University of London, Joanna Bourke, wrote *An Intimate History of Killing*[15] in which she dismisses Marshall as someone who 'did not interview as many men as he said he did and not one of the men he interviewed remembered being asked whether or not he fired his weapon.'[16]

She goes on to suggest that documentary evidence from soldiers themselves, mainly in the form of letters home from the front in World War I which describe in gory detail the pleasures of killing, meant that soldiers loved killing, 'Warfare was as much about the business of sacrificing others as it was about being sacrificed. For many men and women this was what made it a "lovely war".'[17]

At the same time Niall Ferguson, Fellow and Tutor in Modern History at Jesus College, Oxford, was writing *The Pity of War*[18] in which he takes a fresh look at World War I. He too makes the case that soldiers enjoyed killing and quotes personal accounts from World War I to support this theory.[19] He concludes by saying that, 'men fought because they did not mind fighting.'[20]

However, at the same time as these two historians were researching their books a former US paratrooper, Lieutenant Colonel Dave Grossman, was writing a book called *On Killing*.[21] Grossman is not only a former soldier, he is also a psychologist and Professor of Military Science at Arkansas State University and in this book he comes down firmly on the side of Marshall.

Both Grossman and Spiller point to the fact that it is only Marshall's methods which have been discredited and that there is still merit in considering whether his conclusions were right. Spiller notes also that Marshall did indeed visit the battlefields immediately after the battles of World War II and that he was a good observer of the human being under fire, despite his lack of accuracy as a historian.[22]

Grossman points to a large body of historical literature and study which supports Marshall's findings that, in any battle, most soldiers will not be firing at the enemy, instead they will be running errands, loading weapons and generally supporting the minority who are fighting.[23] He goes on to state,

There is ample indication of the existence of the resistance to killing and that it appears to have existed at least since the black gunpowder era. This lack of enthusiasm for killing the enemy causes many soldiers to posture, submit or flee, rather than fight; it represents a powerful psychological force on the battlefield; and it is a force that is discernible throughout the history of man.[24]

The question – are human beings natural killers? – is one which has also preoccupied professions other than military historians. According to evolutionary psychologists such as David Buss, Professor of Psychology at the University of Texas, the answer to this question is a simple yes. In his book *The Murderer Next Door* he states,

According to the theory I've developed, nearly all the many kinds of murder – from crimes of passion to the methodically planned contract kill – can be explained by the twists and turns of a harsh evolutionary logic. Killing is surely ruthless but it is also most often not the result of either psychosis or cultural conditioning. Murder is the product of the evolutionary pressures our species confronted and adapted to.[25]

This idea that evolution has forced humans into becoming killers because of the benefits of killing other people in the great competition of life is taken to its logical conclusion by Buss who suggests, after reviewing hundreds of case files of murderers in the USA that, 'Murderers are waiting, they are watching, they are all around us.'[26]

However Buss's theories are flatly rejected by anthropologists who are moving our understanding on by taking a fresh look at the fossil record and the behaviour of other primates. Robert Sussman, Professor of Physical Anthropology at Washington University (St Louis), states,

If murder statistics vary from place to place, one simple evolutionary, biological, universal explanation cannot be correct, when so many cultural ones are so much better. There is no evidence whatsoever from the fossil record or from primate behaviour to support this type of adaptationists' scenario.[27]

Sussman's book *Man The Hunted*,[28] written with fellow anthropologist Donna Hart from the University of Missouri – St Louis, shows where the evolutionary psychologists are mistaken,

We humans are not slaughter-prone assassins by nature. We often act badly, maliciously, cruelly but that is by choice and not by our status as bipedal primates. We can state this because our closest relatives use cooperation and friendship as the most expedient method for gaining what they need and want. Yes, just like humans, chimpanzees occasionally act brutally wacky – usually because of stress, resource shortages or unknown factors that evict them from their comfort zone. Sound familiar? Isn't that exactly why we humans get crazed?[29]

Whatever the arguments about Marshall's methods, on looking at Marshall's work in some detail it quickly becomes apparent from his combat notes[30] that he was indeed interviewing combat soldiers in the aftermath of battle, sometimes as part of a group and sometimes alone. Although his notes do not record the issue of non-firers it does seem likely that Marshall could easily have asked the question without recording it formally, although whether the questioning was in any way scientific is another matter entirely.

This view is consistent with the recollections of First Lieutenant Frank J. Brennan Jr who accompanied Marshall on similar post-combat interviews during the Korean War. After this war Marshall stated that the ratio of fire had improved so that more than half the infantrymen were now active firers.[31] In a recent interview with historian John Whiteclay Chambers, Brennan recalled that Marshall asked a lot of open questions and that he did ask about firing but without pushing the issue.[32] Crucially, however, Brennan recalled Marshall making only occasional notes during these interviews.[33]

Having interviewed Brennan, Chambers concludes that Marshall's ratio of fire figure for World War II, 'appears to have been based at best on chance rather than scientific sampling, and at worst on sheer speculation'.[34] Chambers also concludes that Marshall was writing as a journalist rather than as a historian when he came up with his 25 per cent because, 'He believed that he needed a dramatic statistic to give added weight to his argument. The controversial figure was probably a guess.'[35] Chambers's final thought is that, even if more of

Marshall's field notebooks are found and they contain more interviews like those with Brennan, 'They probably will not contain the kind of data necessary to substantiate the controversial assertions of *Men Against Fire*.'[36]

Since Marshall is no longer alive the best people to ask about his theory that only a minority of soldiers were firing at the enemy are those who fought in World War II. The results are surprising. Many think that there might have been something in what he said. Those who do not agree with Marshall at all are the ones who would be best classified as being in Marshall's 15–25 per cent of active firing soldiers. A typical response comes from Henry Taylor, ex-7th Battalion, The Rifle Brigade,

If you ask me if any of our blokes had a problem with shooting Ted [*Tedeschi*, Italian for German, used in soldiers' slang], then I can only say that everyone I knew would shoot to hit him. If you did not and that Ted went on to kill a mate, you would have that on your mind.[37]

Some of these 'active firers' asked how it was that so many were killed if not many were firing but Marshall's supporters point to the fact that artillery accounted for large numbers of casualties in World War II and that artillery battles are conducted at enough of a distance for the firers not to be so obviously troubled by their consciences. This argument is helped by the fact that the artillery is held to have been the most effective arm of the British Army in World War II.[38]

Some veterans also mentioned the power of emotion. A soldier who might not be taking an active part in the battle might lose control if his best mate were killed next to him and the enemy soldiers who shot him then tried to surrender. The most dangerous time for any surrendering soldiers was the period immediately after they showed themselves as surrendering. And of course when soldiers knew about enemy atrocities, as was the case in the war in the Far East in particular, there was an additional incentive to kill the enemy.

What about the opposite viewpoint? – the idea championed by Joanna Bourke in particular, that men enjoyed killing. The suggestion that most men enjoyed battle met with universal rejection, even from those best classed as the active firers. Certainly in talking to the veterans and reading their accounts of World War II, it is very difficult to find stories about the joy of killing. Of course many of them look back on the war as a time when they enjoyed the comradeship and the shared danger, but killing, no.

Of course there were individual participants in World War II for whom the term blood lust would not be inappropriate. Men such as Anders Lassen VC of the Special Boat Service of whom it was said, 'If he had the opportunity he'd kill someone with a knife rather than shoot.'[39] So such men do exist; it is simply that they appear to be either less common in World War II than in World War I or that fewer of them wrote about it in World War II. So why is there this body of literature, particularly from World War I and the Vietnam War, in which soldiers talk of the joy of slaughter?

For Britain World War I was a different kind of war to World War II. The country entered World War I in a burst of enthusiasm; men joined up fired by a desire to see the Germans put firmly in their place. Perhaps some of them, responding to the public mood, wrote of their experiences in terms which they felt would be welcomed at home rather than to reflect the reality of what they actually saw. Historians always need to be wary of personal accounts which talk up the achievements of the author. The more medals a veteran has, the less likely he is to blow his own trumpet. And if you read Lyn MacDonald's books on World War I[40] or Max Arthur's *Forgotten Voices of the Great War*[41] there is little there to support the idea that men took pleasure in slaughter.

Peter Hart, the oral historian at the Imperial War Museum for over twenty years, recalled that he had come across only one man he could remember who took any real pleasure in remembering the men he had killed in all his long experience of interviewing veterans. He went on to say that,

Most men regarded it as an unpleasant part of the job to be carried out as dispassionately as possible. Many seem to have consciously or

24

unconsciously suppressed the details of the fighting. It was only in letters home, diaries or in slightly vainglorious memoirs that men were occasionally to be found boasting of their killing exploits. Here it appeared there was often the intent of impressing the intended audience and indeed an element of fantasy could creep in – a very real element of 'giving them what they want' – that would provide fodder for the shallow thesis of the future. Such macho posturing was not found in dispassionate oral history interviews where the soldiers' real feelings usually emerged.[42]

Vietnam was a different war again. By using the methods outlined later in this chapter the US Army had managed to make its soldiers far more effective at killing than their fathers had been during World War II and their grandfathers during World War I.

Logically too some of Marshall's arguments make sense. After all peacetime society, both before World War II and since, demands that its citizens live peaceful lives. Killing someone in any civilised society usually attracts severe punishment. It is perhaps therefore little wonder that men found it hard to kill.

Given that there is probably some truth in Marshall's assertion that not all World War II soldiers were firing at the enemy the only question which arises is the extent of this phenomenon. Was Marshall right in suggesting that only 15–25 per cent were firing their weapons at the enemy? Was it as simple as Marshall made out? Did soldiers either shoot to kill or not shoot at all?

There is some evidence to suggest that there was another group of soldiers between the firers and the non-firers, a group not recognised by either Marshall or Bourke and a group whose size cannot be quantified. This group of soldiers did fire their weapons but only in the general direction of the enemy – in other words they fired but did not fire to kill, or they did not know that they had killed. This theory is certainly consistent with British and American fire policies whereby they fought with lots of fire to cover an advance.

Consider this example:

Rifleman Joseph Belzar, 7th Rifle Brigade, Monte Malbe, Italy, 1944

I saw the long grass of the field below parting and I followed the movement of the German observer as he moved towards our position to lie motionless at the edge of the field. He was obviously observing our positions less than 100 yards away; I don't believe he realised how close we were. I drew my rifle forward prior to taking aim but was too late as he scuttled back to his mortar position. In retrospect I am glad I was too late in firing. At that distance I would not have missed and now, looking back over fifty years later, I should hate to have had the recollection of looking down on a person for whose death I had been solely responsible. Generally in any battle situation there is collective action and one could never be sure whose bullet had found the target.[43]

Given that the situation on the battlefield may not have been quite as straightforward as Marshall made out it is also worth remembering that, apart from the ordinary infantry there were also many Special Forces units formed during World War II. Chief among these were the Commandos whose special training regime produced soldiers second to none and who were close to the 100 per cent of active firers.

But there was something else. Some of these Commandos also said that Marshall might have had a point when it came to the ordinary infantry units they belonged to prior to joining the Commandos but their training as Commandos had been so effective that they became 'proper' soldiers. According to David Cowie, who served with the Fife and Forfar Yeomanry in France in 1940 and who subsequently joined No. 4 Commando,

It [1940] was an absolute mess from start to finish, not because of the men but bloody bad officers and a complete lack of knowledge about the German Army ... There was a complete lack of any training and I believe Marshall was right ... The Commandos trained me to be a real soldier.[44]

So what was so special about the Commandos? The answer is that they worked out what made soldiers kill long before today's armies and before even Marshall came up with his theory about ratios of fire. And to understand the Commandos we need to understand what changed after World War II and how it is that soldiers of both the US and British Armies are now approaching a 100 per cent firing rate.

Colonel Grossman's research is particularly valuable because he has identified exactly what it is in modern training which produces soldiers who can kill.

When we look back at the training of most World War II soldiers it is clear that it fell into three categories. Firstly there was drill, drill and more drill. The idea was that soldiers would respond immediately to orders and that drill conditioned them to instant obedience. Secondly there was weapons training which consisted of firing rifles on the ranges against bullseye circular targets. Thirdly there was fieldcraft, the necessary skills needed to move around the battlefield.

Compare this to the training given to the modern soldier as identified by Grossman. Modern soldiers do learn drill, fieldcraft and they obviously have weapons training. But now there are three additional factors: desensitisation, conditioning and denial.

Desensitisation is all about getting soldiers used to the idea of violence and killing through attitudes and language.[45] Some old soldiers from World War II have told me how upset they are when they see modern British Army or Commando training on the television. Whereas these old soldiers were used to a degree of respect and tolerance from their NCOs, today's recruits face a constant barrage of the language of violence including bawling out and bullying.

Conditioning is arguably the most important single factor in producing a soldier capable of killing. Instead of aiming at inanimate targets on a range, today's soldier fires at lifelike pop-up targets which fall over when hit. They do this day in and day out until the whole process is automatic. According to Grossman this is based, either by accident or by design, on what is known as operant conditioning as identified by the famous psychologist B. F. Skinner. The stimulus is the human-shaped target popping up, the response is to fire the weapon, the reward is seeing the target go down.[46] Do it often enough in training and in battle it becomes automatic.

Not sure? Consider the following:

Private Dick Fiddament, 2nd Royal Norfolks, 1939

It's one thing to fire at a target made of paper and wood and it's another thing to deliberately fire at something you know is like you – flesh and blood and bone, who has a family, probably married with young children, a mother and a father.[47]

Private Michael Asher, 2nd Battalion, The Parachute Regiment, 1972

It was our first day on the ranges and we were letting rip at 'figure elevens': pictures of little yellow men who charged at you with gigantic bayonets and menacing snarls. Whang! Whang! Whang! The targets went down . . . we doubled forward to check the targets. Six bullets smack through the target's midriff. 'You zapped him, soldier,' the corporal said. . . We handled the weapons for hours every day, repeating the rituals over and over again until they became instinctive. . . Familiarity was what our training was about. Handling your weapon had to become so instinctive that you could kill automatically.[48]

One of the benefits of this type of conditioning for modern armies is that, because not every response produces a result or reward, it is hard to undo the conditioning. In other words, when a modern soldier misses a target or the enemy soldier, instead of giving up he carries on until he hits the next one and gains the reward. A similar idea is used by breakfast cereal companies in getting us to eat more of their products – have you ever had a bowl of muesli with a few elusive bits of strawberry in it? You keep eating to find the next piece of strawberry.

Another part of conditioning is the battle drill. Although criticised by some historians[49] the World War II Commandos introduced their own and found that it was a useful way for soldiers to react instinctively when a set event occurred, for example the moment when a unit comes under fire. Modern armies make extensive use of battle drills.

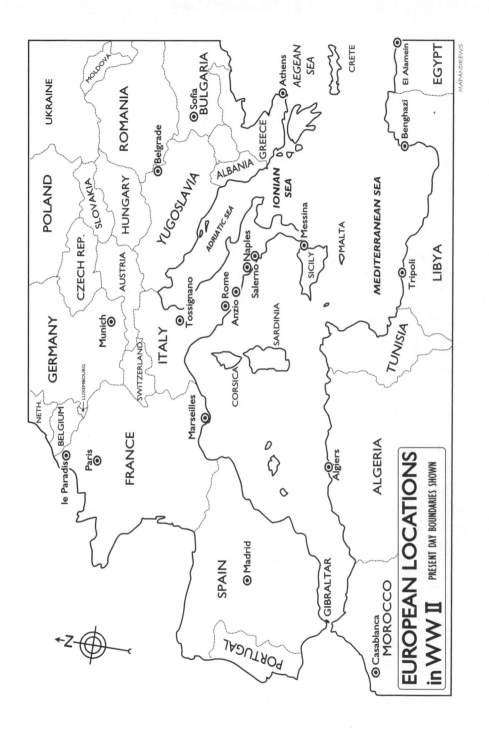

EUROPEAN LOCATIONS
in WW II PRESENT DAY BOUNDARIES SHOWN

The third element identified by Grossman is denial. The idea is that by continually rehearsing the act of killing the modern soldier is able to believe that, when it comes to the real thing, he is not killing a human being but simply another target. Modern armies do not talk about killing enemy soldiers, they talk about engaging enemy targets.[50]

Although the modern British and US Armies make much use of these methods neither was the first to discover them. The Commandos and other Special Forces already used some, if not all of these methods to produce supremely effective killers in World War II.

Elsewhere other perceptive individuals also realised their value. In 1944 Denis Edwards had already seen action at Pegasus Bridge and was a very good sniper even though his training was entirely conventional.

Private Denis Edwards, Airborne Sniper, 2nd Battalion, Oxfordshire and Buckinghamshire Light Infantry

<u>15th July 1944 – my 20th birthday</u>

At midday I went out on a lone sniping trip and the moment I got into one of our 'hides' I realised why things had been so quiet yesterday. The Jerries had been doing a change around and this was obviously a new lot who were wandering around in the open and without a care in the world. It was a reasonably clear day and they presented excellent targets. I contemplated making a fast trip back to our lines and getting out a couple of other snipers but just as the thought passed through my mind a big fat German stopped right in the middle of a wide gap in the opposite hedgerow. The target was just too good to miss and I let fly and the fat man leapt into the air and fell forwards, flat upon his face and still out in the open.

<u>19th July 1944</u>

We [Edwards and a fellow (unnamed) sniper] went out to the sniper hides before dawn. We both spotted a German standing in a gap and yawning his head off. We let fly together and put him back to sleep. Then we peppered away along the enemy hedgerow in the hope of making them think that we were mounting a dawn attack. We may not have hit any more but I guess that we must have caused a fair bit of panic.

We stayed for some while and had just decided to return to our lines to get some breakfast when I spotted a German who must have had the same idea in mind. He flitted past two gaps in his hedgerow and I selected the widest gap in front of him and the moment he appeared I let fly. I think I hit him, but how badly I could not be sure as he hit the ground almost immediately and was lost from sight.

22nd July 1944

Went out sniping first thing and soon realised that a new lot had moved in across the way. Having been 'hit' by us several times in the past and well aware of the dangers, yesterday there was not a German to be seen. Today they were strolling casually around in the open without a worry in the world. It seemed odd to me that the outgoing lot did not advise their incoming comrades of the danger from British snipers but it would seem they never did.

A big fat German ambled leisurely into one of the biggest gaps in the hedgerow and casually raised a pair of binoculars to his face and slowly scanned our hedgerow. Equally leisurely I raised my rifle, took careful aim, gently squeezed the trigger and fired. Fat man crashed backwards and made no further movement.

25th July 1944

Was issued with a brand new sniper rifle straight from ordnance, wrapped in greaseproof paper and covered in a thick layer of grease. I spent a lot of the day taking the rifle apart and cleaning it.

27th July 1944

Mid-morning I scrounged a couple of old biscuit tins, went into a nearby field, propped the cans against a shell-scarred post, lay down about 150 yards away, fixed the telescopic sights to my new rifle and began firing away. Unfortunately the tins kept jumping around so it was impossible to correct the sights. What I really needed was a few obliging Jerries. My chance came when at lunchtime I was allowed to go out to one of the sniper hedgerows and a German kindly presented enough of himself in a small gap, just long enough for me to take aim and fire. Judging by the way that he disappeared backwards I was satisfied that the new rifle was correctly zeroed. Like a kid with a new toy I spent the rest of the afternoon and evening wandering around in no man's land looking for likely targets but none appeared so I guess the first hit must have been good and that the rest of them were keeping down.

Several friends and acquaintances – particularly amongst the generation born after the war ended, who have read this manuscript, have asked me the question, 'What did it feel like when, as a sniper, you looked through your telescopic sights, had a German in view and squeezed the trigger of your rifle knowing that you were taking another human life?' I have thought about this since and the answer is that as a trained soldier fighting in a war where you killed, or could just as easily be killed yourself, you did not regard the enemy as human beings – they were simply targets to be hit and I had no different feelings about hitting these targets as I did of hitting the targets on the rifle range. The only difference was that the targets on the rifle range could not fire back but the ones we met in action could. Thus there was more satisfaction in hitting live targets since it meant one less enemy to fight in the future. One less to kill or wound my comrades.[51]

Denis Edwards also points out that the Commandos and other Special Forces were full of volunteers whereas the rest of the Army was full of conscripts, many of whom had little appetite for war.[52] This is a very important point, one overlooked by some historians. Joanna Bourke dismisses the Commandos as units whose status she says was, 'based largely on very effective self-promotion'.[53] She also refers to a 1941 report which found that, 'A large proportion of men arriving at training centres had not been aware they were volunteering for the Special Service and promptly asked to be returned to their unit.'[54] The fact is, as is outlined in some detail in Chapters 3 and 4, that the Commandos gained their deserved reputation from their operations, and their ability to reject volunteers at any stage during training was key to their success as highly effective soldiers.

Denis Edwards's point about conscripts is also valid today. The modern British and US Armies rely on volunteers, recruited at an age when they are susceptible to the type of training outlined above.[55] Any who are unsuitable do not make it as soldiers and this helps ensure that all soldiers are firers. A conscript army may not be entirely useless but many of its soldiers are.

So what happens if you put an army trained in modern techniques against one trained the World War II way? The answer is that a small modern army can wreak havoc on a much larger force. Colonel Grossman points to Richard Holmes's research into the Falklands War as a prime example of this as explaining how the British Army won a famous victory over the Argentines who were trained in the traditional ways.[56]

So far we have talked about the British soldier of World War II. But what of the German soldier? As has already been mentioned German soldiers spent more time on exercise and used blank ammunition on exercise. This meant they were probably more conditioned and better prepared for battle than the British. But the problem of inactive firers also troubled the German Army. Günther K. Koschorrek fought on the Eastern Front and noted the following of one of his comrades,

Grommel can't aim and pull the trigger. Even when he is forced to shoot, he closes his eyes as he pulls the trigger, so he can't see where he is shooting. Yet he was one of the best shots in the training camp.[57]

But the Germans did have their conditioned killers, many of them to be found in the Waffen SS, crucially an all-volunteer force. Waffen SS training contained all the elements necessary to produce soldiers who were not only ready but also willing to kill. For example members of the Waffen SS Division *Totenkopf* spent 1330–1730 hours each day on battle training and weapons practice and 1900–2000 hours each evening listening to lectures which included Nazi politicising.[58] Crucially the weapons training included shooting at various targets which were either partial or full body shapes.[59]

And, just to make sure they were thoroughly brainwashed, as well as all of this the soldiers of the *Totenkopf* Division spent some time on guard duty at the headquarters of the *Totenkopf* branch of the Algemeine SS at Dachau concentration camp.[60]

This is a book about the reality of fighting at close quarters in World War II. However, we have already seen how it is possible for academics to fall into the trap of painting a picture of the battlefield which is somewhat at odds with the experience of those who were actually there.

Therefore this book will visit the battlefields of World War II and tell the story of some of the actions which were fought in order to see how they support the ideas outlined in this chapter. And in doing so the book will also describe some of the weapons and tactics which were used and which played a part in defeat or victory. Clearly the whole war would be outside the scope of a single book. So for each theatre one or two individual actions have been chosen to illustrate what it was like to fight there.

Notes

1. James Lucas, *Das Reich – The Military Role of the 2nd SS Division*, Cassell 1991, pp. 23–4
2. Brig. Peter Barclay DSO, MC, Imperial War Museum, Sound Archive, No. 8192
3. Robert M. Citino, *The Path to Blitzkrieg – Doctrine and Training in the German Army 1920–1939*, Lynne Rienner 1999, p. 9
4. Citino, p. 110
5. Citino, p. 223
6. Williamson Murray and Allan R. Millett (eds), *Military Innovation in the Interwar Period*, Cambridge University Press 1996, p. 23
7. Williamson Murray, p. 25
8. Major R. H. W Hastings, *The Rifle Brigade in the Second World War 1939–1945*, Gale & Polden 1950, p. xvii
9. General S. L. A. Marshall, *Men Against Fire*, University of Oklahoma Press 2000. Originally published New York; William Morrow & Son 1947
10. Marshall, p. 54
11. Timothy Harrison Place, *Military Training in the British Army 1940–1944*, Frank Cass 2000, p. 79
12. Russell W. Glenn, Introduction to *Men Against Fire*, University of Oklahoma Press, 2000
13. Glenn p. 5
14. Glenn p. 6
15. Joanna Bourke, *An Intimate History of Killing*, Granta 1999
16. Bourke, p. 76
17. Bourke, p. 375.
18. Niall Ferguson, *The Pity of War*, Penguin 1998
19. Ferguson, p. 357 *et seq*
20. Ferguson, p. 447.
21. Lt Col Dave Grossman, *On Killing*, Little Brown 1996
22. Glenn p. 6 and 7
23. Grossman, *On Killing*, ch. 2
24. Grossman, *On Killing*, p. 28
25. David M. Buss, *The Murderer Next Door*, Penguin Press, 2005, p. 9
26. Buss, p. 245

27. Correspondence with the author
28. Donna Hart and Robert W. Sussman, *Man The Hunted*, Westview Press, 2005
29. Hart and Sussman, p. xviii
30. GB99 KCLMA MFF 7, held at King's College, London, original at National Archive and Records Administration, Record Group 407, Entry 427 (Records of the Adjutant General's Office, World War II Operation Reports, 1940–1948) and the Military Reference Branch
31. John Whiteclay Chambers III, 'S. L. A. Marshall's *Men Against Fire*: New Evidence Regarding Fire Ratios', *Parameters*, US Army War College Quarterly, Autumn 2003, p. 115
32. Chambers, p. 117
33. Chambers, p. 118
34. Chambers, p. 120
35. *Ibid.*
36. *Ibid*
37. Letter to the author February 2005
38. Place, p. 4
39. Hank Hancock, SBS sniper, quoted in Roger Ford and Tim Ripley, *The Whites of Their Eyes*, Pan Books, 1998, p. 161
40. Lyn MacDonald, *1914, 1915, They Called It Passchendale, Somme, To the Last Man, Spring: 1918, The Roses of No Man's Land*, all Penguin
41. Max Arthur, *Forgotten Voices of The Great War*, Random House 2003
42. Correspondence with the author
43. Joseph Belzar, unpublished memoir, p. 71
44. Letter to the author 14 January 2005
45. Grossman, *On Killing*, pp. 251, 252
46. Grossman, *On Killing*, pp. 253–5
47. Imperial War Museum, Sound Archive, No. 17354, quoted in Peter Hart, *At The Sharp End*, Pen & Sword 1998, p.19
48. Michael Asher, *Shoot to Kill*, Cassell 2004, p. 31, with the kind permission of David Higham Associates
49. Place, p. 63 *et seq*
50. Grossman, pp. 255, 256
51. IWM 78/68/1 as amended by Denis Edwards in correspondence with author
52. Denis Edwards, email to the author 26 January 2005
53. Bourke, p. 135.
54. *Ibid.*
55. Grossman, *On Killing*, p. 265
56. Grossman, *On Killing*, p. 178
57. Günther K. Koschorrek, *Blood Red Snow*, Greenhill Books, 2002, p. 84.
58. Herbert Brunnegger, *Saat in den Sturm: Ein Soldat der Waffen SS Berichtet*, Leopold Stocker Verlag, 2000, p. 18. With kind permission of the publisher. Translation by the author.
59. Brunnegger, p. 26
60. Brunnegger, p. 61

CHAPTER 2

1940 – The Action at Le Paradis

The Mark III Lee-Enfield Rifle weighs just over 8½ pounds, is nearly 4 feet long and fires a 0.303-inch (7.7mm) bullet, ten of which can fit in the rifle's magazine. This bullet weighs 174 grains or roughly 11.3 grams and once fired it travels at about 2,400 feet per second until its contents of aluminium and lead hit whatever object it is aimed at.

If that object is an enemy soldier then one of two things will happen. The bullet may travel straight through his body without being deflected by bone or other organs. If this happens then the exit wound is of similar diameter to the entry wound. If, however, the bullet hits an enemy soldier and is deflected by bone or other organs then these will cause the exit wound to be distorted. The exit wound will therefore be larger than the entry wound. Given that the human body contains rather a lot of bones and organs most bullets will distort once they hit.

To the present-day historian this fact is of academic value. But on 27 May 1940 ignorance of what actually happened inside the human body when the bullets from Lee-Enfield rifles killed soldiers of the Waffen SS during the defence of the village of Le Paradis was to have terrible consequences.

For all his faults, S. L. A. Marshall did at least identify the factor which wins wars: fire. For Marshall the key to winning future wars was the extent to which an army could get its soldiers to fire their weapons at the enemy.[1]

At the start of World War II the British and German Armies had very different ideas about how to use fire in attack. For the Germans attack was all about the quality of fire rather than the quantity. The emphasis was on staying concealed unless taking part in the advance or in the *Feuerkampf* – the fire-fight. Even then German soldiers were supposed to move at speed and not present an easy target to the enemy. When they were moving forward in a loose-knit single file it was in any case hard for the enemy to find an easy target to aim at. Once the attack was within the killing range of 400 metres then fire was concentrated on to the target and it was this fire which won the assault.[2]

For the British Army in World War II the emphasis was on the quantity of fire rather than the quality of fire. To achieve maximum fire the single file approach adopted by the Germans was out – it meant not all the soldiers could fire. Instead an arrowhead formation was adopted so everyone could fire their weapons at the enemy. Of course the problem with this was that the formation was more vulnerable. However, the planners envisaged that the enemy would be under a constant barrage of fire from the British soldiers and that this would help win the day.[3]

Captain Peter Barclay DSO, MC, A Company, 2nd Royal Norfolks

The first thing is to smother the opposition as much as you can with effective fire. When you've got a demoralised enemy to contend with you're going to capture the objective a lot quicker and with a lot less loss. So the first principle I always reckoned was to shatter their morale with fire – it needn't be all that dead accurate – the noise is generally enough to cow the most brazen adversary. So once you've done that always ensure that you've got an element giving covering fire . . . until you get right up to the assault distance from the position and then the two leading platoons – on a company level – go bashing in together. But the longer you can keep your firing going, until the moment the attacking forces reach the ground and the objective, the more likely you are to succeed – and succeed without heavy loss.[4]

The story of the fighting at Le Paradis is a battle of contrasts. On the British side were the Royal Norfolks who trained their soldiers the traditional way as outlined in Chapter 1 – in other words drill, firing on the ranges, fieldcraft. And then more drill.[5] On the German side were the Waffen SS who employed methods far better for producing soldiers able and willing to kill. As well as traditional drill and fieldcraft these included extensive weapons practice against lifelike targets as well as conditioning in the Nazi creed of hatred and violence.[6]

An additional factor for the Waffen SS was that some 350 years of history separated the Royal Norfolks and the Waffen SS *Totenkopf.* Whereas the Royal Norfolks had nothing to prove, the Waffen SS had everything to prove as World War II was their first time in action. Elements of the *Totenkopf* Division had been in action in Poland before they got to France but for many this was to be their first taste of battle.

General der Waffen SS Felix Steiner

Concerning the fairness of the [Le Paradis] battle in other respects, which was most certainly fought severely but nevertheless with very deep respect, the grim rage of this phase of the battle was generally regretted and the *Totenkopf* Division was regarded even in its own ranks as not yet being equal to the demands of heavy fighting conditions. It was only later on the Eastern Front that it made its name in the Demjansk pocket as a 'Do or Die' Division.[7]

The Royal Norfolks started their war on the Dyle Line in the Bois de Tombeek in Belgium on 11 May 1940. But this was the furthest east they were to travel. From here, as the Germans advanced, the only direction the Royal Norfolks would be going was back towards France again along the route they had travelled to get to the Dyle Line.

Despite the fact that the Norfolks were well dug in on the Dyle the problem for the British Expeditionary Force was that the German advance through the French lines had been so rapid that the Germans were threatening to encircle the British and cut them off from the French Army. To avoid this threat the order came through to withdraw. The format for a withdrawal was usually to take up defensive positions by day and to move by night, although the proximity of the enemy meant that withdrawal was never easy, especially as the Germans also tried to delay the advance by attacking civilians from the air.

Captain Peter Barclay

We never, ever, carried out a withdrawal in contact. If we thought that was likely, we patrolled very offensively against the enemy positions before we pulled out. And gave them something to think about and then extricated ourselves without fear of interference. This in fact occurred every time – we were never once molested in our withdrawal which I was thankful about – because nearly always I was a rearguard company and you had a horrible sort of feeling of getting one up the pants as you were coming out. But it never came to that.[8]

Private Ernie Farrow, Pioneer Section, 2nd Royal Norfolks

After a few days we had to withdraw again. As soon as we started to withdraw three of the Stukas came over. Now they took no notice of us, [but] we dived out of the lorries because we expected them to blow us to hell. But they didn't, they simply went over the top of us and disappeared in the trees. We heard the machine guns, we heard the sirens, we heard the bombs dropping. On our left flank we had the Belgian Army and we naturally thought they were going after the Belgian Army. But after we had driven down the road three or four miles we found what they had done. They had come over us, left us but to stop us they had machine-gunned and bombed these poor people. It was a massacre. All along the road were people who had been killed, with no arms, no heads, there was cattle lying about, dead, there was little tiny children, there were old people. We couldn't stop to clear the roads because we knew that this was what this was done for – for us to stop and the Germans to surround us. We had to drive our lorries over the top of them. We couldn't do anything about it.[9]

Captain Peter Barclay

The initial advance of the Germans was bound to come up the road and our first contact would invariably be along lines of communication. They were very bad at deploying off roads – in fact at deploying off main roads. I found this later on, after D-Day that two or three times I'd put an attack down some little, tiny side road and avoided all heavy enemy artillery fire and in fact achieved remarkable surprise on all those occasions because they only thought in terms of guarding the main road approaches to their positions. They were very inflexible.[10]

By 20 May the Royal Norfolks had retreated as far as the Escaut canal near Tournai and here they received orders to stand and fight. They took over positions previously held by the Royal Berkshire Regiment which were located on a wide front, too wide really for the soldiers of the Royal Norfolks to defend effectively. Added to this there were buildings on the Norfolks' side of the canal and a forestry plantation on the other side where the Germans were expected.

By the time the Norfolks had reached the canal they were exhausted. The previous night they had marched nearly thirty miles to reach their new positions and when the morning of 21 May dawned they were in direct contact with the Germans. Not just any Germans either. For the Norfolks this was to be their first taste of fighting the Waffen SS. And in the ensuing fire-fight they were to notch up another first for the regiment – their first Victoria Cross of the war in an action where one man took on the enemy.

This sort of one-man action is entirely consistent with General Marshall's view of the battlefield where you have a minority of individuals taking responsibility for the fighting.

Captain Peter Barclay

Having satisfied myself on the company layout, my batman reported that he'd seen some black rabbits in a park – there was a château in the grounds of which some of my positions were – and not only that but he'd found some ferrets in a box in the stables. I'm ashamed to say there were also a couple of retrievers kept shut up in the stables and all the occupants of the château and everybody round about had departed except in a little convent where two nuns remained. So we thought we'd get in a little bit of sport before the fun began.

I had a shotgun with me and popped these ferrets down a big warren and we were having a rare bit of sport as rabbits bolted out of these burrows when after about half an hour of this the shelling started along the river line generally. And we came in for a certain amount of this and we thought, 'Well, we'd better pack this up now and deal with the other situation.' So back we went to company headquarters and waited for the next pattern of activities.

After a few hours some Germans appeared on the far bank. They were totally oblivious of our presence in the immediate vicinity. And I told my soldiers on no account were any of them to fire until they heard my hunting horn. And an officer appeared and got his map out and appeared to be holding an O group with his senior warrant officers.

Then they withdrew into the wood and we heard a lot of chopping going on and we saw tops of trees flattening out. And in fact what they were doing was cutting down young trees to make a long series of hurdles to lay over the top of the blitzed bridge which was in the middle of my sector. There were bits of concrete lying across the canal, you couldn't walk across, but they were so placed across the canal that with suitable lengths of hurdles, pedestrians had been able to get across.

Eventually they emerged from this plantation with a number of long hurdles made of these saplings and they proceeded to lay these across the rubble and the remains of the concrete blocks in the canal. So we kept quite quiet and they still had no idea we were there.

I reckoned we'd wait there until there were as many as we could contend with on our side of the canal before opening fire. They were SS with black helmets and they started to come across. We waited for a posse of them to accumulate on our side (they were still convinced that there was no problem about adversaries in the area and they were standing about in little groups waiting for guide parties to get across) and then I reckoned we'd just enough to manage and contend with.

I blew my hunting horn and then of course all the soldiers opened fire with consummate accuracy and disposed of all the enemy personnel on our side of the canal and also the ones on the bank on the far side, which brought the hostile proceedings to an abrupt halt, and then of course we came in for an inordinate amount of shelling and mortar fire.[11]

Private Ernie Leggatt, A Company, 2nd Royal Norfolks

We saw the Germans coming at us through the wood and they also had light tanks. We let them have all we'd got, firing the Bren, rifles, everything. I was on the Bren gun firing from the cover of these old benches, tables and God knows what on this veranda. We killed a lot of Germans. They came up almost as far as the river and we gave them hell and they retreated. They attacked us again and the tanks were coming over their own dead men, to us that was repulsive and we couldn't understand why they did that.[12]

Captain Peter Barclay

Not long after that I was wounded in the guts and in the back and in my arm. And we'd had several casualties before this and all the stretchers were therefore out. My batman, with great presence of mind, ripped a door off its hinges and in spite of my orders to the contrary, tied me to this door. In fact if he had not done this I probably wouldn't be here to tell the tale. They took me round on this door to deal with what had become a very threatening situation from our right flank. Instead of a friendly unit being there, suddenly we were fired on by Germans from our side of the canal. So I had to deplete my small reserve which was sore because I had such a wide front to hold.

I put my Sergeant-Major Gristock in charge of this small force which was about ten men including a wireless operator and a company clerk and various other personnel from company headquarters to not only hold my right flank but deal with a German post that had established itself not very far off to my right. He placed some of his soldiers in position to curtail the activities of that particular post, so effectively that they wiped them out.

While this was going on fire came from another German position on our side of the canal on the bank. He spotted where this was and he left two men to give him covering fire. He went forward armed with a Tommy gun and grenades to dispose of this party which was in position behind a pile of stones on the bank of the canal.

When he was about twenty or thirty yards from this position he was spotted by another German machine-gun post on the enemy side of the canal who opened fire on him and raked through and smashed both knees. In spite of this he dragged himself until he got within grenade lobbing range of this German post on our side of the canal. Then he lay on this side and he lobbed a grenade over the top of this pile of stones, belted the three Germans, turned over on his side, opened fire with his Tommy gun and dealt with the lot of them.[13]

Both Barclay and Gristock were evacuated through Dunkirk. Gristock was awarded the Victoria Cross for this action but sadly he died in Brighton on 16 June 1940.

On 22 May the Norfolks were ordered to retreat once more. After a short period as divisional reserve they were on the move again, this time to the La Bassée canal in front of the small village of Le Paradis near Béthune. The idea was for them to hold the line to buy more time for the retreating BEF. But this time their enemy was the *Totenkopf* Division.

In fact advance elements of the Waffen SS had reached the area on 24 May, a day before the Norfolks took up their positions on the canal in the early hours of the 25th. Intelligence reports given to the Waffen SS suggested that there were two elite British units holding the line and that there would be a hard fight.[14]

This other unit referred to in the German intelligence reports was the Royal Scots whose positions were next to those of the Royal Norfolks. But in taking up their positions the Norfolks had made a mistake because, while A and C Companies were in their allotted positions, B and D Companies had mistakenly deployed on a subsidiary loop in the canal, exposing a large gap in the defences. Orders were given to the Pioneer Section to fill the gap.

Private Ernie Farrow

What they told us to do was to go up on to the top of this canal bank and make sure that every round we fired got a German. After we had fired a number of rounds we had got to scramble back down the bank and then back up again to try and bluff the Germans that there was a whole company of us there. We were told then that we were getting short of ammunition and we had to try and make every round count. We were being hard pressed by machine gun, mortar and artillery. It was the most terrible thing I think I have ever experienced. We were dug in on our little foxholes but we couldn't stay in them all the time; we had to get up to fire at the Germans on the other side who were trying to get across the canal to get at us. Our artillery was doing their best to keep the Germans from getting across – they were even driving their lorries into the canal to get their tanks across. Our artillery was managing to keep them at bay. I was using my .303 rifle, occasionally we took turns in firing the Bren gun but there again we had to be very careful because we were running short of ammunition. We found that by using our rifles we could save ammunition quite a lot. We could pick a German off with our rifles just as well as we could with the Bren gun. The Bren gun used twenty rounds to hit the same German.[15]

The Bren gun weighed just over 22 pounds and was nearly 4 feet long. It was air-cooled and gas-operated and fired the 0.303-inch bullet. Its magazine could hold 30 rounds and could be changed in less than five seconds. It was a reliable and accurate weapon. The Bren gun was ideal for the British philosophy of laying down fire for any attack. However, it was outclassed by the German MG34 (and later the MG42) machine gun (known as the Spandau to Allied soldiers). The MG34 could fire at at least twice the rate of the Bren – a 250-round belt of ammunition lasted just 30 seconds. This made for a devastating fire even at difficult targets although for this set-up the Spandau needed a supporting bipod or tripod. This came with sights enabling accurate fire up to 3,000 yards. Used on the move it could be fitted with 50- or 75-round drums.

In a typical German company there would be more than thirteen Spandaus which made them a formidable opponent. These weapons had a distinctive sound when fired – a high speed ripping noise, like canvas tearing according to some – which the British soldier soon learned to recognise. But for the defenders of Le Paradis the best chance of survival was not with the main body of soldiers, but rather when they were captured on special missions.

Private Ernie Farrow

I remember Corporal Mason shouting to me, 'Come on over here,' he said, 'Right, you, you and you, we've got to go and blow a bridge up.'

I said, 'We're just back.'

He said, 'Never mind about that. Go and find some amatol, gun cotton, whatever you can find and bring it across.' He then went to try and find a vehicle to take us in because we couldn't carry all this stuff around with us.

The CO had already been sent back and Major Ryder had taken over as the CO. He had been wounded as well. He told Corporal Mason that his driver had already been detailed to take us to this bridge; he didn't want any map reference, he knew exactly which bridge to go to, it was only a short distance away.

The vehicle the CO had was an old Humber car. His driver's name was Hawker – he came from King's Lynn and we all knew him. He opened the back of the old car and we put the gun cotton, the primers and whatever we had in the back. The sergeant-major came along and he said, 'Right here lads, here's something to be going with', and he gave us a big tin of Bluebird toffees. He said, 'When you come back there'll be a hot meal for you.' I'm afraid we never got the hot meal. But the Quarter-master came along and said, 'Right, it's just a few rounds.' Three rounds of ammunition we were issued with. Three rounds of ammunition to fight the German Army! We thought, 'Oh Gawd!'

With this we all piled into this old car and we were away. I couldn't tell you how far it was because we were so busy trying to get this tin lid off to get the toffees out and we were being shelled and machine-gunned all the way, not too badly but the occasional shot or burst of machine-gun fire. We knew that one bullet through the back of our car and we could all get blown to pieces.

We hoped to God that the driver would get there as quick as he could. In no time at all the driver turned round and said, 'Here's the bridge coming up!' We all looked up – the lid was still on the toffees, we hadn't got that off – but we looked up. This happened in seconds not minutes. We heard this machine-gun fire; we could see the bridge in front of us and directly to our left-hand side there was a big house and on the right was the canal. At that very instant that he spoke the machine gun opened up and the whole top of this old car was riddled by machine-gun bullets. But not one of us was touched. We were still all alive.

We didn't wait for the second burst. We dived out of this car because the Germans were firing from this house directly in front of us. There was no point in us trying to get to this bridge because they were already over it. The first place we went was straight into the canal. We dived in. The driver was trying to turn his vehicle round to get back to headquarters to warn them that this bridge had already been taken by the Germans. I suppose that was what was in his mind.

By the time we got into the canal we heard this hell of an explosion and we were splattered by bits of metal as the poor old car was blown up and the driver with it. We tried to climb up the edge of the canal bank and fire at the Germans. Somehow we managed to get a footing. How we did it I don't know because as you know the canal bank is all mud. We managed to get there somehow and we fired our few rounds off at these Germans in the house and along the side of the bridge, hoping that every bullet would kill a German. In no time at all we had no more ammunition left and there was no way we were going to get back to headquarters.

There was no way we could get out of the canal where we were. So Corporal Mason said, 'Right, bolts out of your rifles, get rid of them, there's no way they're needed any more. The only thing we need is safety for ourselves.' Our tin hats, everything went off into the canal. Luckily for us we were all good swimmers; we swam under water across the canal.

The Germans were on both sides so it made no difference where we went but we felt it was safer to go on the other side. We couldn't get out of the canal because the banks were too high to climb and if you started to climb the banks you'd be picked off. We wanted to find somewhere where the dyke ran into the canal – we hadn't thought of this but the corporal had.

We swam across and on the other side of the canal there was a bed of river plants. There we kept still to stop even the ripples in the water for fear the Germans would put their machine guns into where we were. The corporal said, 'Right, stop where you are, keep your heads down. I'm going to swim down the canal and find somewhere where there's a ditch runs into the canal where we can climb out.' Then he disappeared.

The three of us in these rushes were very close together. The young fellow on my left-hand side, almost touching me, [was] a fellow called Porter from Beccles in Suffolk. He'd been in the Army with me from the time we'd joined up, a very nice young fellow. He said, 'I'm just going to have a peek over the top.'

At that very instant I hear this machine-gun or rifle fire and I thought that they'd fired across into the bank of this canal. I turned and looked up and this poor fellow had been shot right through the middle of his head and the back of his head was missing. He was then sinking back into the water. I was trying to hold him up which was no good because he was dead. I was telling the fellow on my right – his name was Reeve from Dickleburgh. He was an old soldier who'd been in India and he had two gold teeth.

I was talking to him and I felt something hit my face. I put my hand up automatically and I was covered in blood. I thought, 'God!' I looked at the blood and thought I had been hit. I felt again but I was still all there. When I turned round to look at this poor fellow it was him. They had shot down the river and had shot his jaw and it was his jaw which had hit me in the face.

He was then disappearing; the last thing I saw of him was these two gold teeth in the top of his head. In a few minutes the water round me was red with blood but the poor boys had gone. A few minutes afterwards the corporal came back and there was just the two of us. He knew exactly what had happened. He said, 'Right we can't fret about the poor boys, let's go!' We dived under and swam – how far we swam I have no idea.

Eventually he pulled on me and said, 'Right here we are.' There was this ditch right beside us. The first thing I wanted to do was to get out of that damn canal, to get clear of it. I'd seen enough damage already. He said, 'You stop where you are, that's an order, keep your head down.' As I was standing in this canal I looked down this ditch and on the left-hand side of this dyke I could see a bush and I was almost sure I could see this bush moving. At the same time he said, 'Stay where you are, I'll go and look see if there's anything on this meadow.' With those few words I heard this mouthful of Army language.

I looked at him and he had been shot through the shoulder, and the bone of his arm was sticking out of the top. He was still alive and he put his arm round my neck to keep himself up and again everything happened in seconds. This bush I had seen, there was a German behind it, probably the one who had shot Mis [Mason] just then. He came from behind this bush, jumped into the ditch and he came down running towards us. When he was about twelve yards from us he stopped and put his rifle up to his shoulder.

I said my last prayer because I knew I was going to die. But the Lord was with me again,. There was a loud click, [but] he'd run out of ammunition or his breech had stuck; there was no bullet came out, no bang. He jumped down towards us. We couldn't move.

He turned his rifle round, got hold of the barrel and as he got close to us he took a swipe at my head. I put my arm up to stop him hitting me and the first blow smashed my hand up. The next blow came down and I still had the strength to hold my elbow up to stop him and he smashed my elbow and put my shoulder out of joint. One more blow and I'd have been dead but at that very instant I heard this loud shout and lots more Germans came into sight. One of these was an officer who had shouted.

They jumped into this ditch and he ordered them to pull us out of the canal. They pulled poor old Mis out first. They had to be very careful because if they had pulled his wrong arm they'd have pulled it off he was in such a state. But he was still alive and they put him on a stretcher and took him away. Then they pulled me out.[16]

May 26 saw more hard fighting in and around Le Paradis. The Germans made several determined attempts to cross the canal and succeeded in getting units into the village of Le Paradis itself. Counter-attacks with the help of 1st Battalion, The Royal Scots, ensured that the Germans did not win the day completely on 26 May but the situation was obscure and getting more desperate.

Lance-Corporal James Howe MBE, *1st Royal Scots*

We were with the Royal Norfolks; they had one end of the village and we had the other end. We had some mortar fire for a day or two. Then the Germans attacked, actually the area I was in first. We were about fifty yards from the centre of the village. We were in this house tending our wounded, the regimental aid post, with the medical officer and the padre, about six of us attendants, and maybe twenty wounded. But my first sight of the Germans was [as] they came down this small road towards us. The first thing I saw was a hand preparing to throw a hand grenade through the window of our regimental aid post. This hand grenade came in, blew up and we all dived in the corner. Of course the building caught fire so we had no option but to get out as quickly as we could.

We came out and here were these Germans, SS troops. They screamed at us to get down in the road where there was a Bren gun carrier, one of ours. We sheltered by this Bren gun carrier, at the same time under the muzzles of the German Tommy guns. But the Germans screamed at us and then they began firing on our regimental headquarters which was further down the road. They were using us as a shield.[17]

On the evening of 26 May calm descended on the village of Le Paradis. Sometime during the night battalion headquarters was moved to Druries Farm on the Rue de Paradis, 500 yards to the west of the crossroads which bisected the Merville–Loubleau road. This crossroads was about a hundred yards to the south of the main collection of village buildings, the shops and the church. A Company, 2nd Royal Norfolks, was holding the neighbouring hamlet of Le Cornet Malo.

It was at Druries Farm that the order was received to hold the position to the last man and to the last round.[18]

At 0330 hours on 27 May the calm was broken by a determined German attack against Le Cornet Malo, the brunt of which was taken by B Company which was holding the ground next to A Company.

Private Arthur Brough, 2nd Royal Norfolks

We set our mortar up and it was getting a bit hectic round there. Lots of tanks and heavy gunfire. We were putting as much stuff down the mortar as we could to get rid of our ammunition. We were trying to repulse them but we knew it wasn't a lot of good because there were so many there.

It was a 3-inch mortar, the No. 1 was looking through the clinometer sight, focusing roughly on whereabouts the tanks were situated (I was the No. 1). You say, 'Right on!' and tap No. 2 on the shoulder. He taps Number Three who's passing the bomb over. Then they put it in the barrel. Fire. And that was what we did. The mortar must have been red hot, anything they could get hold of we were putting down the mortar until it got so bad that we even resorted to rifles.

There was only about three of us left by that time and [the] PSM [platoon sergeant-major] had been killed. They were throwing pretty heavy stuff at us. We resorted to rifle fire which was absolutely stupid but I suppose it was instinct to try and do your job until we saw that it was absolutely hopeless so we just chucked the bolts out of the rifles and dived and scattered.

Why you do these things, don't ask me why, it must just be instinct. It was what we were taught to do: immobilise our rifles, take the bolts out. We just ran for it; what can you do when you see all tanks coming at you? There were no officers. The mortar platoon seems to have been isolated there. Johnny Cockerel was with me and we scattered and we dived into a dyke.

There were tanks by the hundred coming up, it was frightening really. As we scattered we got stopped dead in our tracks because there was a bomb that dropped quite near us from the tanks and I could feel something in the back of my leg, my upper right leg and Johnny Cockerel got a piece out of his knee, pretty bad. I looked after him as much as I could, just the field dressing. Mine was just a superficial cut, two or three cuts on the back of my leg and a lot of splinters.

We were in this dyke and all of a sudden the tanks were right on top if us and the next thing we saw was a German officer standing there telling us, 'The war is over Tommy!' That's what he said. We were left there to our own devices for a while and their infantry was coming up behind the tanks. By that time there were a lot of them – just tanks and men. Made you wonder how you really could repulse them.[19]

By now the main German attack was under way but because there were only two survivors from the Royal Norfolks from the main part of the day's fighting the details concerning exactly what happened on the British side remain obscure, even to this day. What we do know is that the Royal Norfolks, or some of them at least, were fighting hard according to their orders to fight to the very last. Given that most were killed during or after the fighting the main witnesses to what happened on 27 May 1940 were members of the Waffen SS.

Sturmbannführer (SS Major) Werner Zorn, Commanding Officer,
1st Battalion, 2nd SS Infantry Regiment

The battle was generally described as having been particularly severe. The enemy resisted stubbornly and losses were, therefore, considerable. With the exception of the 1st Battalion and a few troops of the 3rd

Regiment who, with the SS Heimwehr of Danzig, had taken part in the Polish campaign, the division was not seasoned in battle. Nothing is known to me about cruelties or other dirty business during the battle. On account of the losses incurred, 26 May was occasionally referred to as the black day of the division.[20]

Herbert Brunnegger, 2nd Battalion, 2nd SS Infantry Regiment

The attack is renewed. A weak sun is rising out of ground mist. A signpost points to Le Cornet Malo. Mortars and submachine guns move into position on the edge of the wood and fire at recognisable enemy targets in a village a couple of hundred metres in front of us. While they do this our soldiers move forward on both sides of the path. I come across a young Englishman. His face is distinctive and brown but the proximity of death is making his skin go pale. He is standing up and leaning against a wall made of earth. In his eyes there is an indescribably hopeless expression while the whole time bright spurts of blood are coming out of a wound at the base of his neck. In vain his hands try to press on a vein in order to try and keep the life in his body. He cannot be saved.

Onwards! A surprise as bursts of machine-gun fire hit a section as it moves out of a cutting. The bursts toss them into a tangle of bodies. One stands up and sways past me to the rear – he has a finger stuck into a hole in his stomach.[21]

Unterscharführer (SS Corporal) Edmund Gluma, 2nd SS Infantry Regiment

On the morning of 27 May at about 0500 hours, 1 and 2 Platoons (I belonged to 2 Platoon) received the order to clear the terrain in front of us of the enemy. We came across a group of houses supposed to be near Le Cornet Malo. Here we received heavy fire from machine guns and rifles from the houses. Right at the beginning of the battle we had considerable losses in dead and wounded. Our section reached a water ditch about seventy-five metres away from the houses. Here, however, we were forced to remain inactive, as every movement brought us under fire.[22]

Herbert Brunnegger

Before long the machine-gun nests of the invisible defenders suddenly open up on us. The enemy soldiers are able to make best use of the terrain which is made up of ditches, windbreaks, straw bale dumps, isolated farmsteads, tall grass and newly grown wheat. Snipers and machine-gun nests are hidden in the extensive area over which we plan to attack. Our supporting mortars cannot be used to their full effect. The countryside in front of Le Paradis is wide and flat.

The English defend themselves with incredible bravery and doggedness. Again the losses in terms of wounded and dead pile up. Again we are completely pinned to the ground in front of the enemy who are totally invisible and whose ability commands our admiration. We have to adapt ourselves completely to the enemy's tactics. We work ourselves forward by creeping, crawling and slithering along. The enemy retreat skilfully and without showing themselves. However, it is a thousand metres to the place which we have been ordered to attack. After the meadow, which does afford us protection, there are broad, deep level fields. Any idea of crossing this without support would be totally suicidal. I am reminded of doing this on exercise – then the artillery supported us wonderfully! I conjure that manoeuvre in my mind today in recipe book terms, 'You need such and such a thing . . . ' But I have not seen anything of our big Skoda guns. Where are they dug in?[23]

The guns had a problem. They had been supplied with the wrong ammunition and were in any case too busy changing position to assist the SS infantry in any useful way. This had resulted in the regimental commander Standartenführer (SS Colonel) Hans Friedmann Götze having an argument with the divisional commander Gruppenführer (SS Major-General) Theodor Eicke, about the order to continue fighting without the artillery. The feeling in the ranks was that as a direct result of this Götze was careless of his safety and ended up being killed.[24] But for the time being the troops were unaware of the problem and the artillery did fire the odd shot from the odd gun it managed to get into action.

Herbert Brunnegger

Behind us a howitzer has been brought into position in order to break the resistance of Le Paradis' defenders. After a short time the first shell whooshes right over our heads and crashes down in their presumed positions. Now it must be enough and white flags must soon appear. Rubble, fire and thick smoke show where the shells have landed. Onwards over the last hundred metres!

But then the machine guns open up from a large building which is several storeys high. At the same time the infantry set up a withering fire which sends our comrades to the ground. We try to use every small elevation and small dip in the field. No one digs in, in order to avoid the attention of the snipers. Dammit, they must see our predicament. Is the howitzer no longer to be used? But soon the shells resume their attack on the main buildings of the village. It is where the defenders' return fire is the fiercest.

From my position I can see that motorcycle troops are getting into the village from the far side during the artillery bombardment. Once there they are taking up the fight.

Captain Knöchlein gives the signal to attack. The artillery gives us effective cover and we make it to the village without any further losses. In the village the motorcyclists are already fighting to good effect.

White flags appear hesitantly. We watch them carefully and suspiciously as they emerge into captivity. Most of the British are wounded. The costly fight for the La Bassée Canal and for Le Paradis is at an end.[25]

Private William O'Callaghan, 2nd Royal Norfolks

After connections with the brigade had been cut we were entirely surrounded and the CO told us to destroy and break up telephones, wireless sets, etc. We destroyed all correspondence and made our way one at a time from the cellar into a barn. We were subjected to mortar fire and had some casualties. To save further loss of life the CO, Major Ryder, ordered us to surrender. At this time it was early afternoon.

We hung a towel on the end of a rifle and shortly afterwards all firing ceased. We opened the door and started to file out with our hands above our heads. The first dozen men were cut down and then the firing ceased.[26]

Private Albert Pooley, 2nd Royal Norfolks

After some fifteen minutes we were ordered to form up on the road with our hands clasped behind the back of our heads. During this process we were struck with rifle butts while standing in the ranks. The guards who did this were not reprimanded by their officers or NCOs.[27]

Private William O'Callaghan

We started off again to march along the road and met German troops who behaved in a very brutal manner towards us, hitting us with their rifles and pushing us about. On the march we halted once or twice and it is possible that one of these halts occurred just before we turned off a gateway leading into a farm. On passing through this gateway I noticed a pasture on our right and a farm building on our left.[28]

Herbert Brunnegger

I see a large group of English prisoners by a farmhouse. Those that are not wounded are standing up; the wounded are sitting and lying down in front on the ground. Many of them reach out in despair towards me with pictures of their families. Perhaps they think we are going to send them on leave?

As I look more closely I notice two heavy machine guns which have been set up in front of them. Whilst I look on, surprised that two valuable machine guns should be used to guard the prisoners, a dreadful thought occurs to me. I turn to the nearest machine-gun post and ask what is going on here. 'They are to be shot!' is the embarrassed answer. I cannot grasp this and think there is some stupid joke behind these words. Therefore I ask again, 'Who has ordered this?'

'Captain Knöchlein.' Now I know that this is deadly serious. I quickly hurry to catch up with my own section so I do not have witness the shooting of the prisoners who are waiting for death with pictures of their families in their hands.[29]

Hauptscharführer (SS Sergeant-Major) Theodor Emke, 1st Battalion, 2nd SS Infantry Regiment

At the time when the prisoners were being marched on to the meadow, Antons said to me something to the effect that it was right that they should be shot, the were *franc-tireurs* – *Heckenschützen* – soldiers who, having surrendered by displaying a white flag or raising both hands, allow their enemy to approach to within a short distance and at the last moment use their weapons again.[30]

Private Albert Pooley

We left the road and went into the field through the gate and I noticed at the foot of the wall a large hole which was at least five feet deep, fifteen to twenty feet long and about eight feet broad. When the first prisoners reached the far end of the hole the firing commenced. I was just then entering the gate. It seemed that as the men were hit they fell inside the hole.

When I reached the hole the man nearest to me, Private Ward, was hit and I felt a sharp pain in my left knee and fell into the hole. I fell on top of some men who were already lying there and others fell on top of me. Firing continued for a few seconds during which time I noticed Major Ryder sitting inside the hole with his back to the side nearest to the wall. He seemed to me to be very badly hit.[31]

Hauptscharführer Theodor Emke

As the prisoners reached the house front Knöchlein as well as Schrödel remained behind, leaving a clear distance between them and the marching column. As the column was within four to five paces of the right-hand corner of the house and the last prisoners had just reached the left corner, so that the group was completely covering the front of the house, Knöchlein shouted suddenly, 'Fire!' Because of this shout Schrödel and Petri almost simultaneously gave the order, 'Open Fire!' Both guns opened fire immediately. I involuntarily looked towards the guns and noticed Mai and Pollak on the gun nearest to me (Mai in charge of the gun and Pollak No. 1). I was prevented by the hedge from seeing the second gun to the right of the first. I presume, however, that Wenda was No. 1. My attention was naturally taken up by the prisoners who collapsed from right to left and fell forward. The whole business was over in a few seconds.

We were silent during the return march since members of the section as well as me were very much affected.[32]

Private William O'Callaghan

When I saw the men falling I threw myself forward and fell into a slight depression in the ground and in falling stretched my hands out in front of me and sustained a slight flesh wound in the left arm. After the firing stopped I heard my comrades shouting and screaming in their agony. I then heard what sounded to me like the fixing of bayonets and shortly afterwards I heard screams and shrieks from more of my comrades which sounded to me as if they were being bayoneted.[33]

Hauptscharführer Heinrich Wenda, 2nd SS Infantry Regiment

I heard that British soldiers had been shot. As far as I can remember the comrades did not speak much about it. It certainly distressed them all. It was said that the sights had not worked properly and that the shots had therefore gone too low.[34]

Private Albert Pooley

Groans were coming from men lying in the hole and it was at this point that three Germans jumped down into the hole near Major Ryder, evidently for the purpose of finishing off any prisoners still alive with bayonets. These Germans evidently climbed out of the hole again because further shooting then started with revolvers and rifles from the edge of the hole. One of the men beneath me moved and two shots were fired into the heap of bodies, both of which hit me in the left leg. At the sound of a whistle firing ceased and all the Germans appeared to move away.[35]

Unterstürmführer (SS 2nd Lieutenant) Hinrich Schinkel, 13th Company, 2nd SS Infantry Regiment

Meanwhile another two or three men had come up by the victims of the shooting. I do not know who they were. I am almost certain one of them was an officer. I saw first one and then the other bend down and how shortly after, odd shots kept being fired from a carbine or pistol.[36]

In total ninety-seven British soldiers were massacred that day by the Waffen SS.[37] Not all were men from the Royal Norfolks; there were also signallers and gunners killed that day.

The reasons given by the Waffen SS for the massacre were twofold. Firstly they argued that the British had behaved badly by shooting on German soldiers who were responding to white flags of surrender. This is a dangerous argument and simply a distraction from their own crime. After all in any battle there may well be groups of soldiers surrendering while others nearby continue to fight.

However, it is perhaps worth noting that Marshall's arguments about firers and non-firers might come into play here. It did appear that different groups of British soldiers were surrendering at different times. Perhaps what was happening was that the minority of active firers were continuing the battle despite the best efforts of some of the others to surrender. And if the active firers were the ones refusing to surrender then they would clearly be shooting to kill the Germans who might be moving to accept the surrender, causing the resentment on the German side.

Secondly the Waffen SS argued that the British had used dumdum bullets. However, the 0.303-inch bullet could easily cause the sort of damage associated with a dumdum bullet, depending on the way in which it travelled through the human body. And of course not all the SS were agreed on whether the British were using dumdum bullets.

Hauptscharführer August Leitl, 2nd Battalion, 2nd SS Infantry Regiment

I was detailed by Hauptsturmführer [SS Captain] Knöchlein to patrol the battle area with some men and collect our dead. On this search such bullets would have been bound to have fallen into my hands. I myself am a sergeant-artificer and ammunition expert and in this capacity I can say that the dead men, who without exception had been shot in the head because they had been shot from the front while lying on the ground, in several cases had rather large holes in their heads which were caused by the fact that the shot on striking the steel helmet flattened itself at the point and thus caused a larger wound than would have been the case if it had not struck against steel. I can assert this a specialist, and as I personally saw every single German corpse I must have known better than any other member of the company whether or not dumdum bullets were used and I hereby declare that this was not the case.[38]

There was a third factor in the massacre, mentioned at the start of this chapter. And that was the need for the *Totenkopf* to prove itself. If the Waffen SS was to be the elite unit envisaged by Eicke and Himmler then the message would have been victory at all costs.

Obersturmbannführer (SS Lieutenant-Colonel) Paul Werner Hoppe, adjutant to Gruppenführer Eicke

No official pronouncement was made on the subject and thus apparently a deliberate effort was made to keep the circle of those acquainted with the facts as small as possible. From Gruppenführer Eicke's point of view this is understandable when one considers that the reputation and tradition of the *Totenkopf* Division, their proving their mettle as new and young fighting troops, was jeopardised by such action. And it was precisely in order to prove themselves that the *Totenkopf* Division, especially, had to struggle hard, being the junior unit of the Waffen SS.[39]

After the French surrender the *Totenkopf* Division stayed in France. Although it had shown it could massacre ninety-seven men in cold blood, later when stationed in the south of France it also had no hesitation in executing one of its own members who had assaulted a French woman.[40] In a way the massacre of the British soldiers at Le Paradis tells us something else. If soldiers are conditioned to kill, as were the Waffen SS, then perhaps one of the by-products of that willingness to kill is a lowering of the defences against atrocity. This is a factor which is also a problem for modern armies in places like Vietnam and Iraq.

Justice was finally served out to Haupsturmführer Knöchlein on 28 January 1949 when he was hanged at Hamburg by the British military authorities for his crime. Pooley and O'Callaghan, the only two British survivors of the massacre, had been instrumental in convicting him.

Notes

1. Marshall, ch. 6
2. Stephen Bull, *World War II Infantry Tactics – Squad and Platoon*, Osprey, 2004, p. 30

3. Bull, p.42
4. Imperial War Museum, Sound Archive, 8192, transcript, p. 21
5. Hart, ch. 9
6. Brunnegger, p. 18
7. Statement by POW, Le Paradis file on Knöchlein trial, Royal Norfolk Regimental Museum, also National Archives references WO 208/4685, WO 235/571, WO 235/582A, WO 235/790
8. Imperial War Museum, Sound Archive, 8192, transcript, p. 77
9. Imperial War Museum, Sound Archive, 16813
10. Imperial War Museum, Sound Archive, 8192, transcript, pp. 78, 79
11. Imperial War Museum, Sound Archive, 8192, transcript, pp. 85, 86
12. Imperial War Museum, Sound Archive, 17761 quoted in Hart, pp. 53, 54
13. Imperial War Museum, Sound Archive, 8192, transcript, pp. 86–8
14. Cyril Jolly, *The Vengeance of Private Pooley*, Heinemann, 1956, p. 17
15. Imperial War Museum, Sound Archive, 16813
16. *Ibid.*
17. Imperial War Museum, Sound Archive, 10320, transcript pp. 4, 5
18. Lieutenant William Murray-Brown, 2nd Norfolks, *Britannia* magazine, quoted in Hart, p. 59
19. Imperial War Museum, Sound Archive, 16972
20. Statement by POW, Le Paradis file on Knöchlein trial
21. Brunnegger, p. 75
22. Statement by POW, Le Paradis file on Knöchlein trial
23. Brunnegger, pp. 76, 77
24. Statement by POW, Le Paradis file on Knöchlein trial, Sturmbannführer Werner Zorn interview
25. Brunnegger, pp. 77, 78
26. Affidavit by William O'Callaghan, Le Paradis file on Knöchlein trial
27. Affidavit by Albert Pooley, Le Paradis file on Knöchlein trial
28. Affidavit by William O'Callaghan, Le Paradis file on Knöchlein trial
29. Brunnegger, p. 79
30. Statement by POW, Le Paradis file on Knöchlein trial
31. Affidavit by Albert Pooley, Le Paradis file on Knöchlein trial
32. Statement by POW, Le Paradis file on Knöchlein trial
33. Affidavit by William O'Callaghan, Le Paradis file on Knöchlein trial
34. Statement by POW, Le Paradis file on Knöchlein trial
35. Affidavit by Albert Pooley, Le Paradis file on Knöchlein trial
36. Statement by POW, Le Paradis file on Knöchlein trial
37. Hart, p. 71
38. Statement by POW, Le Paradis file on Knöchlein trial
39. Statement by POW, Le Paradis file on Knöchlein trial
40. Brunnegger, pp. 93, 94

CHAPTER 3

Enter the Commandos

The defining symbol of the World War II Commandos was and remains the Fairbairn Sykes Commando knife. But for all the glamour which surrounds this weapon the stark fact is that using it in anger could be a bloody and horrible business.

The knife itself had a 7½-inch blade and early models had a ricasso (a flat area on the blade next to the cross-guard). The early cross-guard was longer than later versions – it was 2¼ inches across and in the shape of an S. Later versions lost the ricasso and the cross-guard was shortened to the familiar shape known today, which helped in mass production. The key difference between this knife and daggers of old was that the FS knife was designed not only to thrust but to cut and slash as well. Despite popular myth, the Fairbairn Sykes Commando knife was not a product of the war but was originally designed and made in the pre-war years in Shanghai.

William Ewart Fairbairn and Eric Anthony Sykes had first met as members of the Shanghai Municipal Police, the force which maintained law and order in the International Settlement on the Shanghai waterfront until World War II. Before joining the police, Fairbairn had come to China as a Royal Marine and had been an enthusiastic member of the RM Bayonet Fighting Team. Later he rose to be Assistant Commissioner of Police and head of the Riot Squad. Sykes was a reserve police officer in charge of the sniper unit.

In 1931 Fairbairn established the Shanghai Police Armoury

under Nikolai Solntseff and it was here that the Fairbairn Sykes knife was first conceived and made. According to Fairbairn's son, Major John Fairbairn, the starting point was a hunting knife and a couple of bayonets.

In 1940 Fairbairn and Sykes returned to England and were immediately recruited by the Special Operations Executive (SOE) – Fairbairn to be chief unarmed and armed instructor to the SOE and the Commandos. Immediately both the SOE and Commandos saw the need for a fighting knife but there were none available. In 1940, at the suggestion of the Chief Inspector of Small Arms, Fairbairn and Sykes paid a visit to the Wilkinson Sword company in London. Although at this stage there were no firm orders for the FS Commando knife, Fairbairn and Sykes managed to persuade John Wilkinson-Latham of Wilkinson Sword to manufacture a quantity of the knives for sale. In order to demonstrate the correct use of the knife, Fairbairn astonished Wilkinson-Latham by suddenly grabbing a ruler and engaging Sykes in a mock knife fight. The knife would be made. For Fairbairn it remained one of his favourite weapons.

Captain W. E. Fairbairn

In close-quarters fighting there is no more deadly weapon than the knife. An entirely unarmed man has no certain defence against it, and, further, merely the sudden flashing of a knife is frequently enough to strike fear into your opponent, causing him to lose confidence and surrender ... There are many positions in which the knife can be carried. Selection of this position depends on individual preferences based on length of arm, thickness of body, etc. The following considerations, however, should always be borne in mind. A quick draw (essential in knife fighting) can not be accomplished unless the sheath is firmly secured to the clothing or equipment. Moreover, speed on the draw can only be accomplished by constant daily practice. The author favours a concealed position, using the left hand, for in close-quarters fighting, the element of surprise is the chief ingredient of success.[1]

Major R. F. 'Henry' Hall MC, The Dorset Regiment

Now the Fairbairn Sykes knife. Fairbairn and Sykes developed the knife in Shanghai – incidentally they never mentioned Shanghai at all at Inverailort, I didn't discover they had come from Shanghai until years afterwards.

When they got back to England they went into Wilkinson's in Pall Mall and got hold of one of the directors and explained exactly what they wanted and what they wanted was a 7½-inch blade made from one piece of metal right from the tip of the haft right down to the point and then with the guard put on and then the handle, the grip. The grip was to be checkered so that you could hold it whether it was wet or bloody.

Each was individually hand-made; sharpened and honed so that your knife should be able to cut a piece of paper. I bought mine, one of the original Number 1 knives, in Pall Mall for thirteen shillings and sixpence. Later on they developed various other models for economy purposes. They only made 2,500 original No. 1 shiny knives – now worth over £3,000 each!

The Fairbairn Sykes knife is straight. If you are using it for slashing cuts you use it like a paintbrush, stroking it so that when the blade hits the surface you are trying to cut, it cuts at an angle, on the principle of the curve of the samurai sword.

You held the knife between the thumb and forefinger just behind the guard. The knife was perfectly balanced and so you could throw it from hand to hand. As you carried it in your left-hand pocket, if you were right-handed you could draw it with your left hand, throw it to your right hand and catch it quite easily, no problem at all.

The guard was not to stop the other chap's knife from cutting your hand but to stop your hand going down and being cut on the blade when you made a thrusting blow.

On the battlefield you probably had your boots on for three or four weeks and you were filthy, dirty, mucky and probably splashed with blood and the last thing you wanted to do was to draw any more blood and so the favourite blow that Fairbairn and Sykes taught was the sub-clavian thrust. They taught many other blows, vulnerable points and so on, but the snag is that with a man with equipment on or doing it in the dark you just don't know what equipment he has got on and you can't find a vulnerable point or somewhere to stick the knife.

With the sub-clavian thrust it is much simpler – the chap will be dead in about – well the book says three seconds – it's difficult to say when you do it yourself but I reckon about five seconds, without drawing any blood at all.

Whenever I approached an enemy soldier I would have my gun in my right pocket and my knife in my left pocket. Then when I got to within five or six yards I would draw my knife with my left hand and throw it across to my right hand and then approach the chap and give him the sub-clavian thrust.[2]

There were two principal training centres for the Commandos and other soldiers who needed specialist instruction. The first was at Lochailort but this was not as well known as the one at Achnacarry where most Commandos had their training.

The Special Training Centre at Lochailort began life in 1940 after an abortive attempt to raise a ski battalion, the 5th Battalion, The Scots Guards, to fight in northern Europe. However, the mission never took off and instead a couple of officers retreated to the Scottish home of Captain Bill Stirling who had been a member of the battalion. There they came up with the idea of a training school to teach irregular warfare. Stirling managed to interest his cousin, Lord Lovat, in the idea and between them they managed to requisition a large area around Lochailort for the scheme.

The instructors were all to become well known and read like a roll call of famous names during World War II – Lord Lovat, Brigadier Mike Calvert, Colonel Spencer Chapman, Major Peter Kemp, the Stirling brothers, plus Fairbairn and Sykes, newly arrived from Shanghai.

Each course was made up of thirty officers and sergeants and took three weeks. Lochailort was a pioneer in the type of conditioning explored in Chapter 1 and a key part of the course was that anyone not up to scratch was straight back to their unit. Actually arriving at the training camp was an ordeal in itself.

Major R. F. 'Henry' Hall MC

One day I was ordered to go and see our commanding officer and when I arrived in his office I found a sergeant, John Davidson, there as well, whom I had never seen before. We were told that he had selected us to go on an 'Advanced Assault Course' in Scotland and that we were to pass it with distinction for the Honour of the Regiment.

In early 1941 we went to Inverailort in the Western Highlands of Scotland. We went up there by train from Canterbury all the way to Fort William and then we got on the little puffer train that used to go from Fort William to Mallaig, now called *The Jacobite*.

We were sitting there comfortably in the train when all of a sudden the train came to an abrupt halt. We were all thrown forwards, our kitbags came off the luggage racks and the place was a shambles. Then we realised the train was under fire and that explosions were going off all around us. Then instructors leapt out of holes in the ground and shouted, 'Get out of the train! Get out of the train! Grab your kit and follow us!'

So of course we all scrambled out, grabbing everything we had and we were doubled, ran all the way to the big house clutching our belongings. We were shot at all the way as we were running the mile and half to the big house and when we arrived there we were shown some Nissen huts on the lawn and told, 'Find yourselves a bed, that's where you're going to live.'

The ablutions were outside, also on the lawn, just a plain wooden bench with taps, cold water only and when we were lucky enough to sleep in the Nissen huts we had to clean, wash and shave ourselves in the morning with cold water whether it was raining or not. When we did feed, we fed in the big house.[3]

The big house was Inverailort Castle which had its own links with irregular warfare, having been used by Bonnie Prince Charlie. The house was the headquarters and the Nissen huts housed the trainees. The courses were not all standard – there were general courses and there were specialist courses, for example in demolition and explosives. But the trainees on the general courses gained the most because they were taught by the specialist band of instructors.

Major R. F. 'Henry' Hall MC

We had lectures in Nissen huts, but these huts were located on the islands of the River Ailort so that every lecture we attended we were wet either up to the ankles, the knees, the waist or perhaps even the chest, depending on the height of the water.

We had lectures in map reading – they insisted on very precise map reading, probably five to ten yard error only was acceptable – on nutrition, on hygiene, on living off the land, stalking, night work, explosives and explosive devices, fuses and so on, timing devices, booby traps and demolitions of anything, bridges, tanks, cratering roads, blowing down trees, the lot.

On the practical side we had demonstrations of all the things I have mentioned. We practised camouflage, sniping, stalking by day and particularly by night, demolitions and bridge demolition on the Glenfinnan viaduct, living off the land, told what was edible and what was not edible and one occasion we stood round a fire where something was being cooked and then we were asked to take a bite of what had been cooked – we were then told they were rats – hygiene, particularly your teeth, keeping your teeth clean after every meal (anything will do to clean your teeth, a stick of heather or anything like that), how to carry out one's natural functions in the field – you obviously can't stand up or squat down.

Every week we went to the top of An Stac, the highest local mountain, and back, up the wall at the back of the house and then back down again, which was the origin of the Commandos going up Ben Nevis every week and the SAS [Special Air Service] doing their endurance trials on the Brecon Beacons.

We started off from Inverailort one day over the hills and attacked Lettermorar on the banks of Loch Morar. We practised assault landings on the beach near the big house all under fire. We had an interesting exercise – we were taken down past Fort William and across the loch to a place near Corran and then we had to make our way from there back to the big house. It was a night exercise and we had to get across Loch Shiel. They did provide us with a small rowing boat, with only one oar. It was a timed exercise, and if anybody didn't get back in the prescribed time they were sent back to their unit immediately.

The final grand exercise was the attack on Skye. We were taken at dusk one evening in assault boats from Inverailort across to Skye. We landed on the west coast of Skye, blew a gap in the barbed wire with bangalore torpedoes and then crossed the island and attacked Portree (it was raining all the time). Having attacked Portree we advanced down Skye attacking various places on the way, eventually attacking Broadford and ending up near Kyle where we got on a destroyer and were brought back to Inverailort and landed on the jetty probably about midday the following day.

There was no psychology as such taught at Inverailort, but everything was done with such confidence and such expertise and devil-may-care atmosphere, all the instructors were wonderful chaps, you came away from everything feeling that you knew the lot and you were better than anybody else and that the other chap was dead before you even saw him. Anyone who showed any sign of weakness was sent back to his unit immediately.

We were monitored and assessed all the time and anybody who showed any lack of confidence, lack of trying to do something, any idleness or anything of that sort, was straight off the course and back to his unit.

We were wet, tired, hungry, being shot at all the time, exhausted and it was really a test of endurance and absorbing the knowledge that was given to us.[4]

As mentioned earlier, one of the interesting elements of Lochailort emphasised by Major Hall is the fact that students could be and were thrown off the course for any real or imagined weakness. This was also a feature of the Commando training at Achnacarry and was crucial to the success of units like the Commandos which were to be made up only of soldiers who could, and would, kill. This is also a feature of modern volunteer armies – recruits who do not measure up and perform are rejected and this is a crucial part of getting close to 100 per cent of men being active participants in a battle. However, this was not generally realised in World War II and conscripted men continued to be used in the front line as infantry without anyone realising how ineffective this policy was.

Apart from the knife-fighting skills mentioned earlier there were two other elements of close quarter fighting which were taught at Lochailort. Firstly there was unarmed combat and secondly pistol shooting, both of which areas benefited from the specialist knowledge Fairbairn and Sykes had acquired in Shanghai.

In the pre-war years Shanghai was probably the most violent city the world has ever seen, either before or since. The Shanghai Municipal Police Force, which patrolled a small waterfront area around the docks, seized more illegal drugs each year than all the American police forces combined. Murder, kidnapping, corruption and drugs were all commonplace and the police routinely had to arrest criminals armed with guns, knives and an expert knowledge of the Chinese and Japanese martial arts.

After Fairbairn had an encounter with a gang of criminals in 1908 in which he was beaten up and left for dead, he enrolled at a jiu-jitsu school and became the first foreigner outside Japan to gain the black belt from the Kodokan Jiu-jitsu University of Tokyo. He also trained under Tsai Ching Tung who taught martial arts to the Empress of China's bodyguard. As a result of this expertise Fairbairn took on the training of all police recruits and used his experience in dealing with the thugs and bullies of the Shanghai waterfront to teach them unarmed tactics.

In May 1925 Fairbairn was given the job of dealing with the Shanghai riots which threatened to overwhelm the city after the police fired on a mob. His answer was the Shanghai Reserve Unit which successfully contained all subsequent violent disorder without any further shots being fired.

In 1925 Fairbairn wrote *Defendu* (also known as *Scientific Self Defence*) which was the name he gave to his system of unarmed tactics. It quickly became the standard police manual for the Shanghai, Singapore and Hong Kong Police Forces.

By the 1930s Fairbairn's fame had spread and he extended his teaching of unarmed tactics and combat to units of the United States Marine Corps in the Far East.[5] Fairbairn's syllabus of unarmed combat for the British Commandos, SOE and other students at Lochailort, and later in America, was designed to be short, deadly and effective.

Major R. F. 'Henry' Hall MC

On the first morning after our arrival we met 'Dan' Fairbairn and 'Bill' Sykes. We were taken into the hall of the big house and suddenly at the top of the stairs appeared a couple of dear old gentlemen (we later discovered one was fifty-six and the other fifty-eight). Both were wearing spectacles and both were dressed in battledress with just a plain webbing belt. They walked to the top of the stairs and fell, tumbling, tumbling down the stairs and ended up at the bottom in the battle crouch position with a handgun in one hand and a fighting knife in the other. A shattering experience for all of us.[6]

Colonel Rex Applegate, Office of Strategic Services

I first met Fairbairn when he came down from Canada and we soon sized each other up, a lieutenant and a captain. That evening there was a demonstration for assembled COI dignitaries in the mess hall building. He called me out on stage and said, 'I want you to attack me.' The thought of a 28-year-old 230-pounder going against a 57-year-old 160-pounder was incredible to me. He continued, 'Just like you were going to kill me.' I let out a roar and went for him and wound up sailing through the air into the audience. I had been in some bar room brawls and held my own, but it got my attention.[7]

Lieutenant George Langelaan, SOE

Off duty his conversation was limited to two words: yes and no. I never once saw him pick up a newspaper or open a book. All his interest, all his knowledge, all his intelligence – and he was intelligent – concentrated on one subject and one subject only: fighting. His knowledge of anatomy was surprising, though, apart from the main organs of the human body, he had never attempted to find out the names of various bones or muscles and throughout his short, jerky explanations, he would merely refer to 'this bone' or 'that muscle' and point it out or touch it with his finger.[8]

Major R. F. 'Henry' Hall MC

Fairbairn was the elder of the two. He was about five feet ten, lean faced and lean bodied, a tough leathery looking man, a taciturn character. He never spoke very much, except to say, 'Stick a knife in here'' or 'Hit him here" or 'Put your thumb in his eye', or whatever. He kept himself to himself and I think he considered himself to be a little better than Sykes.

Sykes was a much more gregarious character, slightly shorter than Fairbairn, average build, certainly not on the lean side, he looked more like a bishop than anything else. He was easy to talk to, a pleasant character. One of the things he did for me – I asked him one day about sharpening my fighting knife – he said, 'Come up to my room, I'll hone it for you.' Which he did. Two completely different characters, they hated each other's guts but they worked together as a wonderful team and they both taught exactly the same things.

Their speciality was close combat fighting and silent killing. They had learnt their trade on the waterfront of International Shanghai. They had absolutely no respect for the Geneva Convention. They said, 'If you think our methods are not cricket, remember that Hitler does not play this game!'[9]

Captain W. E. Fairbairn

There will be some who will be shocked by the methods advocated here. To them I say, 'In War you cannot afford the luxury of squeamishness. Either you kill or capture, or you will be captured and killed. We've got to be tough to win and we've got to be ruthless – tougher and more ruthless than our enemies.'[10]

Major R. F. 'Henry' Hall MC

First of all they taught how to fall – a continuation of their falling down the stairs – they taught handgun and knife work and neck breaking. Now, when you are attacking somebody the clothing that they are wearing and their equipment must be considered. For example if a fellow is wearing a greatcoat you can't kick him in the parts because the blow won't have any effect. You've got to hit him somewhere else.

If you suspect that someone is wearing body armour you can't stick a knife into his chest, although the favourite place for sticking knives in, taught by Fairbairn and Sykes, does work even with body armour. We were taught releases. If you are grabbed by somebody from the back, front, side or whatever, how to get out of his grip.

We were taught 'come-along grips' – how to take a prisoner along safely without him being able to escape. We were taught the use of sticks, anything from four inches to six feet long; a four-inch stick is just held in the hand and you can strike with the end of the stick and give a chap a nasty knock with it.

And of course a stick can be anything, an actual stick, a rifle, something you pick up in a farmyard. A clipboard for example is a stick – you can strike somebody with it across the side of the neck, on the head, on the nose, under the nose, you can hit him in the parts, you can hit him in the solar plexus, almost anything is a stick. A stick is always held in two hands as exemplified by Robin Hood and Little John.

They taught the use of coshes – they preferred the spring type best – longbows, crossbows, catapults, garrotting, with anything that happens to be handy – a scarf, string, wire, anything you like; the use of shovels – every good soldier always carries either a pick or a shovel and you simply use it to chop off a chap's head, or whack him on the shoulder, or just use it like a battleaxe.

You can do the same with a tin hat, just whip the tin hat off and use the side of it to hit him in the face or whatever part happens to be handy . . . how to tie up a man – tying his wrists with a good old fashioned sailor's handcuff knot and they also taught a way of tying the fellow's wrists behind his back and pulling his ankles up and tying them with the same piece of cord and then putting a loop round his neck so that if he struggled he strangled himself.

They also taught the grapevine where a fellow is fixed to a thin pole by the forced bending of both legs round the pole, then he will lose his grip, fall backwards and eventually kill himself.

All these actions and holds were sometimes demonstrated by the two of them or with somebody else acting as a stooge and then after that they were practised on your own, supervised by Fairbairn and Sykes, and if you did anything wrong you were severely ticked off and very often thrown about a bit and shown how to do it properly. It was one-to-one instruction on how to fall correctly or how to impose a particular grip or a particular release or how to use a particular instrument in the correct manner to achieve the result required. It was a personal touch and personally done. If you didn't show keenness or enthusiasm you were thrown off the course.[11]

Lieutenant George Langelaan

We learned how to roll downstairs easily alone, or with an opponent so that he takes all the bumps, how to jam people in doors or behind heavy furniture, how, when pursued, to slam and reopen a door so that the person chasing you takes the edge of it full on, [choosing] which form of counter-attack [is] required necessitates a cool head, a good ear and nice timing . . . by the time we finished our training, I would have willingly tackled any man, whatever his strength, size or ability.[12]

Lieutenant Ernest van Maurik, SOE Instructor, Czechoslovak Section[13]

Unarmed combat was taught by two ex-Shanghai Policemen, Sykes and Fairbairn. Sykes played the leading role and although a hefty man he had the face and manner of a benevolent clergyman. But when he caught you in a hold or demonstrated how to disable if not to kill a man there was nothing benevolent about him. One dodge which I felt sometimes perhaps might be useful was how to escape from someone who had taken you prisoner and then made you walk, holding a gun to your back. You had to swing round unexpectedly encircling your captor's arm with your own so that, assuming he had time to fire, the bullet passed harmlessly behind your back, simultaneously putting the man out of action with one, if not two of Sykes's and Fairbairn's fancy tricks. Practising this amongst ourselves we found that the captor invariably fired too late. The corollary to this, of course, was finding yourself in the role of captor: you must always hold your gun a foot or more away from your prisoner's back. Don't copy the way they do things in Hollywood, said Sykes, scornfully.[14]

Able Seaman Albert Cattell, Royal Naval Commando G

He [Fairbairn] was about forty- or fifty-odd then and he threw us about like rag dolls. He gets a gun, bullet, Webley .45 and says to stick it in his back, 'Now when I move, you pull the trigger.' Sodding mad he is I thought. 'That's an order. As soon as you see me move you pull the trigger.'

I said, 'I'll blow your spine apart.'

He said, 'You'll be too late.'

I thought, he'll never get out of this.

'What I'm trying to demonstrate is you never push a gun into the enemy's back, you never get that close.' And as soon as he moved I pulled the trigger, my arm was over there, bang. We couldn't fathom out how he did it, he did it with all of us. The trick was, before your brain could get to your trigger finger, the signal, he'd turn round, if you were right-handed he'd turn to the left, so as he came round his left arm knocked that away, his right hand at your throat or your eyes. If the bloke with the gun is left-handed you do it opposite – you don't knock the gun across his body, that would kill him because it would take a second or so and the trigger finger would work. So you knock it away from the body. We fancied ourselves, in our twenties, fit as fiddles, hard as nails and this chap was grey haired, close cropped. With stubble. He chucked us about. He was old enough to be our father but he was fit.[15]

Captain W. E. Fairbairn

I should like in conclusion to give a word of warning. Almost every one of these methods, applied vigorously and without restraint, will result, if not in the death, then certainly in the maiming of your opponent. Extreme caution, then, should be exercised in practice, care being taken never to give a blow with full force or grip with maximum pressure. But, once closed with your enemy, give every ounce of effort you can muster, and victory will be yours.[16]

Although unarmed combat did not in fact take up much time there was an effect on all those who took part in Fairbairn's training, whether delivered by himself personally or by the cadre of trainers which he set up. Fairbairn noted an increase in general confidence and ability to carry out duties beyond those for which a simple knowledge of unarmed combat was required.

Captain W. E. Fairbairn

In initiating training in close-contact fighting, 'gutter' methods in offensive and defensive tactics were taught to personnel assigned for such training. With the building up of a natural confidence in the ability of each man to perform duties of this nature, their training began to show results and their efficiency continuously increased. From reports from overseas theatres it has been noted that, irrespective of whether or not the personnel who have undergone this type of training make use of it in the missions to which they are assigned, the mere fact that they have been so trained and have been imbued with the confidence which comes with it, [means that] their efficiency in other types of combat operations, and their morale, is greatly increased.[17]

> Pistol shooting was the other area of speciality for Fairbairn and Sykes. They had been quick to realise the effect that taking students away from the range and into real-life situations could have on their ability to fight well in battle. They were well qualified to give this instruction – the Shanghai Police Force had recorded no fewer than 666 armed encounters with criminals in a period of twelve and a half years.[18]
>
> Fairbairn and Sykes introduced the idea of instinctive shooting to the British and US forces in World War II – the idea that with the pistol you point and shoot instead of aim and fire, much like the fast draw cowboys of the American West. But this is an idea which has not survived World War II – look at any army or police force today and they use the two-handed grip on a pistol and they take careful aim before firing. Fairbairn and Sykes would have none of this.

Captain W. E. Fairbairn and Captain E. A. Sykes

We must consider the essential points which emerge from our analysis. These appear to be three in number and we should set them out in the following order:

1. Extreme speed, both in drawing and firing.
2. Instinctive, as opposed to deliberate aim.
3. Practice under conditions which approximate as nearly as possible to actual fighting conditions.

In commenting on the first essential, let us say that the necessity for speed is vital and can never be sufficiently emphasised. The average shooting affray is a matter of split seconds. If you take much longer than a third of a second to fire your first shot, you will not be the one to tell the newspapers about it. It is literally a matter of the quick and the dead. Take your choice.

Instinctive aiming, the second essential, is an entirely logical consequence of the extreme speed to which we attach so much importance. That is so for the simple reason that there is no time for any of the customary aids to accuracy. If reliance on these aids has become habitual, so much the worse for you if you are shooting to live. There is no time, for instance, to put yourself into some special stance or to align the sights of the pistol and any attempt to do so places you at the mercy of a quicker opponent. In any case the sights would be of little use if the light were bad and none at all if it were dark, as might easily happen . . . Everyone is familiar with the fact that he can point his forefinger accurately at an object at which he happens to be looking. It is just as easy, moreover, to do so without raising the hand so high as the level of the eyes . . . We cannot claim that the system produces nail-driving marksmanship, but that is not what we look for. We want the ability to hit with extreme speed man-sized targets at very short ranges under the difficult circumstances which have been outlined already.[19]

SOE Syllabus of Lectures

Picture in your mind the circumstances under which you might be using the pistol. Take as an example a raid on an enemy occupied house in darkness. Firstly consider your approach. You will never walk boldly up to the house and stroll in as though you were paying a social call. On the contrary your approach will be stealthy. You will be keyed up and excited, nervously alert for danger from whichever direction it may come. You will find yourself *instinctively* crouching; your body balanced on the balls of your feet in a position from which you can move swiftly in any direction. You make your entry into the house and start searching for the enemy moving along passages, perhaps up or down stairs, listening and feeling for any signs of danger. Suddenly, on turning a corner, you come face to face with the enemy. Without a second's hesitation you must fire and kill him before he has a chance to kill you.

From this picture the facts are clear:

a) You will always fire from the crouch position – you will *never* be in an upright position

b) You have *no time* to adopt any fancy stance when killing with speed

c) You have *no time* to use the sights

Any method of firing which does not allow for all these factors is useless. Gun fighting at close quarters is a question of split seconds.

The best method of firing under these circumstances is by what is called 'instinctive pointing' . . . the natural way that any man points at an object when he is *concentrating*.[20]

Lieutenant John K. Singlaub, SOE

Sykes's method of instinctive firing involved creeping around a blacked-out cellar and shooting at moving targets, illuminated by the muzzle flash of our first shot. Once we could hit the targets with absolutely no hesitation, Major Sykes pronounced us 'improving'.[21]

Colonel Rex Applegate

My first meeting with Sykes was short on conversation. Sykes outfitted me with a brand new Sten gun and a Webley revolver and had me run through a combat course in a medieval Scottish castle. He had installed a comprehensive combat range complete with targets in German uniforms that fired blanks at the trainee, booby traps and other devices.[22]

Sergeant Bill Pilkington, Close Combat Instructor

Captain Sykes had equal authority and great ability. He was the finest rifle shot I have ever seen, as well as being very good with the 0.45-inch Colt 1911 automatic pistol. Both officers were very skilled in unarmed combat also. I did teach a few hundred people the killing arts and I am grateful for the training I experienced with Fairbairn and Sykes, they were really masters of their craft.[23]

Major R. F. 'Henry' Hall MC

Fairbairn and Sykes also taught the use of the handgun. They favoured the 9-mm Browning. Now if you hit a man with a 9-mm bullet, it will not stop him. If you use a 0.45-inch or anything larger, such as a shotgun, that will stop him dead, maybe blow him backwards. With a 9-mm round you need two shots to stop a man dead and so Fairbairn and Sykes taught the Fairbairn Sykes 'double tap'.

You draw your handgun, two shots, pom–pom, and the chap is dead. They carried their handguns in the right-hand trouser pocket. The normal opening of the trouser pocket is a little bit higher than where your hand naturally hangs and so they modified the trouser pocket so that your hand could go into the pocket with your arm at its normal length. The holster of the handgun was sewn into the inside of the pocket. The inside of the pocket was sewn to the trouser so that when you drew the handgun it came out without snagging on the pocket.

They carried the fighting knife in exactly the same way, in the left-hand trouser pocket. I carried my handgun and fighting knife that way during the whole of the war.

As I mentioned they taught us to use the 'double tap' with the handgun. We were not taught to hold the gun out at arm's length or with two hands but to draw the gun and hold it tucked into your navel with the gun pointing straight ahead so that wherever you looked your gun moved round towards the target you were looking at. So you either drew your gun straight into your navel, pom–pom, the chap was dead, or you advanced as I did on one occasion in the mystery shooting house that 'Dan' Fairbairn had made at Inverailort – with my handgun drawn, held into my navel, firing at the various targets that appeared here and there.

With that particular exercise which was supervised by Dan Fairbairn, if you were not a good shot, you were out, back to your unit. One thing they did emphasise, particularly with the handgun, was to count the number of shots you had fired so that you were never caught with an empty magazine and therefore unable to get a round off at your enemy.[24]

Lieutenant Ernest van Maurik

I had also seen Bates {an instructor} in action at Arisaig House. He was good and had been trained as an instructor by Sykes and Fairbairn and therefore taught their system. For our work these experts recommended a 0.38-inch Colt as reliable, not too clumsy in the pocket or shoulder holster and with sufficient stopping power for close work. Just as you can point instinctively at a given object, so you shot with your Colt rapidly and instinctively, forgetting any idea of deliberate aim. You fired two quick shots at each target just to make sure you well and truly stopped your opponent. If you relaxed and followed instructions it worked remarkably well.[25]

The famous shooting house invented by Fairbairn and Sykes was to be adopted all over the world by units such as the SAS as well as police forces and other army units. As an aid to conditioning soldiers for street fighting and for battle it was invaluable – it was a real situation and the targets were all life-size and dressed in the same way as the enemy.

SOE Syllabus of Lectures

HOUSE 'A'

This house comprises one large room with two doors.

Three targets represent Nazi officers sitting round a table. The table is situated in the corner farthest away from the main door. All the targets are hinged so that they can fall backwards out of sight. In front of the main door there is a partition extending into the centre of the room and a wire is stretched from the wall behind the partition around the end of it to a position on the wall on the right of the main doorway. A running target is attached to this wire.

The operation of all the targets is by means of a series of weights actuated by a 'master' weight on a shelf behind the door.

As the student attacks into the room through the main door he sees the three targets sitting round the table and he proceeds to 'kill' them. As he is in the process of doing this, the running target races round the corner of the partition straight towards him and simultaneously the three targets at the table disappear from view.

The whole action from the time of entry has taken approximately three to three and a half seconds and the student has had the task of 'killing' four targets during that period.

The lessons brought out are: firstly the necessity for sheer speed, and secondly, the necessity to utilise to the fullest those first few seconds when your opponent is motionless through shock of surprise.[26]

Apart from House A there was also House B and House C and the student might then find that in moving between the three he would be called upon to shoot running targets which would appear and disappear very quickly. Taken together with the other training at Lochailort it all added up to battle training which was ideal for the conditioning process.

Major R. F. 'Henry' Hall MC

I think the great advantage of the advanced assault course at Inverailort was that it gave you so much confidence. You knew so many more tricks of the trade and methods of attack, demolition and causing havoc and destruction that you became super-confident.

Whatever you did, you did it automatically, subconsciously. The answer to whatever attack you were up against would be an instinctive reaction. You didn't have to think about things, you just took it as something as natural as drinking a cup of tea or making a sandwich – you would do it instinctively, just like driving a car. As regards your emotions when you stick a knife into a chap, you just don't have any because, as I say, it's just like driving a car or making a cup of tea.[27]

> Having graduated from Lochailort, officers such as Henry Hall were sent back to their units to disseminate the same type of training which had made such an impact in Scotland. This led to pockets of outstanding practice being established in main-stream infantry units of the British Army, although such methods were never going to take over the whole Army, especially when they involved practices which were unorthodox, to say the least.

Major R. F. 'Henry' Hall MC

When Sergeant Davidson and I returned to Canterbury I was made battalion bombing officer. In World War I any officer who conducted trench raids was given that title, I was told I was to command a battalion battle patrol. Our commanding officer, Harold Matthews, had selected three experienced corporals and thirty men for the patrol.

Our first task was to train and teach them all we had learnt at Inverailort to the commanding officer's satisfaction. After training was completed he tested us by doing all our demolitions and dirty tricks himself!

We had each been issued with a bicycle and a mass-produced blackened Fairbairn Sykes fighting knife. Sergeant Davidson and I had been issued with an escape compass. My blackened knife and compass are in the British Resistance Organisation Museum in Suffolk. My No. 1 knife was taken by the RAMC when I was wounded!

We also had gun cotton, 808 [explosive], primers, detonators, safety fuse, cordtex, time pencils and all types of switches. We were administered as an ordinary infantry platoon and part of a rifle company, but I was in command, not the company commander.

Our first task was to get to know Kent by heart – we went off for days on end exploring every nook and cranny, living off the land. I was then given our operational tasks which were:

1. A secret one – to go to ground if the enemy invaded and then, on my own initiative, cause as much havoc against troops and communications and dumps as possible, our true role. We never had any holes in the ground like the Resistance Organisation had – simply because I'd never heard of them because they were so secret.

2. Our second task was to act as the enemy on battalion or brigade exercises, to test the security of Headquarters and dumps and to test the vulnerability of communications in the brigade area.

3. A propaganda role. We practised on a mock landing craft on the beach near Deal for a raid on Dieppe and were encouraged to talk about our 'raid' in pubs and public places.

We had a wonderful time swanning about Kent doing just what I wanted us to do, improving our training and perfecting our techniques for these tasks. We gave demonstrations of our skills to battalions in our brigade and to various training schools.

Then one day I was ordered to do an exercise umpired by our brigade. We landed at dusk on a remote beach near Herne Bay and had to rendezvous with an 'agent' at a map reference (in an allotment hut near Ashford) with a battalion in our way to stop us. We were given orders by the agent to attack a farm below Charing Hill at dawn, lay up during the day and get back the next night, again through a battalion, back to the beach where we had landed.

All went well. After a few days I was told by Harold Matthews that I had won the brigade battle patrol competition! Up to that time I had no idea there were any others anywhere. I still don't know how many others there were – I never met nor had anything to do with any, nor heard of any. But each battalion must have had one.

I carried on learning more about Kent, giving demonstrations, testing security, etc. and one day I was told to meet an officer at a map reference

(Norman Field, I learnt just a few years ago) who told me he commanded the XII Corps Observation Unit and we were to lay on a demonstration for 130 Brigade, which we did near a gravel pit (which I used for grenade work) near Canterbury. He then asked me to help him train his men in dirty tricks; I would meet unknown men at map references at night for several months.

So things went on very happily for me and we achieved a high standard of efficiency. I had introduced the use of a bird call which I used in Kent instead of a whistle and in action to identify ourselves when returning through our own lines, also a Totem – a six foot holly pole with a brass jug which we had pinched from a pub in Sandwich and my whole patrol had scratched their names on it. On top of the pole was the skull of a cow!

I had learnt the *haka* when umpiring a Maori battalion on Salisbury Plain so I modified it into a Dorset/Maori war cry and used it as our war cry – it went, 'Te na ta tong ata, cora cora, comity comity Yaaaaaaaaaaaaaaaahhhhhh!!!!!'

We used it in Kent and in action as a normal war cry, when the enemy looked up to see what was going on you could shoot him, as a hoax war cry to keep them on their toes, very useful at night. Just a few men, or small groups spread over a wide area, to disturb the enemy's rest.[28]

Meanwhile, back in Scotland, Fairbairn and Sykes continued to teach at Lochailort until the centre closed and they went their separate ways. However, the training they had laid down continued at Lochailort's more famous successor, the Combined Basic Training Centre at Achnacarry, home to the Commandos and the US Rangers. The World War II Commandos were to continue this early tradition of battle conditioning, one of the key elements in producing soldiers who are both ready and able to kill.

Achnacarry itself was the hereditary seat of the Clan Cameron, further east from Lochailort and just eighteen miles from Ben Nevis, whose summit was one of the final challenges for the Commando trainees. The training centre started life in early 1942 under the command of Lieutenant-Colonel Charles Vaughan, a veteran of World War I and the Coldstream Guards in which he had been regimental sergeant-major. Vaughan set the standard for the training. He was concerned not just to produce fighting Commandos but he was also keen to ensure their moral fitness and general disposition as first-class parade soldiers. Indeed even going to the pub was frowned upon in this push for clean-living Commandos.[29]

In his introductory address to new arrivals he was keen to make them understand that he did not want anyone who went to pubs and got into fights, 'Give them two pints of beer and the smell of a barmaid's apron and they'll fight anyone. We don't want them, we don't need them, we won't have them.'[30]

Unlike modern soldiers, who face bawling out as well as bullying behaviour designed to desensitise them to violence and killing, the Commandos at Achnacarry were put under a regime where instructors pushed them hard but were prepared to help, rather than bully them. Lord Lovat's philosophy for the Commandos was simple – officers and NCOs relied on leadership to achieve results.[31] James Dunning, a former instructor at Achnacarry states, 'No matter how hard the training or how frustrated and exasperated the instructors were, they never "lost their bottle" or became sadistic. At Achnacarry Charlie Vaughan would never have allowed or tolerated it.'[32]

Achnacarry was also to see another development which is still used today in the British Army – milling. This was a scenario where two opposing teams of ten men attacked each other without weapons. The two teams were paired off against each other by weight and then each pair was put into the ring with only one instruction – Attack![33] This was different to a boxing match in several respects. Firstly there were no rules, the winner was whoever landed the most strikes on the target area on the top half of the opponent's body in sixty seconds. Secondly the audience were encouraged to yell their encouragement, unlike normal Army boxing where the onlookers had to contain their support.

Surprisingly no one was seriously hurt during these bouts and they were found to be a useful way to encourage aggressiveness within the rules set by the Commandos. After all, what the Commandos needed were men who could fight and kill but only within the limits laid down by their commanders. To assist with this process Vaughan also insisted that the men spend time on drill, turn-out and personal administration – the last thing he wanted was for anyone to think that the Commandos were anything like the popular myth that they were savages. As Vaughan said to a group of visiting reporters, 'I would like you to tell your public that we are not a band of "cut-throats".'[34]

This provides for an interesting contrast to today's soldiers. The Commandos managed to become effective fighters with really only one of the factors identified by Colonel Grossman and discussed in Chapter 1 – conditioning. They did not indulge in the other two, desensitisation and denial, and yet still managed to become conditioned killers. Clearly this indicates that the most important part of training for a soldier is the conditioning for battle and in this area the Commandos were second to none.

They had already realised that banging away on the ranges against bullseye targets was a waste of time unless the Army was in the business of training competition shooters. Therefore the Commandos set up firing exercises against lifelike human targets or parts of targets. Out went the lying down on the range, in came realistic scenarios resembling battlefield conditions. And even in cases where the range was the only place they could practise they improvised by using metal plates as targets which pinged when hit.

As exercises developed, eventually the totally realistic exercise was brought into play. Alongside the firing came being fired at.

Colonel Rex Applegate

A spectator watching one of the famous British assault courses in which live charges, live grenades and live rounds of ammunition are fired around the man participating in the course, asks himself if he would actually be able to take such a course. From the spectator's viewpoint, it looks very spectacular and the element of danger thrown in by live ammunition striking close to his feet, charges bursting around him and all the other real battle effects is very impressive.

This same spectator, once he enters such a course, is so intent on firing his own weapon, throwing his own grenades and reaching his objective that he does not heed or notice the various charges bursting around him while he is going through the course. In a large way this explains a soldier's reaction in combat. He is so intent on his own job or mission that, after the initial effect, he is not bothered and does not think about what is going on around him.[35]

The live-firing exercises at Achnacarry were famous for their realism. As one Commando said to the then Major Peter Young during the Dieppe raid, 'This is nearly as bad as Achnacarry.'[36] However, not all live-firing exercises conducted by the Army as a whole in World War II were as realistic. Major Tom Bird DSO, MC, recalled that, 'There is nothing new about exercises with live ammo, we had them all the time when I was at the Barnard School of Infantry in 1944. It was dangerous but not much like the real thing.'[37]

Why did the Commandos produce such lifelike exercises? Perhaps it was in the attention to detail, especially on the opposed landing exercises — the whine of the Stukas on loud-speakers, clusters of thunderflashes going off simultaneously, firing and bayoneting dummies against a backdrop of explosions and fixed Bren fire. The opposed landings also had another purpose — to reinforce to the Commandos that the overwhelming principle when attacking an enemy coast was the need to get off the beach as quickly as possible.[38]

The syllabus of training at Achnacarry had a very definite bias towards weapons which comprised nearly one third of all training conducted there. Fieldcraft took up thirteen per cent, unarmed combat and ropework ten per cent each, with the remaining third spent on boating, map reading, speed marches, night training, demolition and drill.[39] Achnacarry provided the opportunity for trainees to get to grips not only with all the available British weaponry but also foreign arms as well and this was a popular part of the training there.

However, even on the British weapons the Commandos were expected to excel. Although the Lee-Enfield magazine held only ten rounds the Commandos were expected to achieve a standard of fifteen aimed rounds per minute, and in practice, under instructor Captain Wallbridge, they often achieved twenty-five rounds. Wallbridge's aim was to get at least twenty rounds per minute from most squads with just an hour's practice per day over a period of six days.[40] After 1941 the Mark III Lee-Enfield was replaced gradually by the Mark IV which was identical in most respects except for the bayonet and the backsights. These made it a favourite with the Commando snipers and it also had the useful feature of being able to fire the No. 36 grenade from a special discharger.

The Commandos also preferred the American Tommy gun to the British Sten gun although its high rate of fire meant that ammunition was easily wasted in long bursts which tended to go high because of the recoil. Bursts were therefore ideally limited to three or four shots at a time, all well aimed.

The most hated weapon was the Boys anti-tank rifle which had a fearsome kick and was found to be more use against enemy fortifications than against tanks. This was later replaced with the PIAT whose only disadvantage was that the bombs weighed in at 2½ pounds each. Along with the 2-inch mortar it was a formidable weapon.

After practising their skills, the Commandos started to notice that their responses in attack and defence situations were starting to consolidate into set moves. With this in mind the Commandos evolved their own battle drills. Battle drills did not start with the Commandos. They are probably as old as armies themselves – soldiers long ago realised they were developing routines which worked well during battle. For the modern British Army they actually had their origins in World War I when commanders realised that the infantry practised every stage of an attack right up to the moment the attack started – and not beyond. In 1918 Lieutenant-General Sir Ivor Maxse, Inspector General of Training, set out tactical battle drills and these were embraced enthusiastically by commanders.[41]

Once World War II started battle drills started to make an impact and they became a feature of the battle schools which were responsible for improving the quality of British infantry training through World War II. However, these battle schools did not always use realistic battle situations – where resources were limited they might practise on the parade ground in an imaginary scenario.[42]

The value of battle drills during World War II is a controversial issue for historians and it was controversial at the time. What is best – a set sequence of moves on a pre-determined stimulus (for example the moment a squad comes under fire) or the exercise of initiative by the junior commander on the spot?

Modern armies like battle drills because they are a logical extension of the conditioning process. Once a man is used to shooting down life-sized targets then the next stage is to pre-rehearse all the stages of war which can be rehearsed. Once a unit goes into action they will be firing and acting according to a set series of stimuli.

The historian Timothy Harrison Place probably has the most incisive view of the effectiveness or otherwise of battle drill during World War II. He takes the view that the British approach to attack with pre-timed fire plans stifled initiative because it was supposed to take over the minor tactics practised as battle drill. Because this infected all battle drill training in mainstream infantry schools during World War II it had an effect of reducing the training carried out. He concludes, 'It was not too much battle drill that deprived the British infantry of the power of initiative, but too little.'[43]

Fortunately for the Commandos they were unaffected by the rigidity in the British Army training system. They believed firmly in battle drill and set about devising their own with gusto. They had come to the battle drill philosophy without any prompting from other mainstream developments inside the Army – Captain Dawson of No. 4 Commando was convinced that the Germans must have used battle drills in order to operate the Blitzkrieg.

Discussion within No. 4 Commando led to American football where set drills are used during games. The first battle drills revolved around the smallest unit, the sub-section. Within each sub-section the Bren unit would be the fire unit and the Tommy gunners would be the movement group ready to assault. A typical drill was the response to enemy fire. Once the section came under fire immediate cover was sought and the source of the enemy fire located. Having done this the Bren group would engage the enemy position and the assault group would find the best route to the enemy position and attack once within range with grenades and guns and bayonets.[44]

These drills helped the Commandos prepare for their role as raiding parties on the enemy coastline. But what was the effect of all this training on the execution of an actual operation? The answer is simple – in many cases, resounding success. The US 1st Ranger Battalion went through Achnacarry where it was given, if anything, a harder time than the British Commandos. Later, after one battle in Italy, its commander, Colonel Bill Darby, said, 'The achievements were due entirely to the training at Achnacarry.'[45]

One of the best examples of Commando success was the No. 4 Commando operation to destroy the battery at Varengeville as part of the Dieppe raid. And it was a success which was all the more deserved because the Commandos worked so hard to make it happen.

Notes

1. Captain W. E. Fairbairn, *Get Tough*, Paladin Press, 1979, p. 96, quoted with the kind permission of Paladin Press
2. Major R. F. Hall, correspondence with the author, autumn 2004
3. Hall, correspondence with the author
4. *Ibid.*
5. William L. Cassidy, 'Fairbairn in Shanghai', *Soldier of Fortune*, September 1979, p. 68
6. Hall, correspondence with the author
7. Colonel Rex Applegate and Major Chuck Melson, *The Close Combat Files of Colonel Rex Applegate*, Paladin Press, 1998, p. 42, quoted with the kind permission of Paladin Press
8. George Langelaan, *Knights of The Floating Silk*, Quality Book Club, 1959, p. 65

9. Hall, correspondence with the author
0. Fairbairn, p. v
11. Hall, correspondence with the author
12. Langelaan, pp. 67–8
13. Van Maurik trained the Czech SOE Agents who atacked Reinhard Heydrich on 27 May 1942
14. E. H van Maurik, unpublished memoir, p. 4
15. Author interview, also appeared in David Lee, *Beachhead Assault*, Greenhill Books, 2004, p. 52
16. Fairbairn, p. vi
17. From Captain W. E. Fairbairn's personnel file in NARA, quoted in Applegate and Melson, p. 48
18. Capt W. E. Fairbairn and Capt E. A. Sykes, *Shooting to Live*, Paladin, 1987
19. Fairbairn and Sykes, pp. 5–6, quoted with the kind permission of Paladin Press
20. Anon. (Public Record Office), *SOE Syllabus*, 2001, I. 5, p. 371
21. Major General John K. Singlaub, *Hazardous Duty*, Summit Books, 1991, p. 39
22. Applegate and Melson, p. 50
23. Bill Pilkington, quoted in Applegate and Melson, p. 50
24. Hall, correspondence with the author
25. E. H van Maurik, unpublished memoir, pp. 2–3
26. Public Record Office, *SOE Syllabus*, I. 5, pp. 414–5
27. Hall, correspondence with the author
28. *Ibid.*
29. James Dunning and Irving Portmann, ex-No. 4 Commando, interview, Emyr Jones archive
30. James Dunning, *It Had To Be Tough*, Pentland Press, 2000, p. 105
31. *Ibid.*, p. 107
32. *Ibid.*, p. 107
33. *Ibid.*, p. 123
34. *Ibid.*, p. 101
35. Applegate and Melson, p. 51
36. Peter Young, *Commando*, Ballantine Books, 1969, p. 128
37. Major Tom Bird, letter to the author 16 January 2005
38. Dunning, *It Had To Be Tough*, p. 81
39. *Ibid.*, p. 102
40. *Ibid.*, p. 70
41. Place, p. 49
42. Place, p. 52
43. Place, p. 79
44. Dunning, *It Had To Be Tough*, p. 83
45. Quoted in James Ladd, *Commandos and Rangers of World War II*, BCA, 1979, p. 168

CHAPTER 4

No. 4 Commando – Dieppe

The 2-inch mortar was probably one of the simplest weapons to see combat in World War II. All it consists of is a short steel tube on a base plate which weighs 4.1 pounds. It is operated by two men – one (the No. 2) drops the mortar bomb down the barrel. This bomb weighs 2.25 pounds and can travel up to 500 yards, although its optimum range is up to 250 yards, and it is fired by the No. 1 by means of the trigger on the base plate. Aiming the 2-inch mortar is not a scientific process. It sits on the base plate and has no independent support and so has to be held in the firing position by hand. Because this mortar had no sights, it was simply a case of point and shoot. Practice was the key to successful operation of the 2-inch mortar. In training the Commandos managed to get nine out of ten bombs inside a box ten yards by ten yards at 250 yards range.[1]

It was a good job that No. 4 Commando was proficient in the use of this mortar because a single shot from one of their 2-inch mortars was to turn the tide of the battle for the Hess battery at Varengeville.

The No. 4 Commando action to capture the Hess battery, code-named 'Operation Cauldron', stands out from the rest of the Dieppe raid because it was the only action on the day which went according to plan and achieved its objective.

Why did No. 4 Commando succeed and the other units at Dieppe fail? It is interesting to listen to the Commandos themselves talking about the Dieppe raid. Whilst No. 3 Commando had the bad luck of running into a German convoy en route to their objective on the other side of Dieppe they did manage to land, although they did not succeed in silencing the coastal battery at Berneval.

The main landings at Dieppe were a failure and some of the No. 4 Commandos ascribe this, at least in part, to the failure of the attacking forces to put every effort into getting off the beaches.[2] This principle was fundamental to No. 4 Commando and every Commando knew that to hesitate on the beach was an invitation to disaster. Any natural instinct to dig in on the beach under heavy fire had to be resisted.

As far as the No. 4 Commando achievement goes there was one factor which was instrumental in their success – training. Lord Lovat, who commanded No. 4 Commando, had several weeks' notice of their part in the raid and immediately put this time to good use. Although his senior officers knew what was going on the rest of the men in No. 4 knew nothing of their destination until the night before they sailed.

Their principal objective was the Hess battery with its six guns at Varengeville which was to the west of Dieppe, about 1,000 yards inland from the beach. These guns were big 15.5-cm Filloux guns which had seen service with the French on the Somme in 1940. Each shell fired from one of these guns weighed a massive 94.7 lb and had a range of over 20,000 yards. Given that a shell could be fired every thirty seconds, the battery was clearly a danger to the main allied assault on Dieppe and silencing the guns was going to be of crucial importance.

The Commandos had aerial photographs of Dieppe and knew what they would face from the beach to the battery. The plan which was devised was simple and based on standard fire and movement techniques. No. 4 Commando would split into two groups for the assault. Group 1 under Major Mills-Roberts was the fire group and would land on Orange Beach 1 at Vasterival and take a direct route to the battery. This group consisted of eighty-eight men from C Troop and a fighting patrol from A Troop. They would climb the cliffs from the beach, make their way inland and engage the battery. Group 2 under Lord Lovat was the assault group and was made up of B Troop, F Troop and the remainder of A Troop. They would land at Orange Beach 2 at the mouth of the River Saane and make their way round to the rear of the battery for the actual assault. There were 164 Commandos in this larger group. They would have to work harder because this route would cover 1½–2 miles.

Training took place at Lulworth Cove in Dorset and was split into two different types. Although the Commandos mostly did not know their destination they were used to training and training hard. Of course some did put two and two together and worked out from the fact that they were practising a raid that they would shortly be going on the real thing.

The first part of the training was the general training which everyone had to undergo and the first element of this training was battle fitness. Every Commando was on foot for this operation and had to be able to get to the beach, across the beach, up the cliffs and along to his objective carrying full kit and weapons. Training was laid on accordingly in both wet and dry clothing. The second element was boat and landing drill. These early exercises did not go well because of navigational errors. It was a salutary lesson – on the day itself the landings were made on the right beaches. The third element was weapons training; everybody had to refine their skills with rifles and Bren guns.

The second type of training was specific to individual groups. For Group 1 this mainly involved getting them prepared for their role as the fire party. Mortar training was critical and included work on both the 2-inch and 3-inch mortars. The 3-inch mortars had been added to the Commando armoury because of the need for heavier support weapons. Then there was sniper training for the designated snipers. In addition the Commandos had to be trained with bangalore torpedoes which would blow the obstacles in the gullies as they moved off the beaches, and the demolition teams needed to make sure they could blow the guns once they reached the battery.

For Group 2 training was concentrated on movement and fighting at close quarters. All the members of this group had to be completely fit to move across country carrying their weapons and then fight once they reached their objective. Their weapons training therefore concentrated on the rifle, bayonet, Bren, Colt automatic and Thompson submachine gun as well as grenades. For the purpose of this training targets were improvised so as to give realistic firing opportunities against the sort of targets which they would come up against on the day – firing on the ranges was not going to be helpful.

By the time of the Dieppe raid itself No. 4 Commando was fully prepared for the operation. On the evening of 18 August 1942 No. 4 Commando assembled in Southampton where they were addressed by Lord Louis Mountbatten, Chief of Combined Operations, and this was the moment when most members of No. 4 Commando found out exactly where it was that they were going.

Troop Sergeant-Major James Dunning, C Troop, No. 4 Commando

I do want to emphasise because I have been asked many times about security that at no time did we know, in C Troop or I believe among No. 4 Commando other ranks and junior officers, the exact destination of the raid.

People have often bandied about the idea that everybody knew but we did not and I have subsequently seen, in the records at Kew, that a security officer did come, prior to the raid, to Weymouth and went around the civilians there trying to find out if anybody had spilled the beans but we had a clean sheet and it was quite obvious because *none of us knew we were going to go to Dieppe*. We didn't know until Lord Louis came on board the *Prince Albert* on the night before the actual raid that we were going to Dieppe . . .

We carried two extra LMGs [light machine guns – Brens] making six in all. The No. 1 and No. 2 on the gun had twelve magazines and then every rifleman carried a spare Bren magazine. The riflemen each carried 100 rounds of .303 in bandoliers, their bayonets had been sharpened and darkened and the rifle bombers carried EY cup discharger and ballistite charges so they could fire 36 grenades if possible. I was in charge of the 2-inch mortar team – Privates Horne and Dale – whom I had got up to a very high pitch throughout the year. They had been the regular Nos. 1 and 2 and had been under my orders and training throughout the year.

We carried twelve rounds of HE and smoke, it wasn't a lot but the twelve rounds of HE and smoke could make quite an impact as indeed it did. The 2-inch mortar men carried Colt 45s as I did. We also had the Boys anti-tank rifle and Gunner McDonough carried sixty rounds and did a marvellous job with it.

We wore cap comforters – we had discarded our steel helmets and as the green berets had not yet been issued we wore the cap comforters. We were only in light raiding order. This was very important because at the time there was a lot of clamour for a Second Front and a lot of misguided people maintained that it was going to be more than just a daylight raid. But the very fact that we went in raiding order (we didn't carry any emergency rations and as far as I remember we didn't have any water bottles) dispelled the suggestion that it was more than a raid because we couldn't afford a sustained battle or survive there more than a few hours without emergency rations and water.

In C Troop we did have entrenching tools, just to scrape holes, if we needed to in a defensive role in front of the battery. In the event we didn't need to use our entrenching tools. Underneath all our equipment we had the Mae Wests so that in the event of a wet landing we had something to keep us afloat because you have to remember that, even if you were a good swimmer, with all that ammunition and your weapons it was quite a load to carry and swim inshore as well.

I vividly remember Lord Louis Mountbatten coming on board the *Prince Albert* about 6.00 p.m. on the evening prior to our sailing and giving us one of his inimitable pep talks. He really was very inspiring, the easy, confident way in which he spoke to us, told us about the support we should be getting from the air and wished us well. He impressed upon us the importance of our task which was to knock out the battery supporting the defences at Dieppe.

We sailed later that evening from Southampton and it was quite an eerie sensation for me to sail from my own home town, only a mile or two away from where my mother was then living. The journey across was quite eventful. We prepared everything, our ammunition, our explosives.

We were well briefed once more and we turned in for a few hours' kip while the boat was sailing across the Channel. We had a very early reveille, about 1.30 a.m. We had breakfast and then we went to our boat stations to embark in our landing craft.

This had all been well rehearsed; we all knew exactly what seats to sit in and what order to go in and we did this very quietly in the dark and we were lowered into the water some nine or ten miles offshore and then we went in to the landing beaches.[3]

On the final run in to the French coast the sky was illuminated by starshell and tracer fire which was over to the left of the Commandos. This was the moment when No. 3 Commando ran into a German convoy and the operation was blown. However, at the time the No. 4 Commandos did not know what was going on; all they knew was that No. 3 Commando had come up against the opposition.

The two groups landed at slightly different times. Group 2 under Lord Lovat was the first to land at 0430 hours on Orange Beach 2 while the Group 1 Commandos were due to land at 0450 hours on Orange Beach 1 and they managed to land only two minutes late. Although Group 2 was not faced with cliffs on the same scale as Group 1, it did have to contend with opposition.

Captain Pat Porteous VC, No. 4 Commando, Orange Beach 2

We hit the beach, which was a steep shingle beach with a belt of, I suppose, three or four yards of wire at the top of this bank and a steep drop down the other side. We knew this was there from the air photographs and every boat had some rolls of ordinary chicken wire to roll over the barbed wire which made a sort of bridge which one could stagger over. While we were getting that on they [the Germans] opened up with mortars which they had obviously ranged very closely on to the beach and caused about a dozen casualties. The whole training had been, to get off the beach just as quickly as possible, regardless of anything, so we left a medical orderly with the wounded who were on the beach.[4]

Lance-Corporal John Flynn, No. 4 Commando, Orange Beach 2

We hit the beach and almost immediately there was heavy gunfire and then aircraft seemed to be diving on to the gun battery firing cannon shells. I looked to my left and I could see Lord Lovat standing up about thirty yards away and someone was trying to put the rabbit netting over the very high defence wire (rolls of barbed wire).

That was all I remembered for a while [he had been stunned by a mortar bomb] and then I remember there didn't seem to be anyone else around. The bodies of the two mortar men were there and I knew I needed to get to Captain Webb. I followed the tracks and eventually caught up with F Troop. I wasn't really aware that I had been hit and pushed on.[5]

Sapper K. C. Kennett, Signal Section, No. 4 Commando, Orange Beach 2

I joined the headquarters group of Lord Lovat. I carried a spare battery for the wireless set as well as a rifle and a bandolier of .303 ammunition. I was joint operator of the wireless set . . . The beach was very narrow; we were fired upon by machine guns on leaving the landing craft. There was a lot of wire to be cleared just off the beach. We lost quite a few men doing this. Daylight came very quickly. The colonel was magnificent and showed great leadership.[6]

Fusilier George Cook, No. 4 Commando, Orange Beach 2

When we landed there was some barbed wire and another chap and myself we had a roll of wire netting which we threw over the barbed wire so we could run over it. They were firing tracers from some pill boxes and as we went over the wire we finished up near Lord Lovat and he said, 'They're firing too high,' quite casually. Lord Lovat was about six feet and I'm five foot four so I thought, 'If they're firing over his head there's no danger they're going to touch me', but they did fire some mortars and four or five blokes were killed on the beach.[7]

Across on Orange Beach 1 Group 1 had an easier time than Group 2 had had on Orange Beach 2. But for them, timing was crucial. The Commandos in this group had landed at 0452 hours and were due to bring down concentrated fire on the battery by 0615 hours which was fifteen minutes before the main assault from Lord Lovat's group was planned to begin.

Troop Sergeant-Major James Dunning, Orange Beach 1

We touched down on the right beach at the right time and, as we had so often rehearsed, we went across the beach as fast as possible. This was absolutely imperative as it was vital not to stop on the beach where you were a target for enemy fire.

We got under the shelter of the cliffs where [Lieutenant] David Style was responsible for selecting which of the two gullies we would climb. From the aerial photographs we had expected both the gullies to be wired and mined. We had brought bangalore torpedoes to deal with these.

David Style decided that the wire was too dense in the left-hand gully and would take too long to clear so he tried the right-hand one and decided to blow holes in that one for us to scramble up the loosened chalk face. Just as we were about to go up the gully just prior to blowing the bangalore torpedoes some fighter aircraft came in and the noise of these aircraft drowned out the noise of the explosions. This helped to preserve the secrecy of our landing.

We were lucky that there were no mines in the gully although I understand that it was later reported that there were some. Our climbing skills came in quite useful as we made our way up the gully. We were using new rubber soled climbing boots which later became standard issue for all Special Forces.[8]

Private Alan Coote, A Troop, No. 4 Commando, Orange Beach 1

I had the Boys anti-tank rifle, a brute of a weapon to fire with terrific recoil. My only previous experience with this weapon was half a dozen shots on the field firing range. I did also have a Colt 45 automatic pistol as a personal weapon for close-quarter use should it be required. The Boys anti-tank rifle weighed 37 lb, fired a 0.55-inch armour-piercing round, was over 5 feet in length, was supported by a single short leg and was designed to fire at ground level. Blast from the muzzle, particularly on dry ground, raised a considerable dust cloud. The gun gave a very easily identifiable flash and bang.

On reaching the beach the landing craft ramp was on the shingle but the swell was running up the beach so we on my craft hesitated to let the water run back before stepping ashore with completely dry boots. Not what you would expect at such a moment and quite different to the D-Day landings which were much more like the movies.

As we landed the RAF came screaming in and there was an extraordinary amount of noise. We had some minutes clustered at the base of the cliffs, waiting for the bangalore torpedoes to do their job. This they did most successfully and allowed us to make our way up the steep gully in single file and heavily loaded, something which would have been impossible against even the lightest of defensive fire.[9]

The next task for the fire group, Group 1, was to get into position to engage the battery. However, for the Commandos in this group it was not just a case of rushing over the thousand yards distance to their position. The Commandos also came across signs saying 'Achtung Minen!' and 'Danger Mines!' – it amused the Commandos to think that the Germans had so kindly warned them of the danger in their own language but some realised that the French and English words for this warning are the same.

A defensive screen was put out around the bridgehead under Sergeant Langland, and members of C Troop started making enquiries and searching some of the houses in the vicinity. But then events started to overtake them.

Corporal Raymond Robouhans, Free French Commando, attached
C Troop, No. 4 Commando

Our duty was to search houses and to talk to French people in order to gain information on the German troops stationed in the vicinity of the battery. Our second duty was a frontal shelling by mortar, rifle and automatic weapons, directed on to the battery and its exterior defences from a distance of 130–150 yards to prevent the battery opening fire on to the ships approaching Dieppe.

About 5.47 a.m. the battery started to open fire on the British armada in front of Dieppe. Immediately the order came from Mills-Roberts to stop searching the houses and to move quickly to take up firing positions. It was at this time as we moved in single file taking cover along a hedge that an isolated German sniper, hiding in a farm building, shot a British

Commando in the shoulder. This man was just behind me, he was the last man in the line as we moved to take up firing positions by an old barn about 130–150 yards from the battery.

A field of oats separated us from the German gunners. During the next thirty-five minutes the mortar section of Mills-Roberts and Lieutenant Starr's section with rifle, machine gun and anti-tank rifle opened a demoralising and deadly barrage of fire on to the battery. During this devastating attack I saw two or three Germans trying to run away from the battery across the oat field but they were immediately shot down by men of our section.[10]

Troop Sergeant-Major James Dunning

Our orders were that we had to be in position and start engaging the enemy in the battery not later than 6.15 a.m. The main assault under Lord Lovat would go in at half past six and this would be preceded by an air strike. However, as a result of the battery opening fire and the message from the IO [Intelligence Officer] that the main flotilla seemed to be in range Major Mills-Roberts, who was in charge of all our party in this part of the raid, decided to speed things up.

He was in visual contact with David Style who had the Bren guns in his command and also the snipers, so they pressed on as fast as they could through the wood to the farm buildings where they took up positions overlooking the battery. They were just about in ideal range, just a couple of hundred yards away.

We, meanwhile, had gone up to headquarters, to the front of the wood which was to the right of the farmhouses as you looked at the battery. I crawled forward to the edge of the wood with my 2-inch mortar team to within sight of the battery. I remember seeing a cook dressed in white in the battery.[11]

Sergeant H. Lindley, No. 4 Commando

We eventually got into a position on the forward edge of a wood. Dawson said to me, 'Take the snipers out,' so I took six snipers out. The aircraft had been zapping them before we got in. I was lying next to Dickie Mann when I saw a man in white overalls and I said to Dickie Mann, 'There's a sitting target for you,' he ups with his rifle, bang, and we saw him go down.[12]

Troop Sergeant-Major James Dunning

We got into position and the order was that when we were in position and ready to engage the battery, Robert Dawson would blow and whistle and we would start firing. The whistle went, well before the deadline of 6.15 a.m. – it must have been about 6 o'clock. All the sections were ready in their positions; the snipers were ready. The snipers were under Dickie Mann, a great shot, a butcher in peacetime. He was a dead shot, no mistake. He was going through the long grass, ready to take up a firing position right in front of the battery, an ideal position in which to start sniping. The Bren gunners were up in the first floor of the farm building overlooking the battery, we were down on the ground at the edge of the wood. Everyone was ready to start to engage the enemy battery.

Robert Dawson blew the whistle, the Bren gunners opened fire and we started to range. I had got my 2-inch mortar team and I reckoned that it would be best to pick the centre of the battery as the best target area because the 2-inch mortar is not exactly a weapon with pinpoint accuracy so if I aimed at the middle it would allow for any errors left or right and would probably hit something.

The first shot didn't seem to provide anything, [though] we heard the explosion. Then I decided to group shots in threes, one to the right, one to the left and one in the centre. The third shot must have been the luckiest mortar shot of World War II because it hit the cordite stack, there was a blinding explosion, a fire and the guns, to my knowledge, didn't fire again. It was seven minutes past six.

The Germans were obviously taken by surprise, there was fire coming back at us, particularly the flak tower was firing at us and after a few minutes an enemy mortar started firing at the wood. We engaged the battery until 6.20 a.m. and the 3-inch mortar and us started to put smoke in the battery site.

Dead on 6.25 a.m. a flight of Spitfires roared in to rake the battery with cannons. We had the distinct feeling, only a few hundred yards away, that it was a bit too near for errors. By now the flak tower had been put out of action by McDonough (he had fired something like sixty rounds from his shoulder with his anti-tank rifle) and that's a fair whack because the Boys anti-tank rifle had a vicious recoil. Dickie Mann accounted for quite a few Jerries with his sniper rifle.

Exactly on time we saw the white over white over white Very lights of Lord Lovat and we ceased fire. Once we ceased fire our major role was over. We reckoned we had done a pretty good job.[13]

Private Alan Coote

My memory of this and other actions is how little you see of both your own force or the enemy. It is almost as if you and one or two others close to you are the only people involved, more so when you come under fire. Sound yes, but sight minimal, and the feeling of being completely isolated. We did, however, eventually have quite a volume of fire cracking around us. This was thought to be from the flak tower, although I could neither pick up a weapon nor flashes from the weapon slits visible at perhaps some 200 yards.

The problem of returning fire was one of elevation – without a pit or hole in the ground it was impossible to raise the barrel sufficiently to engage the target. Unless some form of high support was available the Boys anti-tank rifle could not be brought to bear. There was no such support available so my No. 2 had to become the human bipod. This he managed and I fired a few rounds but both he, myself and the weapon were completely exposed and it was totally impractical to continue for any prolonged reply. I could see no fire coming from the tower and ground fire was cracking over us and around us. So we returned to cover and sought a new position and new targets.[14]

The single shot by James Dunning's mortar team was probably the most important round of the entire action. The shell had landed right on the bagged cordite charges which had been left out by the side of one of the guns in the battery – a foolish mistake by the Germans and a fortunate one for the Commandos. As it turned out, after this shot the Hess battery did not fire again and the main attacking force coming into Dieppe was certainly spared heavier shelling as a result.

Although the battery had been silenced there were still plenty of Germans ready to fight Lord Lovat's group, which needed to get into the battery to make sure none of the other guns were going to be used. After their landing on Orange Beach 2 Lovat's group split up, with A Troop heading off towards the Group 1 positions. This fighting patrol, under Lieutenant Veasey, made its way to its position at a nearby crossroads where its task was to intercept any move by a German company from the other side of the River Saane. The remainder of Lovat's group made their way up the River Saane on the east bank, protected from enemy fire by the steep banks and the woods. They had cleared the beach in just thirty-five minutes after they had landed.

As the assault force ran inland they heard the massive explosion caused by the 2-inch mortar from the fire group. At the Blancmesnil le Bas woods near the battery, F Troop under Captain Pettiward went left to the western end of the battery while B Troop under Captain Webb went right to attack the battery at its most southerly point. Lovat and his HQ party took up position between the two troops.

The full complement of German soldiers at the battery at Varengeville was 130 men under Hauptmann (Captain) Schöler. However, on the day of the Dieppe raid there were some ninety-seven actually present at the battery. Some of these men had seen service on the Eastern Front but others whom the Commandos captured and brought back to England turned out to be conscripts from Poland and the east.

Therefore the quality of the opposition facing No. 4 Commando was mixed. Some were battle trained and some were still in their initial training period. The fact that only one of the prisoners brought back by the Commandos had been born in Germany speaks volumes about the quality of the two opposing forces – the better trained German soldiers were either killed or escaped, whereas the less well trained Eastern European soldiers were easily captured and brought back.

However, the Commandos did not yet know exactly where the soldiers they were attacking came from. At this stage they were attacking the battery as two separate groups which had the advantage that the two troops would not be getting mixed up and firing at each other, but it did also mean that, of the two approaches, F Troop would be more exposed.

Captain Pat Porteous VC

We swung left across open ground behind the German defences. We had no opposition at all crossing that bit of open ground which brought us round to a little wood at the back of the battery where we were to assault . . . we went in, luckily we found a spot in the wire. The battery had barbed wire entanglements around it but there was a spot where obviously the German soldiers had been coming home late from leave or something of the sort and had trampled a pass down through this bit of barbed wire at the back. We managed to get in there without any problem at all. Where we got into this area of the battery was typical *bocage* country with masses of little hedges, cottages, farm buildings, hedges, bushes – it was very close country.[15]

Fusilier George Cook

Somebody shot a bloke out of the ack ack tower . . . he did a lovely swallow dive off the top . . . Sergeant Horne and myself went to cut some barbed wire. Sergeant Horne said to me, 'Come on!' because we had wire cutters, 'You cut there and I'll cut here.' So we started cutting and I heard an 'Ugh,' and when I looked there was Sergeant Horne with blood spurting out of his chest. I had a look at him and it looked as though he was dead which was a bit of a shock to me because he was about the toughest fellow I knew . . . Anyway I cut the wire and I went back to Porteous and I said, 'Sergeant Horne's dead, he's been shot.' The next thing I knew, bonk, that was me. I got hit . . . I woke up, kind of came round and the sun was shining on me. I had lots and lots of flies. I tried to move and couldn't, tried to gather my senses together and three Germans came round the corner, one of them stuck his bayonet right on my throat.[16]

Sergeant J. Halliday, F Troop, No. 4 Commando

We came under sniper fire which was when Sergeant Horne was wounded rather badly. He had been shot through the stomach and it had blown out quite a large part of his back and for the first time in my life I administered morphine. He was in a fairly poor state and swearing at the guy who had got him. We propped him against a wall.[17]

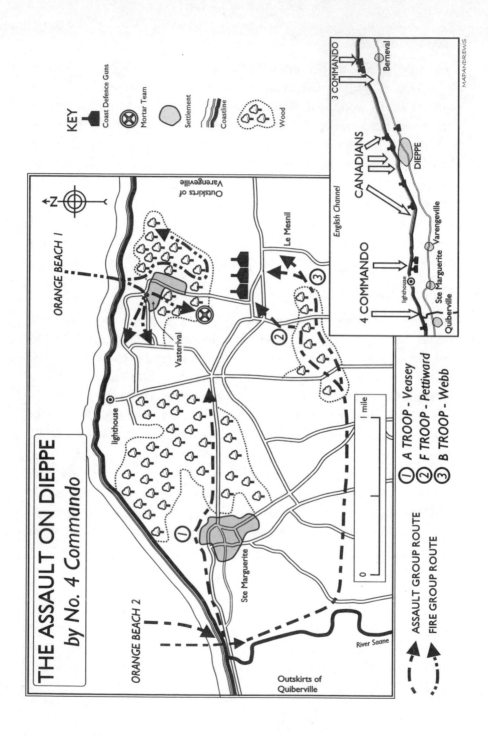

THE ASSAULT ON DIEPPE
by No. 4 Commando

KEY

⬚ Coast Defence Guns

⊗ Mortar Team

⬠ Settlement

〜 Coastline

🌲 Wood

ORANGE BEACH 1

ORANGE BEACH 2

Outskirts of Varengeville

Outskirts of Quiberville

lighthouse

Vasterival

Le Mesnil

Ste Marguerite

River Saane

N

① A TROOP - Veasey
② F TROOP - Pettiward
③ B TROOP - Webb

ASSAULT GROUP ROUTE
FIRE GROUP ROUTE

0   1 mile

3 COMMANDO

Berneval

CANADIANS

DIEPPE

English Channel

4 COMMANDO

Varengeville

Ste Marguerite

lighthouse

Quiberville

MAP ANDREWS

Sergeant Irving Portman, F Troop, No. 4 Commando

Most of the men in the troop were quite capable of blowing the guns but they gave the job to the corporals and the sergeants because they wanted to make sure they were going to be blown. The last thing Lord Mountbatten said to us before we set off when he came on board our ship was, 'Now look, I don't give a damm what Germans you kill or what you do to kill or whatever you take but don't forget, you have to get the guns.' I had eighty-odd pounds of explosive on my back – they were all primed charges, they all had primers and detonators.

We were looking round for a route to get into the battery and Pat [Porteous] came round [and] said, 'Try this hedge,' so I dived through and a grenade landed – it was only a stick grenade so it wasn't bad but I got this piece stuck in my eye so I rolled behind a tree and like a twit I was looking towards the battery which was a couple of hundred yards away – I should have known that no one can throw a grenade 200 yards. But this Jerry flung a grenade and it landed in the branches behind me and pieces went through my rucksack without setting anything off. I was carrying a rifle but I also had a Colt automatic. I pulled round the side of this tree and I could see a helmet appearing just out of the ground about twelve yards away.[18]

I was a marksman, a pretty good shot, and I got him pretty plum centre . . . when I got there I saw there were two of them in a dog-leg trench. The one I had shot had half his head blown off, but the other one was looking the other way, his rifle poking through the bushes. He hadn't noticed his pal was dead. He turned and saw me at the same time as I noticed him. I can see his face now, turning. I stabbed him in the neck with my bayonet, then I was so scared I shot him about three times to make sure.[19]

Captain Pat Porteous VC

We bumped into a truck of German soldiers who were just disembarking. Obviously they had come up from Ste Marguerite or somewhere down in that direction. We managed to knock them off before they got out of the truck, killed the lot of them virtually with Tommy guns.

We then started working our way through this very dense bit of country, all these little cottages and hedges and so on. Roger Pettiward, who was troop commander, was killed by a sniper and the other subaltern, John MacDonald, the other section commander, he was killed by somebody who threw a stick grenade, which left me in command of the troop.[20]

Sergeant J. Halliday

There was a signals store near where we were in the orchard and we decided to move to cover at the side of this store and then make a charge round because we suspected there were some Germans there. They turned out to be in some slit trenches behind the hedge and they were using stick grenades against any movement.

We decided to group at the side of the wall and then charge as fast as we could. Captain Pettiward was in front and led the way and I was behind him. The moment we turned the corner there was a stick grenade came over and it got Captain Pettiward and blew him to bits. So we had to regroup again. I had gone into the store which was empty and we were looking to see if we could go through the store and deal with this menace.[21]

Corporal Pat McVeigh, F Troop, No. 4 Commando

We got to the end of this building and Jerry dropped a grenade on his rucksack and he [Pettiward] had gone. It blew his head off.[22]

Captain Pat Porteous VC

I was going along a little lane towards the battery with a bank on the left and I suddenly saw a German popping up on the other side of the bank. I threw a Mills grenade at him, and he threw a stick grenade at me. As soon as they went off I popped up but unfortunately he popped up a little bit quicker and he shot me through my left hand so I withdrew a bit and put on a field dressing. We passed on and there were several other casualties, chaps who had got sniped or blown up with grenades.

We lined ourselves along a bank which was giving us a little bit of cover from where the actual guns were, low bank about four feet high. We lined right along this. I made contact with Commando headquarters who were in the centre of the battery area or approaching the battery area and he said, 'Come on, it's time we went in', so we did a little bayonet charge into the gunpits themselves.

It seemed to be a hell of a long way but I think it can't have been more than about eighty yards or a hundred yards. The guns were fully occupied dealing with the chaps from the other party of Commandos who had landed and we got very little opposition coming in. I got another bullet in my thigh which slowed me up.

We got into the gunpits. The first gunpit I came to was the one which had the mortar bomb in it and it was just full of corpses. I staggered on to the next gunpit and then I rather gave up the ghost.[23]

Sergeant J. Halliday

Fortunately there was a raised road which offered cover for our attack on to the gun positions. Unfortunately behind the road there were two bunkers so, keeping the troop under cover, Captain Porteous and myself went down to clear out the two bunkers. The bunkers only contained some French civilians and we moved into position for the final assault. During this time we were just assembling when we came under fire again. This was a great motivator and we went into the attack with bayonets fixed and all guns firing. It seemed to be a bit of an anti-climax because our mortars had hit the cordite store and a lot of damage had already been done.[24]

For his actions at Dieppe in rallying F Troop after the loss of two of its officers and leading it in the bayonet charge despite being wounded twice, Pat Porteous was awarded the Victoria Cross. His bayonet charge was also joined from the other side by B Troop under Captain Webb whose Commandos had also been making their way to the battery. This group included Lance-Corporal Flynn who had been hit on the beach and who had been determined to get to Captain Webb with his wireless set.

Lance-Corporal John Flynn

Eventually I reached him and as soon as I got to him I opened up the set. To my amazement I still had the three aerial rods. I got through immediately and the first response I got was, 'Attack at once!' I gave that to Captain Webb and followed on.

Once at the battery one of the Commandos was searching one of the buildings when a German from inside shot him and jumped out and butted him with his rifle. Needless to say the German did not live for very long after that.[25]

Private Charles King, B Troop, No. 4 Commando

The 3-inch mortar changed from high explosive to smoke, I fixed my bayonet, then three white Very lights, one after the other, were fired, the signal for the attack. We got up and charged across open ground swept by machine-gun fire, through barbed wire, overrunning strongpoints, ending up on the gun sites. The gun crews were bombed and bayoneted into total submission. Quite a lot of Germans hid in the underground tunnels containing stores and ammunition, as well as in the office, cookhouse and the outbuildings. Quite a number of Commandos were killed or wounded in the charge and in the mopping up in the buildings and the isolated resistance.[26]

Private William Spearman, B Troop, No. 4 Commando

It was total confusion really because anybody who wasn't a Commando you recognised, you just killed them. People were running out of buildings, running into buildings.[27]

In the fire-fight the German commander, Hauptmann Schöler, was killed by a Commando who burst into his office and raked him with submachine-gun fire. With the Commandos inside the battery there remained the mopping-up operation. The Commandos went from position to position making sure the enemy were neutralised as well as collecting anything of intelligence interest. However, in clearing one machine-gun post they would come under fire from the next and this was while the most important task of the whole operation – blowing the guns – still needed to be carried out.

Sergeant Irving Portman

We charged in and I was very lucky because I got away with it. I finished up at the gun position and I pitched a 36 grenade in and there were two Jerries dead with their clothes burnt off and there were these other couple and I sorted them out. Vic Ford jumped into the gun position behind me, I cussed him and said, 'Come 'ere you and give me a hand here!' I wanted him to give me a hand to put a shell in the breech. 'Eff you,' he said, 'I'm not going in there.' So I threatened him.

Later in Blighty Vic Ford said to me, 'You bugger, you would've shot me, wouldn't you!' 'Course I would,' I said but of course I wouldn't but I had to threaten him. He was scared but so was I, to be honest. When I pulled that cordite out of that gun I had to put the charge in behind the shell. When I opened the breech there was already a shell in there so I pulled the cordite out that was there (I didn't know what to do with it because it was live and there were bits of flame around so I didn't know what to do with it). Vic was quite right actually but I had to get this damm thing in. This was Number 3 gun.

We had made up the charges in the rucksacks, primed them all and all we had to do was open the breech, slam the charge in, making sure there was a shell in the breech to take the blast of the explosive and that would do a really good job on the gun. The one I did I stuck a limpet on the side as well, just an ordinary limpet mine. They had little magnets on them and were originally intended to use on ships.[28]

With the charges in place it was time for the Commandos to withdraw. This was potentially as dangerous, if not more so, than the assault itself and the Commandos had therefore practised withdrawal drills back at home. As they started to withdraw the Commandos heard the charges they had placed on the guns in the battery explode behind them. Lord Lovat's group passed through C Troop which was covering the retreat.

Troop Sergeant-Major James Dunning

We had worked out a staged withdrawal, by thinning out and leaving some groups, withdrawing some and leap-frogging back so we were protecting our rear all the time. We took up a position between the wood and the bridgehead and waited for the assault parties to go in.

We only found out how it had gone once the assault parties came through us. It was just about 7 o'clock when they started to jog down the track. I can vividly remember Pat Porteous being carried down on a stretcher which was just a door being carried by some German POWs – little did I know at that stage what deeds he had done and that he was going to be our VC.

Once the assault parties had gone through we thinned out once more right to the top of the cliff. We hadn't been counter-attacked although there had been some mortar fire coming down in our area. As we approached the cliff top I remember seeing a couple of cows which had been hit by mortar bombs, lying either dead or dying. I remembered how, when I had been going in, I had looked at the cows and thought, what a lovely, peaceful scene.[29]

Private Alan Coote

When the general noise of the action was subsiding, TSM [Troop Sergeant-Major] Williams who was nearby, was obviously quite seriously wounded. There were no medical personnel around and we had been issued with large shell dressings as well as our personal issue of first field dressing. I used mine and another shell dressing to cover the wound. TSM Williams, 'Pinkie', refused to go on a stretcher but was obviously incapable of making his own way back to the beaches.

I was ordered to see the sergeant-major safely back to the beach. We made extremely slow progress with no chance of taking cover despite the crack of rifle bullets repeatedly hitting the hedgerows and trees. Every obstacle was a painful and hazardous manoeuvre for the TSM. The TSM had his left arm around my shoulders and I held him up by the back belt thong on his trousers. It was very tricky going down the gully. The TSM wanted me to leave him on numerous occasions but I managed to persuade him to keep going. After a number of stops we finally made the beach and I handed him over to the medical staff.[30]

Sergeant Irving Portman

As we were coming down the cliffs one of the German prisoners tried to run away; if he had just kept quiet he'd have been brought back to Blighty to be a prisoner but given the sort of shots we were he was riddled.[31]

Sergeant J. Halliday

We re-assembled and headed back to the beach through C Troop who were doing a bridgehead operation. Coming back on to the beach there was all sorts of mayhem. The RSM [regimental sergeant-major] was standing in the beach controlling things as if it were a sunny afternoon on the beach. We got back on to our LCAs [Landing Craft Assault] and headed for home.[32]

Troop Sergeant-Major James Dunning

Down on the beachhead the large smoke generators, which had been prepositioned by the beachhead party to screen the re-embarkation, were being lit. We began our final thinning out (by this time the assault parties had re-embarked). Robert Dawson then sent up the red over red signal which meant the bridgehead parties (some of which were still on the cliff top) and any stragglers would have to re-embark within the next thirty minutes.

The re-embarkation was a bit wet because the LCAs did not come very far inshore and we had to wade out quite a way and that's where Lord Lovat was shouting, 'Come in you buggers and pick us up!' There was some sporadic sniping but it wasn't very accurate.[33]

Troop Sergeant-Major Lou Chattaway, B Troop, No. 4 Commando

We covered the rear of the Commando on the way out. I was the No. 2 but I was firing the gun. I remember Lovat coming down and saying, 'Come on, get out of it!' We were more or less the last off the beach. I lost my Bren gun in the water. I was trying to get it out but Lovat shouted at me to leave it and get back on the boat. I had just about had it by the time I got to the boat and I had to be hauled in.[34]

Troop Sergeant-Major James Dunning

Over the town we could see quite a few dogfights going on and there was much activity. We didn't realise at that time what a battle was taking place. We got on board and started to pull offshore. We waited quite a while, while we decided if we were needed elsewhere (we also had a reserve role in case we were required).

At about 9 o'clock we were told we were no longer required and we made our way back. We picked up some American airman on the way who had been shot down. We had a relatively peaceful journey back to Newhaven.[35]

At this stage the Commandos did not know what a disaster the Dieppe raid had been. All they knew was that they had carried out a successful mission. Behind them the Commandos left the dead as well as some of the wounded and with the wounded was the Commando medic, Jim Pasquale, who had volunteered to stay behind to look after the wounded in the full knowledge that he would be spending the rest of the war as a prisoner. His brother Ted had also been on the raid but he was killed during the D-Day landings, a fact Jim learned only when he was released in 1945.

Medical Orderly Jim Pasquale, No. 4 Commando

There was a chap called Mercer and he was in a terrible state. He was blind, one of his eyes was hanging out and all I could do was to push it back and put a patch on it . . . The Jerries were very good to us really, they took the wounded and took us up to a hut. We were lined up and [when] one of our planes came over we were told to scatter, and this German officer said, 'For you the war is over!'[36]

The Commandos did take a number of German prisoners back to England and the issue of what happened to these prisoners has stirred controversy among historians. On one side is John Parker who quotes the account by William Spearman in the Imperial War Museum where he states that because there was no room in the boats, 'They found that the only thing they could do was to shoot some of the prisoners.'[37] On the other hand Parker also quotes Pat Porteous who said,

We only had three or four [prisoners] and we certainly didn't tie them up . . . This story has got around that No. 4 Commando killed prisoners on Lovat's orders but this is absolutely not so.[38]

However, Parker points to the fact that Porteous was wounded and perhaps not aware of everything around him.[39]

Will Fowler, whose book *The Commandos at Dieppe* is perhaps the definitive work on the No. 4 action at Dieppe, disagrees. He points to the fact that no one else could recall there not being room on the boats plus the fact that the Commandos would not have left their wounded behind if they were prepared to shoot prisoners to make room on the boats.[40] Then there is also the crucial fact that no one else on the raid said that prisoners were shot and this is borne out by my own enquiries. It seems that in this case the reputation of the Commandos has been unjustly sullied.

So why was No. 4 Commando successful at Dieppe? In his after-action report Lieutenant-Commander Hugh Mullineux RN, who was the special navigator on the No. 4 Commando operations, stated,

I am convinced that the success of the operation . . . was due, in very large measure, to sound and intensive preliminary training for the job in hand and to the determined leadership by their Officers.[41]

The action by No. 4 Commando was considered so success-ful that a paper was written to capture the lessons from the whole operation. Written by an officer called Martin Lindsay from the Gordon Highlanders it was called *Destruction of a German Battery by No. 4 Commando during the Dieppe Raid*.[42] However, this manual was not well received by officers who considered their units could have carried out the operation equally well.[43] But could they?

The Army as a whole did not put its soldiers though the same training. Could these officers have known who would perform on the day? Who would kill and who would not? Had they routinely rejected soldiers who did not attain the required standard? Did they condition their men to fight like the Commandos? Did they train as intensively? The answer to all these questions is of course no – these elements were exactly those which set the Commandos apart from the main body of the Army.

The end result of the Commando way of war was that the Commandos eliminated, through careful preparation and training, all those elements which other units would have to turn to luck to solve. An Army unit might, if it were lucky, have good men who would perform well on the day; it might, if it were lucky, have men who were fit enough to survive the gruelling route to the battery heavily laden and then fight when it got there; it might, if it were lucky, have pulled it off.

The only factors which the Commandos could not train and prepare for were the matters of chance outside their control which could scupper the whole operation – No. 3 Commando was hit by just such bad luck when it ran into the enemy convoy during the approach to Berneval. But then the thought arises – if the Commandos had been in charge of intelligence gathering and planning at a higher level perhaps they could have avoided even these sorts of problems.

At the end of the day what is important is that No. 4 Commando planned and executed a brilliant operation which proved that its methods of training and organisation really did work and work well. And as they came home the Commandos themselves had a chance to reflect on all of this.

Sergeant J. Halliday

We had always wondered what it was like to come under fire and during our training we had tried to relate it to how it would be in the real thing. All the time at Dieppe we were so occupied in thinking about what we were going to do next and, while the shock of seeing people being wounded or killed had an effect on almost every individual there, it still didn't detract from the objective we knew had to achieve. The fact we had seen the blood and the gore only helped us realise that this was the real event. Perhaps the fact they were all extremely fit helped motivate people. My own personal feelings can be summed up by the fact that when we got back I suddenly realised that I didn't particularly want to talk about it, to go over it again. For a few days I was pretty much to myself.[44]

Notes

1. James Dunning, *The Fighting Fourth,* Sutton, 2003, p. 72
2. Emyr Jones archive of taped interviews and recordings of individual Commandos in No. 4 Commando
3. James Dunning tape, Emyr Jones archive
4. Imperial War Museum, Sound Archive, transcript of Pat Porteous interview, 10060/2/1, p. 8
5. John Flynn tape, Emyr Jones archive
6. K. C. Kennett tape, Emyr Jones archive
7. Imperial War Museum, Sound Archive, transcript of George Cook interview, 9977/3/2, p. 14
8. James Dunning tape, Emyr Jones archive

9. Alan Coote tape, Emyr Jones archive
10. Raymond Robouhans tape, Emyr Jones archive
11. James Dunning tape, Emyr Jones archive
12. H. Lindley tape, Emyr Jones, archive
13. James Dunning tape, Emyr Jones archive
14. Alan Coote tape, Emyr Jones archive
15. Imperial War Museum, Sound Archive, transcript of Pat Porteous interview, 10060/2/1, p. 9
16. Imperial War Museum, Sound Archive, transcript of George Cook interview, 9977/3/2, pp. 15–16
17. J. Halliday tape, Emyr Jones archive
18. Irving Portman tape, Emyr Jones archive
19. Imperial War Museum, Sound Archive, Irving Portman tape 9766/5, quoted in Will Fowler, *The Commandos at Dieppe*, Harper Collins, 2002, pp. 167–8
20. Imperial War Museum, Sound Archive, transcript of Pat Porteous interview, 10060/2/1, p.9
21. J. Halliday tape, Emyr Jones archive
22. Pat McVeigh tape, Emyr Jones archive
23. Imperial War Museum, Sound Archive, transcript of Pat Porteous interview, 10060/2/1, pp. 9–10
24. J. Halliday tape, Emyr Jones archive
25. John Flynn tape, Emyr Jones archive
26. Charles King tape, Emyr Jones archive
27. Imperial War Museum, Sound Archive, transcript of William Spearman interview, 9796/08, p. 46
28. Irving Portman tape, Emyr Jones archive
29. James Dunning tape, Emyr Jones archive
30. Alan Coote tape, Emyr Jones archive
31. Irving Portman tape, Emyr Jones archive
32. J. Halliday tape, Emyr Jones archive
33. James Dunning tape, Emyr Jones archive
34. Lou Chattaway tape, Emyr Jones archive
35. James Dunning tape, Emyr Jones archive
36. Jim Pasquale tape, Emyr Jones archive
37. Imperial War Museum, Sound Archive, transcript of William Spearman interview, 9796/08, p. 52
38. Imperial War Museum, Sound Archive, transcript of Pat Porteous interview, 10060/2/1, p. 13
39. John Parker, *Commandos*, Headline, 2000, quoted in Fowler, p. 196
40. Fowler, p. 196
41. Lt-Cdr Hugh Mullineux, After Action Report, quoted in Dunning, p. 87
42. Notes from Theatres of War No. 11, *Destruction of a German Battery by No. 4 Commando during the Dieppe Raid*, HMSO 1943
43. Fowler, pp. 232–3
44. J. Halliday tape, Emyr Jones archive

CHAPTER 5

The Desert –
Victory at Snipe

From an address by Maj-Gen Raymond Briggs CB, DSO, *at the Empress Cinema, Brixton, 26 March 1944, during 'Salute the Soldier' Week*

On the 26th October 1942 I was commanding an armoured division. The Battle of Alamein had been going on for three hard days and on that Monday it was quite obvious that there were two features held by the Germans that we must have. The code-names of these two features were Woodcock and Snipe. It is about Snipe that I want to tell you.

So that we could have some firm base round which our armour could manoeuvre it was quite essential that Snipe, strongly held by the Germans, should be in our hands. I therefore ordered a battalion of the Rifle Brigade, eighty per cent of them Londoners, to make an attack on Snipe that night. The attack went in with the utmost vigour, and the riflemen were not slow in driving the enemy from their positions.

There was a very yellow moon and the enemy position was on the forward slope of a little ridge. Between my Tactical HQ and Snipe, which was out of sight, was a long valley entirely dominated by German 88-mm anti-tank guns. All night long, the riflemen, who were experienced in desert warfare, bearing in mind their slogan, 'Dig or Die,' were busy digging in their 6-pounder anti-tank guns and converting the enemy's weapon pits to their own use.

Germans and Italians had been in that position some time and the ground was stagnant with filth, and the air laden with flies, and all of this in brilliant moonlight under the enemy's machine-gun fire. Shortly after midnight, the position was reported as captured and consolidated.

About 3 o'clock, next morning, the enemy started attacking this very isolated battalion with tanks. From early morning until dusk, this one battalion withheld eight major tank attacks, each of them varying in strength from five to fifty tanks. I shall never forget that morning listening in on my wireless to the CO of that battalion giving his reports and orders.

That morning I made constant attempts to move forward armour so that it could help those riflemen but any attempt to cross the valley was met by the most intense fire and many tanks were knocked out. It was quite obvious that the battalion could not be supported in daylight without losing a large number of tanks. I had to make the decision as to whether I would put in an armoured attack to support them, or whether I would leave them to fight it out as best they could.

I knew more of the general situation; I knew that, at that moment Rommel was moving the tanks of the 21st Panzer Division from the south to join the 15th Panzer Division and I knew that my tanks would be needed almost immediately for a more important role. Reluctantly, I had to make the decision that the loss of the tanks was not justified.

How magnificently those riflemen supported the decision I had made! All day long they stuck to their position inflicting tremendous damage on the enemy, killing large numbers of Germans and capturing a few. This battalion completely destroyed, 'brewed up', as they used to call it, thirty-five German tanks and damaged beyond repair at least another twenty more. I ordered them to withdraw that night.

They went into that action about 400 strong and how amazed and relieved I was to hear that so comparatively small a price had been paid for their magnificent achievement. Two officers and twelve other ranks killed, twelve officers and thirty-three other ranks wounded. The CO, Colonel Turner, got the VC. Here is an extract from Colonel Turner's citation, 'Throughout the action, Colonel Turner never ceased to go to each part of the front as it was threatened. Wherever the firing was heaviest, there he was to be found.'

An almost finer tribute came from a Sergeant Calistan, who lives at Forest Gate, and who had already gained the Military Medal, and who, for this action, was awarded the DCM. 'Our colonel kept going from gun to gun. How he inspired us! When the first attack came in, the colonel was acting as loader by my gun. He got wounded in the head, a nasty one, and we wanted bind it up, but he wouldn't hear of it. "Keep firing," that's what he went on saying.'

For that one action alone, for those thirty-six hours' magnificent stand, the battalion gained one VC, one Bar to the DSO, one DSO, one Bar to the MC, four MCs, 3 DCMs, one Bar to the MM, and 10 MMs.

Based on my own experience in this war of nearly six months' fighting in France and of two years' command with the Eighth Army, I can assure you that, for sheer guts, determination and willpower, the British soldier has no equal.

I would like to define him as a man who is often grousing, but who never really complains, as a man who has never been known to let his leaders down in battle, a wonderful comrade and a staunch friend who, well led, will perform miracles of valour and endurance. A man we respect and love and one whom we should all be proud to salute.[1]

The Snipe action was arguably the single most extraordinary action of the whole of World War II, perhaps even in the history of the British Army. According to R. H. Haigh and P. W. Turner who wrote a monograph about Snipe, it even outshone Rorke's Drift as a battle against the odds. They point out that the defenders of Rorke's Drift had the luxury of vastly superior weapons (breech loading rifles against spears), a limited defensive front and a good ammunition supply, added to which their attackers failed to make best use of their overwhelming numbers. The men of 2nd Battalion, The Rifle Brigade, on the other hand, were not only vastly outnumbered (one battalion against two divisions) but also outgunned by the German and Italian force.[2]

It is therefore all the more surprising that the Snipe action is not well known in the annals of great British battles, although perhaps the reason for this is the fact that it has been submerged by the rest of the Battle of El Alamein.

Given that Snipe was fought by a regular battalion of the British Army, how does it fit in with the factors already identified as critical for military success in the previous chapters in this book?

We have already seen how fighting at very close quarters requires conditioning if it is be successfully executed by all soldiers in a unit. However, there are different shades of close-quarter fighting which can be seen in the following list which ranks weapons according to how difficult they are to use on an enemy soldier:

- At the top of the list is the fighting knife. Using this weapon requires the soldier to close right in with his enemy. The fact that its use is going be bloody and horrible means that only a strong or well conditioned individual is going to be able to use it in anger. The Commandos were trained to engage from this level onwards.
- Next comes the bayonet. Immediately there is more distance between the attacker and the defender with the length of the rifle. All soldiers were trained to use the bayonet but most soldiers would rather fire their rifle at close quarters than have to use the bayonet and most soldiers, on seeing the bayonet close up, would run rather than stand and be skewered.
- After the bayonet comes the handgun. With the handgun comes more distance and less blood which immediately makes it easier to use than the knife or bayonet.
- Next on the scale comes the rifle and light machine gun and the distance increases so that soldiers can, if they choose, simply shoot in the general direction of the enemy and not know if they have killed anyone or not. Or they can shoot to kill. At Snipe this was the level at which the enemy infantry were engaged.
- After the rifle come weapons such as the heavy machine gun and mortar where the distance may increase yet further.
- After these weapons comes the anti-tank gun. At Snipe the 2nd Battalion, The Rifle Brigade, had the 6-pounder which they used to great effect against the German and Italian tanks. At this level the battle is even more impersonal as tanks are machines, rather than people. The same effect can be seen in road rage where drivers are dealing with machines rather than the people in those machines.

- Finally there are weapons such as heavy artillery and aircraft bombs where the soldiers and airmen do not even see the enemy they are firing at.[3]

Consider this comment from Major Tom Bird DSO, MC, who went through the desert campaign and particularly Snipe with 2nd Rifle Brigade,

When as anti-tank gunners we hit an enemy tank and it started to burn the tank crew would (of course) jump out if they could. Our motor platoons would then shoot at them with small arms fire. It was a pretty mean thing to do, but I don't remember any hesitation . They weren't close enough to be real people perhaps, just little figures in the distance.[4]

In his book *On Combat*[5] Colonel Grossman points to two factors being responsible for killing like this. Firstly he points to the fact that it is much easier to deny an enemy his humanity if his back is turned (you do not have to look him in the eye and kill him). Secondly he points to the psychology of the battlefield in which soldiers behave like hunters and hunted in a confrontation like that of the process of confronting a dog. As long as you face the dog down it will usually stay away but turn and run and it will attack. Soldiers will behave in the same way.[6]

Although distance is important there were other factors in play as well. Another important factor was that the men of 2nd Rifle Brigade, as it was composed at Alamein, had been fighting together for a long time in the desert. After Alamein many of the key officers and men who had fought at Snipe did not go with the battalion to Italy where, as Chapter 6 explains, the battalion was virtually wiped out in the attack on Tossignano.

In *Men Against Fire* S. L. A. Marshall makes the point that a soldier fights much better if he is in a group of his friends, 'It is therefore to be noted as a principle that, all other things being equal, the tactical unity of men working together in combat will be in the ratio of their knowledge and sympathetic understanding of each other.'[7]

The group dynamic was crucial at Snipe because the riflemen on the guns were operating in such small groups. A single rifleman with a rifle has his fate in his own hands to a greater extent than an anti-tank rifleman on a 6-pounder. The single rifleman can decide whether to fire or not, the rifleman in a 6-pounder crew will always fire because of what Colonel Grossman describes as, 'mutual support, accountability and diffusion of responsibility'.[8] This also applied to World War I where the machine-gun crews killed vast numbers on both sides. Grossman also points to street behaviour today to back this up. Two thugs are far more of a threat than a single thug because they can feed off each other in order to commit a crime.

It is also interesting to note that another battalion attempted something similar to Snipe the following night and failed. As part of the relief of 1st Armoured Division (of which 2nd Rifle Brigade, was a part) the 4th and 5th Battalions, The Royal Sussex Regiment, were sent to relieve the Snipe position (they believed that 2nd Rifle Brigade was still there when in fact they had vacated earlier in the evening) and to take the Woodcock position.

This was a disaster. The battalions had only converted to the 6-pounder anti-tank gun the previous month and their training was woefully inadequate. 4th Royal Sussex first of all came under friendly fire from the Gordon Highlanders and then dug in in the wrong place. The spot they chose was very exposed and they found it difficult to dig their 6-pounders in. One company moved off to attack an enemy position and was wiped out. The next disaster to hit the battalion was that radio contact was cut off, for reasons no one knows. As dawn broke they were exposed and surrounded. The German and Italian tanks attacked and wiped out the battalion, killing and capturing virtually all the British soldiers including the commanding officer. Only six officers and sixty men made it back to safety.[9]

This makes the Snipe action even more extraordinary. As we have seen the elements were all in place for 2nd Rifle Brigade. The men had all served and trained together a long time and they were killing at a distance. But it was also the case that the officers and men who fought at Snipe were good at their job.

The man in charge, Lieutenant-Colonel Victor Turner VC, bears some comparison with Lord Lovat. Both were extraordinary leaders who piloted their units through extraordinary actions. Like Lovat, Turner was not just a respected commanding officer; the officers and men thought he was something very special.

Major Tom Bird DSO, MC, S (Anti-Tank) Company Commander, 2nd Rifle Brigade

Turner was a marvellous man. We all adored him and he was incredibly brave and inspirational. We were four experienced company commanders who had been in the desert for quite some time and we all knew our jobs.[10]

Rifleman Horace Suckling, 2nd Rifle Brigade

Colonel Vic Turner was well liked by everyone. One of our chaps in the desert was given detention by Colonel Vic for having a rusty rifle which was the worst crime because it might backfire on you. He later wrote to this chap while he was in detention regretting that he had had to give him detention but explaining it was for his own good. I never heard of any other colonel who would do this.[11]

Sergeant Joe Swann DCM, 2nd Rifle Brigade

Colonel Vic was a wonderful soldier, he was a man's soldier. He could come down to your level and at the same time keep control. I don't think anybody in the Rifle Brigade could ever say a bad word about Colonel Vic Turner.[12]

Turner had been in command of 2nd Rifle Brigade since late July 1942. However, the battalion itself had been in the desert since before the war and had come from duties in Palestine to fight as a motor battalion. It was not an ordinary infantry battalion and only ninety of its men were deployed as infantrymen – instead its strength lay in its Bren carriers in the scout platoons, the anti-tank company with the 6-pounders and the machine-gun platoons. It was a formidable fighting machine and had learnt its craft in a summer of fighting in which it had perfected the art of fast movement and fast fighting and during which Turner himself came to realise the benefits of proper training and conditioning.

Lieutenant-Colonel Vic Turner VC, 2nd Rifle Brigade

Very rarely do battles turn out exactly as they were planned, owing to the fog of war and to the unexpected that crops up. It's therefore extremely important that in peace time you should get the drill, as it were, of conducting a battle, or exercises so that when it actually comes to fighting [and] you are enmeshed in the fog of war, your actions are so automatic that you can adapt yourself to the unexpected and carry on without losing your head.[13]

The story of Snipe starts on 23 October 1942 when 2nd Rifle Brigade had the distinctly unglamorous, but vital, job of providing the minefield task force to guide the Eighth Army's attack through Rommel's defensive minefields. Although unglamorous, this work was still fraught with its own dangers.

Rifleman Horace Suckling

On the night of 23 October our platoon was on the lighting of the lamps, [and] some of our platoons were protecting the mine lifters with small arms protecting their flanks. Myself and my best friend Bill Milligan were in a covered 3-tonner, lighting the lamps and handing them at the back to the lads putting them on stakes marking the safe lanes for the armour to go through. The noise outside with our terrific barrage meant we couldn't know what was coming back from the enemy positions. I said to my mate, this I don't like, let's put our tin hats on and instead of lighting one lamp each time, let's light a few lamps, hoping to save time. We had about six lamps lit when the next thing was, what with the moving truck, one lamp overturned and the next thing was a stream of flame creeping up to the 40-gallon drum of paraffin. We tried to put it out but to no avail. Whoosh! We bailed out. We hit the ground and crawled to a slit trench where we were kept down by enemy small arms fire. The truck blew up and we had accomplished our task of lighting that lane![14]

Sergeant Joe Swann DCM

The minefield task force was on 23 October and we crawled into position that night. The guns were put into position and we had sixteen guns lined up along the enemy front in case of tanks coming through and we just sat there while the infantry, the chaps in A, B, C and Headquarters Companies, went along digging for mines. Nasty job and of course where everything we were laying out was on a wide front so everything that was chucked over from the German side landed somewhere.

I always remember that there was an anti-tank gun on my left and we were sitting underneath our vehicles – we thought, 'Bugger this, we'll get underneath!' There was nothing we could do if a shell was going to hit us. I always remember a big bang on our left and there was an anti-tank gun and there was a chap hanging on the barrel which was pointing up into the air. A shell had gone off over the top and there were two of them lying on the floor and this chap was hanging from the barrel. When we went to get him down he was dead. Horrible.

There were four sections in each platoon.[15] Each section had four guns and each one was supposed to have six or seven men – you were lucky if each had three men because the casualties were coming in all the time. We sat there for 23 and 24 October. On the night of 25th we went forward. We got through the minefields – it was horrific with the bangs from the howitzers. They would nearly blow your scalp off and they weren't even firing at us, they were firing at the Germans! They frightened the daylights out of us when they fired in the darkness!

On 26 October at about 5.00 p.m. we were told we were going to attack Snipe. Colonel Vic hadn't been very happy because we were all jumbled up and nobody was sure where anybody was. We had been put off until the night of 26 October and at about 9.00 p.m. we went forwards to Snipe.[15]

Lieutenant-Colonel Vic Turner VC

About 1600 hours on the 26th I was again sent for by brigade HQ. This time I was told that there was an enemy strongpoint on either end of a kidney-shaped ring contour, named Kidney Ridge. Incidentally, it wasn't a ridge at all, but a depression! The northern end was 'Woodcock' and the southern end was 'Snipe'. Instead of attacking Woodcock in conjunction with the 6oth [Rifles], which we originally intended to do on the 25th, the 60th were to attack Woodcock and we Snipe simultaneously after thirty minutes' preliminary concentration of artillery. In addition to my own sixteen 6-pounder anti-tank guns I was allotted eleven 6-pounder guns from 239 Battery, 76 Anti-Tank Regiment, RA.[16]

> One of the major headaches for 2nd Rifle Brigade was that 1st Armoured Division and the rest of the Army had a difference of opinion about navigation amounting to 1,000 yards. This may not sound much but if 2nd Rifle Brigade was operating on one set of co-ordinates it might find itself being shelled by artillery working on a different idea of what those co-ordinates meant. After further discussions at brigade HQ the outcome was still far from satisfactory. As Turner recorded, his final comment was, 'I must form up as if the armoured division's positioning is right and, if it isn't, I must just march on the flash of the falling shells! Hardly, you will agree, a very satisfactory way to start an attack!'[17]
>
> With the battalion on the start line and ready to go, this difference in navigation duly manifested itself and the artillery started shelling on the wrong bearing for 2nd Rifle Brigade which meant that the whole battalion had to re form!

Lieutenant-Colonel Vic Turner VC

We were now all in position and Z minus 5 arrived and with it the artillery concentration, but did it go down on a bearing of 233 degrees? Not on your life; it was on a bearing of 275 degrees! This meant forming up again on the new bearing and re-setting our compasses, a by no means easy task by the light of a just-rising moon. However, we accomplished it and were only ten minutes late on the start, so I asked brigade for another ten 'whisps,' the code I had arranged in case I required extra artillery preparation, each 'whisp' representing an extra minute's concentration.

We left the start line, therefore, at 2310 hours, my company commanders each mounted in a wireless carrier and I in a wireless Jeep driven by Major Tom Bird. Our start was anything but auspicious, as we drove straight into a German vehicle pit within a hundred yards! However, luckily, there was no danger and we got a carrier to tow us out.

There was a certain amount of AP tracer and MG bullets flying about, but nothing serious, though away on the right we could see a good deal of fire in the north from the Woodcock direction.[18]

Captain F. W. 'Tim' Marten CMG, MC, *adjutant, 2nd Rifle Brigade*

While we were on our start line three Wellingtons came over and dropped bombs over us. Two or three people received minor wounds, I was hit in the back of the shoulder but it did not really penetrate through as I was wearing a leather jerkin, a pullover and a shirt. It just cut my back. The result was that when we started the medical officer with his vehicle was attending to the wounded and never came forward. Consequently we had only Corporal Francis who was medical orderly on the Snipe position.[19]

Sergeant Joe Swann DCM

I was ordered to line up the portees [trucks carrying rather than towing anti-tank guns] with the guns on tow at last light on the track. We then sat there for two or three hours and suddenly we had the command to start up. As soon as the command had worked its way back to me (I was the fifth vehicle in the row, there were four portees in front), we were off at a mighty gallop.

The only way we could keep in line was by heading into the thickest of the dust. The officers had gone on ahead with the colonel and we just pushed on behind. It was awful because there was so much muck being thrown up into the air that you just couldn't see anything. We experienced that all the time in the desert; you had the officers in front in the Jeep and they were guiding everyone along. The road and the sky was clear but if you were at the back you got all their dust. We used to tell them about it but we just had to follow. We opened up our anti-gas stuff and put the visors on so we could continue to see.[20]

Lieutenant-Colonel Vic Turner VC

Presently we came on a series of German dugouts belonging to German engineer personnel. The Germans occupying them made no stand, but bolted, the Riflemen of the motor platoons having great fun lobbing hand grenades into the dugouts. We captured 25–30 prisoners.

After about 1,000 yards we came to a long, low trip wire stretching across our front. I was afraid it was a minefield, so halted the carriers, letting the riflemen of the motor platoons advance on foot, while I sent the RE detachment to investigate. The carrier crews, however, were thoroughly worked up and excited at seeing the silhouettes of the German engineers running westward in the light of the rising moon and were not going to be done out of their fun, so continued to blaze away with their machine guns at the fugitives through the lines of the advancing motor platoons! I ran up and down the line using the most lurid flow of language in an endeavour to stop them, when luckily the Sapper detachment reported that it was a dummy minefield, and I was able to let the carriers loose again before any casualties had occurred.

The change of direction of the attack meant that instead of an advance of 1,300 yards we now had to advance 1½ miles – just twice the length. After about 1¼ miles I saw a long, low ridge in front and decided to halt as soon as we reached it. It was one of those beastly ridges that in the moonlight seem to get farther away the nearer you get to them! So, after going another quarter of a mile, I decided to halt where we were. To confirm that we were correctly on our objective I got the Gunner OP to ask for a round of smoke on to the objective. As this fell within 300 yards of us I thought this was good enough and so sent through the success signal both by wireless and by Very light. This was at 0015 hours.[21]

Captain F. W. 'Tim' Marten CMG, MC

Then the colonel said, stop. I said to him, 'Have we come to the right place?' He said, 'I don't know but this is where we are and here we stay!'

By great good fortune he had found this place, in some accounts described as a German engineering dump, I think myself it was Italian. I found this dugout which could house me, the signallers and the wireless sets. It was twelve feet long by six feet wide, quite deep. There were some steps and the roof was covered with railway sleepers. It was towards the north end of the position . . . We were in a heaven sent position because we were in a very shallow disc, I suppose it only went down about two or three feet, covered with scrub and old bits of engineering stores. It meant that as soon as we were dug in an enemy approaching couldn't see any trace of our occupation. The guns were dug in more or less in a circular ring as decided by Vic Turner and Tom Bird. Between them were the riflemen with their small arms and the Bren guns.[22]

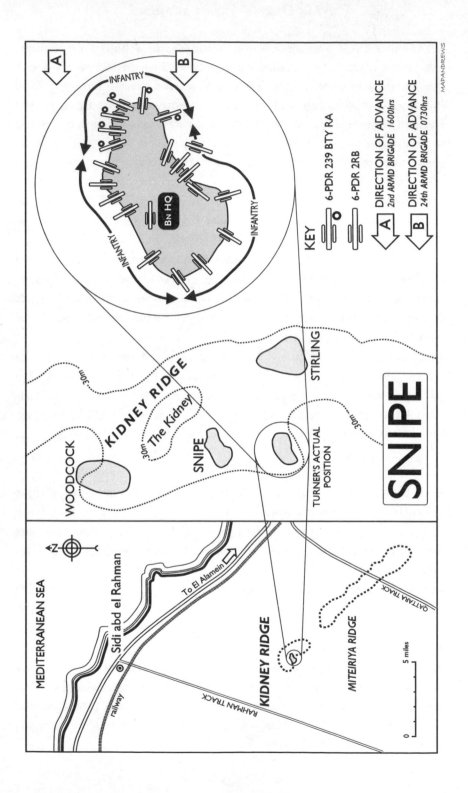

MEDITERRANEAN SEA

Sidi abd el Rahman

railway

To El Alamein

RAHMAN TRACK

KIDNEY RIDGE

MITEIRIYA RIDGE

QATTARA TRACK

N

0   5 miles

WOODCOCK

KIDNEY RIDGE

30m

The Kidney

30m

SNIPE

STIRLING

TURNER'S ACTUAL
POSITION

30m

SNIPE

INFANTRY

INFANTRY

INFANTRY

Bn HQ

A

B

KEY

6-PDR 239 BTY RA

6-PDR 2RB

A   DIRECTION OF ADVANCE
    2nd ARMD BRIGADE 1600hrs

B   DIRECTION OF ADVANCE
    24th ARMD BRIGADE 0730hrs

MAP ANDREWS

The battalion having started to dig in, the scout patoon promptly set off to reconnoitre the terrain around Snipe. This was normal practice for motor battalions and the purpose was not only to reconnoitre forward of the Snipe position but also to cover the riflemen as they dug in both themselves and their guns.

Lieutenant Dick Flower MC, *Scout Platoon, 2nd Rifle Brigade*

Having gone forward about 250 yards we came upon quite a lot of wire which seemed to indicate a possible minefield so rather than riding across a minefield and risk losing the Bren gun carriers we got out of our carriers and waited around to see if we could find a gap through this minefield, which we were lucky enough to find because at this time the moon was coming up giving a certain amount of light – it was quite a good moon. We were able to see a matter of perhaps a couple of hundred yards.

We managed to find a gap through this minefield so I was able to lead the carriers through this gap in line ahead and then when we got through the minefield we were able to deploy again in normal open formation on the other side of the minefield. Then having got through this minefield we saw what looked like about fifty or sixty tanks 200 or 300 yards away so we halted and looked through our binoculars. It was quite clear that this was what we called an enemy tank leaguer where the tanks used to move into close formation during the night for protection.

It wasn't entirely a surprise because we knew at this time that the Germans had a large number of tanks and you have to remember that, by this stage in the battle of El Alamein, we had only just got through the main minefield which was three to four miles in depth. On the other side of the minefield the Germans had a further line of defence which consisted mainly of tanks that were dug in and also their own anti-tank guns and it was this final line of defence that the Germans had, of tanks and anti-tank guns, that was an embarrassment to Montgomery in getting our own armour forward.

We also, having got through this minefield, came across about forty or fifty Germans who we were not quite sure what they were doing but when they saw us they recognised these as British vehicles and we started shooting at them and we managed to take about a dozen of them prisoner.

127

This was a slight embarrassment of course because we were still going forward to investigate these tanks while the rest of the battalion was behind us digging in. We had no way really of keeping these Germans so we had to sit them on the front of our carriers and drive forward with these prisoners virtually in our carriers.

Having gone a bit further forward it was then quite clear that these German tanks were in the process of being replenished and they had a number of lorries there, it was quite clear they were filling up with petrol and being replenished with food and water and ammunition.

So we decided that this was a super target in view of the fact that we could see about two or three hundred yards. We started firing with our Bren guns at these replenishment lorries. Being what we called soft-skinned vehicles they didn't have armour and a number of them very soon caught fire which was very satisfying. As a result of this of course the German tanks started to open up.

They weren't quite sure where we were or who we were but they managed to locate us and started firing not only high explosive shells at us but also machine-gun fire from their gun turrets. As a result one of my carriers was badly hit and caught fire. As a result of this action the prisoners we were carrying, about a dozen or so of them, decided they would run for it and they jumped off our carriers and started running forwards towards their own tanks.

I think the German tanks thought perhaps this was a British infantry attack coming in and so they shot at their own prisoners trying to get back to their own lines. We were also shooting at them.

As a result of this I think the German tanks realised there was some sort of rather serious threat and then the tanks started moving forward to attack us and we therefore decided it was high time that discretion was the better part of valour and that it was high time that we withdrew behind what had appeared to be a minefield we had come through originally. This we did and took up our position on the rear side of this minefield and continued to cover the digging in by the battalion. During this little action of course we had been reporting back regularly on the wireless to battalion headquarters and warning them of these attacks.

Fortunately by this time our own anti-tank guns had had time to dig in. They had been warned to expect these German tanks and shortly afterwards the first of these tanks started to appear and my carriers then withdrew back into the main battalion position. Within a short time the first of these German tanks appeared I suppose not more than about 150–200 yards from the main battalion position and our anti-tank 6-pounder guns got their first shoot of the day, well perhaps not day because it was still night.

They let loose at very short range and they managed to knock out I think it was three German tanks in that little action which caught fire. The German gun crews bailed out of their turrets which was their normal reaction and as they dived out of the turrets we already had our machine guns trained on these turrets and in many cases killed the German crews as they bailed out.[23]

Sergeant Joe Swann DCM

I was supposed to be going back with the four portees and so I went forward to find the second-in-command, Major Tom Pearson, and I said to him, 'What's going to happen, sir, are we going back?'

'No, not yet we're not, not while this is going on,' he said. I then said I would go up on Corporal Cope's gun because he was short handed. It was a most uncomfortable walk because there was tracer whizzing all over the place. Our tracer and their tracer. When you looked (and everything was dark) you saw this yellow stuff and this white stuff.

I was just moving the gun into position when a 76.2-mm [self-propelled] gun came across our front, 200 yards away. There was a road going round the escarpment and this gun was up there firing at us. Colonel Vic Turner, the commanding officer, was at our gun at the time. He said to me, 'Swann, do you think you could hit it?' I was a good shot, I had good eyes. I said, 'I'll have a go.' I swivelled the gun round and laid it on to a butt in the bank so that the nose of the vehicle, as it came into it, would give me the clue to fire, so I fired at it and I hit it. When it was stationary I put another one into it and the people inside bowled out of it and disappeared. So that stopped that one.[24]

After this action the sky over Snipe began to lighten with the grey light of dawn. The riflemen were well dug in, although they were fully aware that daylight might bring with it the need to reposition some of the guns in order to improve their fields of fire. Back at Eighth Army headquarters the weather

129

men were already busy and the forecast they produced was a perfect one: 'Wind light south-east becoming west-north-west. Very little cloud decreasing inland. Slight risk of coastal showers. Visibility 10 miles.'[25]

About a mile north of Snipe the 2nd Battalion, The King's Royal Rifle Corps (60th Rifles), were in trouble. They had been sent to capture Woodcock but they had had problems. Owing to the dust raised both by their vehicles and artillery fire, they had gone astray. En route the battalion had come under heavy fire from mortars and machine guns and managed to capture a hundred enemy prisoners. It did not take long for their commanding officer, to realise that their position was precarious and he promptly issued orders to withdraw to the north-east.

This left 2nd Rifle Brigade on their own. But hopefully not for long. After all, relief had been promised in the form of the tanks of 24th Armoured Brigade. This was not an immediate consideration for the riflemen because dawn had brought with it the first real chance to see exactly where they were and, more to the point, what sort of opposition they were facing.

Sergeant Joe Swann DCM

We were then ordered to stand to at first light, about 0530. As the dawn came up to our right we could see a big concentration of enemy vehicles. I remember just sitting there and looking round and thinking, 'There's a lot of vehicles here!' We had landed right in amongst this leaguer of German tanks, there were ambulances and everything else. It was an amazing sight, like a large car park![26]

By an amazing chance the Rifle Brigade had dug in right in the middle of the German 15th Panzer and Italian *Littorio* Division leaguers. The 15th Panzer Division was to the north of the position and the *Littorio* Division was to the south-west. The leaguers were full of men and machinery and the riflemen knew that the dawn would mean that the enemy would break camp and move out to carry out their orders for the day.

As they moved out they presented perfect targets to the

riflemen dug in at Snipe. Although common sense, their mission and military doctrine might have suggested to the riflemen that they should lie low and not give away their location, this course of action was not followed. Instead the dawn was broken by the sharp crack of the riflemen's 6-pounder guns.

Captain F. W. 'Tim' Marten CMG, MC

At about six, just as it was getting light, the party started. The two leaguers became clearly visible: the range was comfortable (800–1,200 yards). So we opened up with everything, 6-pounders, machine guns and mortars, causing a lot of 'brew-ups'. (Local vernacular: 'brew-up' is the order given when a column of vehicles halt, to brew some tea and cook some bully. Each vehicle does its own cooking on a petrol fire in a sawn-off petrol tin and the 'brew up' makes a little plume of black smoke. This, at close range, looks similar to a vehicle burning at some distance, hence the term 'brew-up' for an enemy truck or tank hit and set on fire.)

This was a most encouraging action, as the enemy were unhappily placed in close formation, and all they could do was to scram as quickly as possible. At the end there must have been twenty tanks and vehicles knocked out and our losses only one 6-pounder knocked out. (Four others had mechanical defects and failed to fire.)

One tragedy: Hugo Salmon, Tom Bird's second-in-command, received a hideous, disfiguring wound in his face, neck and chest. He lived till about midday, and then, mercifully, died.[27]

Sergeant Joe Swann DCM

For my first shot I took on a staff car, then I took on a 15-hundredweight truck. By then as well the gun had bedded down in the soft sand so I took up a Bren gun and I put two panfuls of ammunition straight into the mixture of vehicles which everybody by this time was firing at. Within five minutes the enemy had disappeared so relative calm then prevailed. We then set about getting the gun in a decent position because we were on a slope pointing upwards and we only had a 200-yard field of fire to our front.

We got this done and then for a hour or so there was a little bit of shooting going on which we didn't know much about but we had to keep our heads down because all the time we were there the enemy were sending over shells and so were our own people, none of whom knew exactly where we were.

Then the tanks started coming. On my front I could see two or three tanks but they were too far away to fire. From where we were I was on a height, looking down on a bowl. I had a grandstand view of nearly everything. It was just like being in a football stadium where you sit halfway up and you can see all the way round, although I couldn't see behind me where Charlie Calistan and another couple of guns were on our rear.[28]

Rifleman Owen Pannett, 2nd Rifle Brigade

I was positioned about fifty yards away from Sergeant Calistan's gun but from where I was I couldn't see much. It was the early hours of the morning and there wasn't much going on but suddenly the tanks started appearing. I was on the ground with a Bren gun and my job was to deal with the infantry as well as the crews of any tanks which were knocked out. The German and Italian infantry would arrive with the tanks. We kept them at a distance and didn't give them much chance.[29]

Rifleman Horace Suckling

Come daylight, on came the enemy tanks advancing with infantry behind them, our 6-pounder guns were putting a terrific barrage at the tanks. We were firing at the crews who bailed out and the infantry. What with the shelling and the smoke it was hell on earth. I went in with the Bren at the hip, aiming at the source of the enemy gun flashes, crawling and standing as best it suited my aim. The noise of the artillery was deafening. We had to watch our ammunition and we made sure we were not wasting it.[30]

Rifleman Vic Gregg, 2nd Rifle Brigade

Two medium tanks and an armoured car approached the position to our right, I am talking now as it affected myself, Reggie and Albie. Between us and the anti-tank gun to our right was another carrier section. In front of the anti-tank gun nearest to us was another rifle section, so placed as to defend this particular gun from any infantry assault. The three men crewing the anti-tank gun allowed the three vehicles to approach to 200 yards which was close enough to see the eyes of the drivers peering through their front vision slits, and then within half a minute the three vehicles, (one light tank and two armoured cars) disintegrated into a fireball of flame. This was a 6-pounder at work.

After that all hell was let loose. Their infantry attacked us with some show of force, unfortunately for them that five or six metres height advantage (which they had to climb in order to get to grips with us) became their undoing, they were just mown down in front of us, some of them no more than twenty feet away from our guns. This folly continued for some short period of time, when as smartly as the attack had come in so it faltered to a close. Then we had one of those lulls; the Germans pulled back and we lowered our sights.[31]

The result of this action was that six tanks were destroyed and two were hit in the north, and eight tanks were destroyed to the south and south-west where two self-propelled guns were also knocked out.

One of the first priorities for the battalion in the light of the dawn was to ensure that all the guns had the best possible fields of fire. This was complicated by the soft sand which required the 6-pounders to be pointing the way that their trails were facing. The guns effectively had their fields of fire restricted by the soft sand. Another restriction was that placed on the guns by the nature of the terrain. The scrub patches and the undulating folds in the ground were useful for defensive purposes as they did a very good job of protecting the riflemen and the guns but these undulations also interfered with the field of fire. This was both good and bad, good because the terrain often forced enemy tanks to attack in single file but bad because it meant that the gunners could only fire at an enemy tank when it had emerged from the natural cover and was almost on top of the position.

The process of readjustment involved repositioning some of the guns, digging in others which had become loose in the sand and moving others, a task that exposed the riflemen to enemy fire and which was to account for many of the Rifle Brigade's casualties at Snipe.

Major Tom Bird DSO, MC

When daylight came we found a number of our guns didn't have a proper field of fire and had to be re-sited. We had shot quite a lot of vehicles during the night so when daylight came there were vehicles all over the place. It was during this general movement that we lost two or three guns and a number of men killed. My second-in-command was killed at this time, Hugo Salmon. He was helping to move a gun and of course he was very visible. Most of the time the guns were not very visible. There was a little scrub and the guns were all dug in but some were dug in too far and had to be moved again. As far I was concerned any gun that could still fire had to be supplied with ammunition and any gunners who had been hit had to be replaced. There was a continual sorting out to ensure that any gun that could fire was manned and had ammunition.[32]

Sergeant Joe Swann DCM

As far as morale went, from what I could see everybody was quite happy. The guns were scoring and stopping the tanks and I think this was the biggest morale booster. If some of these tanks had come straight on after being clouted by one or two shells, well we'd have had to back right out of it. The thing is, they did stop them and I think this was the biggest thing.[33]

With morale high and the battalion scoring hits on the enemy tanks, things were looking up. However, at about 0700 hours a potentially serious problem had raised its head. The Rifle Brigade lost its forward observation officer, Captain Noyes of 2nd Royal Horse Artillery.

Captain F. W. 'Tim' Marten CMG, MC

One tragedy occurred at this time, our gunner OP got lost, God knows how. He was with me in the dugout at 4 o'clock, then disappeared. At half past seven our 7th Battalion (some two miles away) reported that he had arrived on foot. Evidently [he had] got lost, and walked all that way there. Apparently he decided (very foolishly) to try and walk back in daylight, which involved crossing a position strongly held by the Germans. We never saw him again. It was a terrible handicap having no

OP officer with us, as we had innumerable and most deserving targets – and further we had no means of directing or controlling the fire of our own artillery, which fell with accuracy and without let-up in our own position. In battle it's terribly difficult to identify the position of the forward troops on the ground, and cases of our own troops firing at each other always occur (cases of aircraft bombing and strafing our own troops occur even more frequently).[34]

In 1962, after C. E Lucas Phillips's book *Alamein*[35] appeared, Captain Noyes wrote to him and explained that he had been picked up by a German patrol and that he then spent the rest of the war in a prisoner of war camp. His loss was a severe blow to the battalion, the more so because of the way the enemy attacks were developing. Before advancing on the position they were grouping together and these groups of tanks would have made ideal targets for the forward observation officer to direct fire on to.

The Germans were unaware of the importance of their catch. They had other things on their minds. At 0740, about the same time as Captain Noyes was captured, they were making decisions about their own tactics for the day.

Deutsches Afrikakorps telephone message log, 27 October 1942

Feldmarschall Rommel to corps commander 0740 hours
Rommel: Today's policy will be to squeeze out the enemy. Economy on petrol is necessary.
Corps Commander: Ammunition too must be monitored.
Rommel: The only possibility of success is the push up from the south.[36]

In response to the order to move north the 21st Panzer Division was already underway and its Battle Group North arrived just after Rommel put the phone down.

Two riflemen from C Company, Eddie Blacker and Johnny Nelson, had finally arrived at the Snipe position around this time. They had walked there, having become separated from the main body of the battalion during the advance. But if they were under any illusion that they would simply take up position with the rest of their company they were wrong. No sooner had they arrived at Snipe than they were sent on their way again.

Rifleman Eddie Blacker, 2nd Rifle Brigade

We got to where the guns were early in the morning. We walked down and I said to Johnny Nelson, 'We'll have to find the company, I don't know where they've gone!' We went down to one of the guns and found Sergeant Eldo Francise there. He said, 'What are you doing?'

I said, 'Which way is C Company?'

He said, 'Never mind about C Company, see that tank down there?'

I said, 'Yeah.'

He said, 'The two of you, go down there,' and as he was saying this there was a pop pop pop, the noise of machine-gun bullets hitting the front of the 6-pounder. He said, 'Stop them sods firing at us.'

'Alright,' I said, 'we'll get going then. How do we get down there?'

'Use your bloody loaf!' He said. So we went down there, staying pretty low as we went. It took four or five minutes to crawl the eighty yards to the tank. It had been hit by a shell and it looked like it had been there for some time. It didn't look like a fresh hit because it had been on fire at some stage.

When we got to the tank we raked a lot of sand out with our hands, it was so soft. We made ourselves a nice position underneath the tank and we had a good look around because it was starting to get light by then. We turned around and could see what was happening. There was one tank which had come up and the 6-pounders had popped him off straight away.

We could see a good way and we were probably as high as the ridge. We were on fairly high ground and we could see this tank, a shell had hit it but it hadn't burst into flames although it had stopped it. There was no firing from anywhere when they came out of the turret so Johnny said, 'Shall we do it?'

I said, 'We should let them get away a bit further first otherwise we might find ourselves in trouble.'

'Alright,' he said, so as they went we popped them. One of them got away but the other two, they had no chance. The third one need not have had a chance, I think we were a bit soft on him.[37]

It was fortunate for the defenders of Snipe that Eddie Blacker was one of Marshall's twenty-five per cent of active firers because his actions as a sniper that day were to have an important effect on the battle. For now the two riflemen were in a good position. They were invisible to the enemy and they had an excellent field of fire. They had their guns, they had ammunition and they had water. They had plenty of targets to shoot at. But one thing which they did not have enough of was food. And it was in the eventual search for food that the peculiar conventions of the World War II British Army interfered in the smooth running of this particular part of the battle. These were to deprive Eddie Blacker of his fellow rifleman.

Rifleman Eddie Blacker

I had my Lee-Enfield rifle with me – if we had had a machine gun it would have been worse because the Germans would have seen us. We had filled our pouches and side pockets with ammunition from the boxes; I had about 200-odd rounds of ammunition with me. If we had loose rounds we used to use finished clips, fill them up and bung them back into the rifle. We would take the magazine out from the bottom of the rifle, press the rounds in or press them in from the top.

The sequence of firing a Lee-Enfield was simple – bolt back, forward, fire. The sight was just a titbit at the front of the rifle and then you had a clip which came up and this was marked from 200 to 2,000 yards and you just put it to whatever you reckoned it was and sighted up and started shooting. This was pretty good because we were taught to adjust our sights near enough to know where we were.

If you saw an infantry bloke and fired you knew you had hit him, whether he was dead or not you didn't know, but he would go down. In the films they jump but there was none of that, they would just go, bump, down.

The German snipers used to climb on to the sides of the tanks and they used to lay there and they used to fire from the sides of the tanks. The other infantry used to walk behind the tanks, sometimes you could have a go at their legs but the ones on the tanks were the ones doing the firing so you knocked them off first and the others were just a bonus, if you wanted it.

We were about eighty yards away from Sergeant Francise, it was a long way really. We had plenty of water, we had our water bottles. But we had nothing to eat with us. After a while Johnny said, 'I'll go and see if I can get something.'

'OK,' I said, 'but keep down low, otherwise you'll give our position away and we've had it then.'

He went off and that was it. I never saw him again. The next time I did see him it was four or five weeks later. He turned around and he said, 'Bloody cheek, I got up there and an officer says to me – what's your name? So I told him and he says to me – Right! You're my batman. He says – you've got flat feet, you're not fit to be a soldier.' So that was Johnny's job from then on! I didn't know who the officer was, I didn't ask him.

I wished Johnny had left me his ammo because I was having to stop there under that tank – for ever really, the way it was going. It was funny because you'd fire one round and they weren't expecting it from just there; it could have come from anywhere, it could have been a machine gun. They couldn't see me, there is very little smoke comes out of a rifle end. That's the reason I got away with it.

I was right under the tank and I could see right out the front. The British guns were to the right and the Germans were attacking all around. I could see our guns with ease and the way they were dashing about it was like a school party.[38]

Meanwhile the defenders of the main Snipe position had been under fire and not just from the German and Italian guns. The 24th Armoured Brigade had been sent to attack forward through Snipe using the position as a firm base and at about 0730 it made its first appearance. The Sherman and Grant tanks of the 41st, 45th and 47th Battalions of the Royal Tank Regiment made up the attack – it is worth remembering that 24th Armoured Brigade had been engaged in continuous fighting since 23 October.

47th Royal Tank Regiment had also lost its commanding officer, Lieutenant-Colonel Parkes DSO, who had been killed after he had attended brigade for orders at 2100 hours the previous evening. This added to the confusion, because although Major Ward was now in command and although he had also attended brigade for orders the previous evening, he delayed passing them on to the battalion because he was expecting the brigadier to issue revised orders at 0500 hours.

Finally orders to the squadrons were given out at 0530 hours and they stated (wrongly) that the enemy appeared to be occupying Snipe, apart from two companies from the 51st Highland Division. At 0600 hours brigade sent orders through for the tanks to move immediately owing to concern about shelling from the German 88-mm guns as the daylight increased. However, this was easier said than done. Shelling the previous evening had meant that the individual squadrons had scattered on the ground so A Squadron was ordered to move first and B Squadron ordered simply to follow. This was difficult enough given the dust raised by the leading tanks but the urgency and the fact that they had the wrong information meant that individual troops had little idea of what was going on. The stage was set for complete confusion.

41st Royal Tank Regiment also had orders to move towards Snipe in support of the 47th, but at 0630 hours the commanding officer, Lieutenant-Colonel J. B. Whitehead MC, TD, reported to brigade that the 47th had still not set off. Brigade responded by giving him orders to lead the advance. Of course by now the 47th was also on the move and it was not long before the tanks of the two battalions merged on the same track. Added to the confusion was the fact that no one knew exactly where the 45th Battalion was.

By the time the tanks came towards the Snipe position the battle was intense with smoke and dust reducing visibility considerably. The situation was also complicated by the fact that 5th Royal Horse Artillery, which was in close support of 24th Armoured Brigade, had lost its G Battery observation post when it ran over a mine.

As they came out of the minefields many of the tanks in A Squadron, 47th RTR, were hit by enemy guns firing at a range of 2,500 yards. Immediately they turned to meet this threat in irregular line formation. They were also aware of the noise of anti-tank guns firing away towards the enemy. As A Squadron tanks tried to take cover, B Squadron under Major Callan moved forward.

Lieutenant Fulton, A Squadron, 47th Royal Tank Regiment

I moved to the left and heard Major Callan calling his squadron together. He had great difficulty in rallying them and moved over the ridge minus four or five [tanks]. I could hear him calling them, and could see him waving a red flag. I could also see the tank he was calling on my left and moved across to them and led them through behind him. Major Callan had by this time advanced through enemy small anti-tank guns, and was giving magnificent encouragement calling up and saying 'Come through behind me, the bastards are packing in, it's easy.' He was then hit on the turret. He reported this on the wireless and the next I saw of him was on the back of his tank waving us on with his red flag. He was hit again with high explosive and killed.[39]

Visibility was still poor and it was not long before B Squadron tanks were hit as well. Everywhere there were small parties of enemy tanks and guns and many surrendered, although this turned out to be meaningless as there was no way the tank crews could deal with them. Many simply got back in the trenches and carried on the battle.

By 0730 hours the British tanks had made it to within 200 yards of Snipe and it is entirely understandable in the noise and confusion of battle that their first shells (75-mm high explosive) started landing inside the Snipe position itself. As the riflemen themselves realised it was excusable really as nobody knew exactly where they were. There were, after all, a large number of enemy tanks in the area and to the British tanks the weapon pits and guns of the Snipe position seemed like a good enemy target. But the fact that it was excusable did not mean the riflemen had to like it.

Lieutenant Warwick, A Squadron, 47th Royal Tank Regiment

On advancing through the enemy minefield, my squadron was held up by heavy shellfire. We replied to this fire until ordered to advance. We then advanced south-west for almost one mile. During this advance, I was on the right flank of the squadron, and in touch with a battalion of the Rifle Brigade (2nd Battalion), who were holding a position on the slopes of Kidney Hill. Several of our tanks on my left opened fire on these friends, killing several; I screamed over the air to stop this with little or no effect.[40]

Captain F. W. 'Tim' Marten CMG, MC

Our position was two miles in front of all the rest of our troops, and even the OPs couldn't get nearer – at that range it's difficult to identify an isolated packet of troops on the ground. Further a large number of guns and vehicles were destroyed in our area, and there was movement going on among them, so that it must have appeared to any distant observer as if our area was the centre of an enemy concentration (often it was). Anyhow we got plastered solidly all morning by our own guns, and also had two vicious doses of 75-mm fire from our own Sherman tanks, all of which was most unpleasant and made us very angry. Colonel Vic was hopping mad and told me to send all sorts of rude messages over the air, which I didn't do as they don't help.[41]

Lieutenant-Colonel Vic Turner VC

Shortly before 0730 hours we heard the noise of tanks from the east and the Shermans of 24th Armoured Brigade appeared on the ridge 2,000 yards east of 'Snipe' and started to shell us vigorously with 75-mm high explosive and machine-gun fire. There was really some excuse for it as we were surrounded by derelict enemy tanks and self-propelled guns and they themselves were being heavily shelled by 88-mm guns.

I sent Lieutenant Wintour off in a carrier to meet 24th Armoured Brigade. He found the leading squadron commander and said, 'Look here. You're shelling our position.'

'I'm awfully sorry,' said the squadron ccmmander.

'Not half so sorry as we are!' replied Jackie Wintour. The leading squadron stopped shooting, but not so the remainder of the brigade, who continued to roar us up [*sic*] until about twenty-five tanks started forming up about 1,500 yards to our south and south-west, when the armoured brigade began to realise who were the real enemy.[42]

Now that the situation had been made clear to the 24th Armoured Brigade the battle could continue with the help of the Sherman tanks. The gentlemanly discussion between Lieutenant Wintour and the Sherman squadron commander had been a timely one especially because of the arrival of the twenty-five enemy tanks. But before the next part of the fighting there was, briefly, a moment to look around and consider their position.

Captain F. W. 'Tim' Marten CMG, MC

By eight o'clock, when there was a temporary lull, we were able to take stock. The 6-pounder situation was serious, but not critical – there were four left firing to our south and south-west, four to the north-west and north and five to the north-east and east (which was the protected flank, and did not need as many as five, but it was impossible to move them, as attempts to do so with carriers, which were the only vehicles remaining in the position, had cost us several lives and six carriers burnt).[43]

But time to look around was short. The next phase of the battle was about to erupt. The fight for Snipe which had been fierce enough already, was now becoming even more intense.

By 0800 hours things should have been looking up. After all the tanks which had been sent into Snipe now knew who their friends were and, perhaps more importantly, where they were. But time to assimilate this information was short. As the British armour advanced towards Snipe the enemy were also moving. About twenty-five tanks with long-barrelled guns took position hull-down behind a ridge about 1,500 yards to the south and south-west of Snipe. Immediately the defenders of Snipe opened up on them and a gun of 14 Platoon scored three hits at a range of 1,100 yards. The crews of two of these tanks were then killed by machine-gun fire from the Shermans as they baled out.

At 0825 hours Colonel Becker of the German 15th Panzer Division was on the telephone to his divisional headquarters to report that some thirty-two vehicles – carriers, tanks and self propelled guns – were being engaged around Snipe.[44] At 0830 hours the first Sherman tanks came into the Snipe position and the battle became very fierce. Both sides laid down smoke screens which had the unfortunate effect of blocking any possible targets for the British tanks. However, the enemy made full use of the smoke and proved to be very good at firing a round of smoke at an individual British tank and then firing into it with their 88-mm guns. The tank crews had a terrible time.

Lieutenant C. H. Hanna, A Squadron, 47th Royal Tank Regiment

The order came through for the regiment, with A Squadron up, to advance and occupy the ridge from which fire was coming (which was in fact 2nd Battalion, The Rifle Brigade's positions). I brought my troop up to the left flank of the squadron and we advanced under a smoke screen, some of which was falling rather short amongst us. As we came up on the ridge, we were under shellfire, and then anti-tank guns opened up on us from all around, some at less than 100 yards. Most of the time we did not know what was hitting us. At the same time as we were receiving hits on our front, a shot from the rear removed our right idler and another penetrated the rear of the engines. We managed to recover the tank, but lost touch with the battalion.

As we came out, we were a target for every gun around, and smoke would have been very useful (which tanks other than squadron headquarters were not carrying). We were using the Browning machine gun at close range, which put up enough dust to help, when we got a second separated ammunition case. This put the gun out of action, as we had no tool for removing it, and had just used our spare barrel to clear a similar stoppage.[45]

Lieutenant Fulton

About 500 yards from them [2nd Rifle Brigade], the position of the tanks was Captain Crinks in 'Defiant' on my left front, myself followed by the rest of the squadron. 'Arran' and 'Defiant' were hit almost at the same time in front – Lieutenant Warwick just behind me. The spare driver of 'Arran' and Corporal Munn (commander) were blown out of the tank and took cover. 'Defiant' was on fire but still moving in reverse. I could not see the gun or guns which engaged us and withdrew about 100 yards to hull-down to try and spot him. We moved forward a bit to the left and came right on top of a Mark IV Special [German tank]. It was firing across our front. We put three rounds of SAP [semi-armour piercing] through it, and had to withdraw again, but it had ceased firing, and was smoking round the turret ring.[46]

Lieutenant Warwick

Two 88-mm guns then opened up and knocked out three tanks almost immediately. This gun was on the right flank and, although several tanks were behind me, none of them registered or attempted to silence it. My co-driver was killed immediately as the right ammunition sponson was hit and exploded. The projectile then ricocheted round the floor of the turret, killing the wireless operator and wounding the gunner.[47]

By 0845 hours seven Shermans had been set on fire and they started to retreat. For 47th Royal Tank Regiment the attack had been a disaster. Not only had they fired on the defenders of Snipe but they had also taken such a hammering that they were forced to withdraw behind the Oxalic ridge, together with 41st RTR. There they joined 45th RTR which had remained on the ridge giving covering fire.

The defenders of Snipe had not escaped unscathed either. The Shermans had approached the position close to where 239th Anti-Tank Battery was sited in the north-east part of Snipe. Two of their guns had taken a direct hit and Sergeant Smith, one of whose guns was hit, had been temporarily blinded for several hours. One of the Sherman tank drivers, badly burned and screaming loudly, was rescued from his tank and taken to one of the trenches where he later died.

The original 1st Armoured Division plan for 27 October had been for 24th Armoured Brigade to attack through Snipe and for 2nd Armoured Brigade to attack through Woodcock. Although 2nd Rifle Brigade had occupied Snipe there was certainly no way it could be any kind of firm base from which to attack the enemy divisions. Which left Woodcock. Due to confusion about 2nd King's Royal Rifle Corps' whereabouts and the fact that they had withdrawn from their position at dawn, Woodcock was clearly not going to be a firm base for an attack either.

This left 2nd Armoured Brigade in something of a quandary. At 0400 the brigade's tanks had broken leaguer and started to move north-west – at this stage it was still believed that at least one company of 2nd King's Royal Rifle Corps was on Woodcock. By dawn the three armoured regiments were moving cautiously forward. On the right were the Queen's Bays and in the centre were the 9th Queen's Royal Lancers who came up against enemy resistance and took at least fifty German prisoners. The 10th Hussars were on the left. They found that ahead of them the guns of the Snipe position were firing and they moved southwards in order to try and help the riflemen.

Major Douglas Covill MBE, DCM, *10th Hussars*

In 1942 I was a troop sergeant in 10th Hussars. We were equipped with Sherman tanks which we thought were very good because they were the biggest tanks we had been equipped with up until then. The Sherman tank could move fairly quickly and although it wouldn't stop an 88-mm shell it could stop a 75-mm shell.

The biggest trouble with the Sherman was the draught. The engine was air-cooled and the air was brought into the tank through the turret. This meant that, as you stood in the tank, your back was freezing so we would often wear our overcoats to keep out the cold.

The Sherman did have a petrol engine which meant that if you were hit the tank would go up in flames. We couldn't afford to think about that, we just had to get on with the job.

On 27 October 1942 we were positioned on a ridge which overlooked the position occupied by the Rifle Brigade. Our squadron was hull-down which meant we were just below the ridge so that we could observe without ourselves being seen. From where we were I could see the whole area where the Rifle Brigade was being attacked. A couple of hundred yards away to the left and slightly obscured by our own ridge was the Snipe position. This meant that when the Germans came in we were in a good position to be able to shoot some of them up. The whole squadron, fifteen tanks strong and each tank about thirty to forty yards from the next, was strung out in a line firing at the Germans.

To make sure we hit our targets we bracketed our fire. We would line up the tank and I would give the command to my gunner, '1,500 yards, fire!' He would set the sights to 1,500 yards and fire. If the shell went over our target I would say, 'Down 200!' and the gunner would move the sights down. If that shell fell a little short I would give the command, 'Up 100!' And that would get him.

We fired a couple of hundred shells that day, we had fifty shells in the tank and when we ran out we would be resupplied. I know we hit a number of enemy tanks that day but the only way we knew for certain that we had got one was if we set them on fire. Of course the tanks we couldn't hit got under the ridge and we could no longer take aim at them. The Rifle Brigade had to deal with these themselves.[48]

Although the Shermans of 24th Armoured Brigade were retreating back to the Oxalic ridge the Germans were not going to sit back and simply let them get away. The enemy tanks were at the extreme range of the 6-pounder guns on the Snipe position but that did not prevent the defenders of Snipe trying to hit them.

Lieutenant-Colonel Vic Turner VC

As they withdrew the Shermans were engaged by tanks and guns from the north. It was at a Mark IV special out of these tanks that 239 Battery had their first shoot. It was at extreme range, but at 1,800 yards the tank was hit and halted at the third shot, but another immediately came up and towed it away. Shelled as we were by tanks and guns, we sent an R/T message to brigade HQ, 'Our crying need is for an OP.' The reply was that one would be sent shortly, but he never arrived, though one from 4th Royal Horse Artillery tried to get through.[49]

The use of the 6-pounders at the edge of their range threw up an interesting difference in the fighting mentality of 2nd Rifle Brigade and the Royal Artillery. Through the day there were several instances of Rifle Brigade officers encouraging Royal Artillery gunners to have a go despite the fact that their own officers disapproved.

Captain F. W. 'Tim' Marten CMG, MC

We were much more, perhaps undisciplined is the wrong word, but we had some 88-mm telescopic gun sights from Jena-Zeiss which had been adapted for our 6-pounders and we were quite prepared to take an enemy tank on at 1,500–2,000 yards. I don't know that we killed them at that range but we certainly did them a lot of damage. The Royal Artillery gunners were much too disciplined to do that. In one of the intervals we did persuade one of them to have a shot at 800 yards and he did hit it.[50]

By now the situation on Snipe was becoming increasingly serious. Ammunition was running lower and the intensity of the enemy fire after the Shermans had withdrawn meant that even 2nd Rifle Brigade's own support parties were having difficulty in getting through.

In the event, there was only one more chance for the wounded to be sent back. At 0900 a dash by Captain Shepherd-Cross with three carriers managed to get through with the most severely wounded. On the way one of the carriers received a direct hit from a 75-mm shell. The idea was that Shepherd-Cross would return with more ammunition, medical supplies and the medical officer but such was the fire being directed on to Snipe that this proved to be impossible.

Captain F. W. 'Tim' Marten CMG, MC

During the day the fire was so intense on Snipe and on the approaches to it, that no vehicles could drive across to us, though Tom Pearson made an attempt on more than one occasion. This had two serious consequences: first Pic, the regimental medical officer, was never able to get to us (and we badly needed a doctor) and secondly we became critically short of ammunition, but couldn't get any more.[51]

Lieutenant Dick Flower MC

Because of all the fighting that had taken place there were dead bodies lying around as well as the filth that lies around in any battlefield. The flies were almost as bad as the enemy. The flies were simply appalling at

Alamein and during the daytime one was pestered by literally millions of flies. And even if one had time to eat a little food – and we were living at this time just on bully beef and biscuits and perhaps a little bit of jam from a tin if one was lucky – and if you put a little bit of jam on an army biscuit, if you didn't get it in your mouth within a couple of seconds it was simply covered in flies.

One of the other problems that we had and which sticks particularly in my mind was that our splendid doctor, who was the most marvellous fellow called Picton, unfortunately he was never able to get up on to our position at Snipe. As we were cut off for twenty-four hours he was never able to get up to us.

The only medical person we had there was the medical officer's splendid medical orderly, a splendid little man called Rifleman Burnhope, who, apart from being the medical orderly, was also the company barber. He was simply marvellous because we had a lot of casualties in this particular battle and despite the ground being covered by high explosive shells from the enemy and machine-gun bullets most of the time he quietly went about his job, moving from position to position tending and bandaging the wounded. I was so delighted when I heard later he had been awarded a Military Medal for that particular action which was extremely well deserved.[52]

> With the tanks of 24th Armoured Brigade now back in the relative safety of the ridge, the Germans and Italians promptly set about attacking the defenders of Snipe again, not just with tanks but also with infantry.

Lieutenant-Colonel Vic Turner VC

After the withdrawal of 24th Armoured Brigade to hull-down positions on the ridge to the eastward, Italian infantry started forming up as if to attack us from the south. The scout platoon of C Company got their machine guns on to them and dispersed them and also brewed up two British captured 15-hundredweight trucks, towing 6-pounder guns, which were about to come into action.

Two enemy tank attacks now developed. The first was by thirteen M13 Italian tanks from the west. I moved two guns to reinforce this sector, but moving them in heavy sand was very difficult and vehicles and men offered good targets for the enemy, and in doing so I lost three riflemen killed.

This attack was beaten off fairly easily and four M13s were brewed up. Meanwhile, 25–30 German tanks moved forward from their hull-down positions in the south to attack 24th Armoured Brigade. In doing so they moved right across our southern flank at about 1,000 yards. We engaged them, which caused them to detach half their strength to attack Snipe.

This gave an excellent 'cross ruff' as the tanks attacking Snipe presented excellent broadside targets to 24th Armoured Brigade, whilst those attacking 24th Armoured Brigade presented excellent targets to our guns on the southern face. At least eight were brewed up and the enemy tanks then withdrew.[53]

This same attack was described in a captured Italian war diary although some of the facts stated in this account do not match any of those from the British side.

Extract from the War Diary of the 12th Battalion, 133rd Regiment, Littorio *Division*

The battalion attacks. In spite of the violent enemy fire and the resultant initial losses of tanks and men the battalion advances firmly but keeping a certain distance from the anti-tank guns which are extremely well dug in and camouflaged. Suddenly there is most violent fire from another eight or ten anti-tank guns hidden on our left and in depth. A number of victims in the battalion, which halts too suddenly. Enemy fire becomes more and more violent. The survivors then give incredible proof of valour. 2nd Lieutenant Camplani from outside his turret urges his own tanks on to the attack and at the head of them, drives his own tank at full speed on the most forward anti-tank gun. He is stopped by a belt of mines in front of the anti-tank positions and by a shell which breaks his tracks.

2nd Lieutenant Stefanelli has his tank hit by an armour-piercing shell which penetrates and explodes. Lieutenant Pomoni's tank at the head of his company is hit in the engine and the crew miraculously saved. Lieutenant Bucalossi's tank is hit and set on fire. Lieutenant Zilambo is wounded in the right leg and saved by Lieutenant Luciano (the adjutant). 2nd Lieutenant Delfino continues the attack and is only stopped by the minefields.

Colonel Teege's adjutant and his interpreter follow the action from their own tank and report the actions of the battalion in battle to their commander. Colonel Teege expresses his admiration for the magnificent courage shown by the battalion and for the way in which Captain Preve commanded the movement of his own tanks and the Semoventi [self-propelled guns].[54]

> In the original war diary the time of this attack is given as 0700 whereas in fact it was carried out more than two hours later. Secondly the account exaggerates the opposition. At no time in the battle could ten guns engage the same targets at the same time. Even if the riflemen had wanted to, the nature of the ground would have meant it would have been very difficult to start moving the guns around quickly. For most of the time a single gun covered a single approach although for this Italian attack three guns were brought to bear.
>
> The Italian attack had been carried out under the direction of Colonel Teege of Panzer Regiment 8 who commanded the Stiffelmeyer group of German and Italian tanks on 27 October. The Italian war diary records a loss of nine tanks burnt and three tanks immobilised and four killed and eleven wounded. This is more than the four observed by 2nd Rifle Brigade and in the confusion of the day it is entirely possible that the actual number destroyed was somewhere between the two. Not that most of the riflemen had the opportunity just at that moment to ponder such questions.

Captain F. W. 'Tim' Marten CMG, MC

We caused a lot more casualties to the enemy, as did our tanks when they got back to hull-down positions. The banging and noise was terrific, shells were landing all round my dugout and each one caused a most unpleasant concussion inside. I think it was conspicuous because of the two wireless aerials, but we couldn't take these down without losing our communications.[55]

Although the tanks presented a serious danger to the defenders of Snipe, the riflemen who were not manning the anti-tank guns were busy fighting off infantry attacks. There was also the threat presented by the enemy machine gun nests which were a constant and ever present danger. Added to this were snipers who were using the tanks as cover to try and pick off the defenders of Snipe. But still in position under his burnt-out German tank was Rifleman Eddie Blacker. Apart from witnessing the tank attacks, he was ideally placed to take on the machine gunners and the snipers.

Rifleman Eddie Blacker

From where I was I could see German tanks everywhere. There was one that came within eight yards of where I was. I kept dead quiet and dead still – that was about 9 o'clock in the morning. Eldo Francise had hit a tank but the shell didn't stop it. It was so close to me that the sand as it turned came up over me. Then it went away and the next one was a lot further away.

I was mainly going after the snipers and the machine guns. From where I was I could see the machine guns and that was a simple job because I could pick them off. They were sitting up firing their machine guns and there were some of our blokes from one of the companies going round shooting grenades at them. There were quite a lot of machine guns. People say that there weren't lots of infantry there but there was.

The sun was up, bright and hot. They said it was cold the night before but it hadn't felt cold to me. You do get a bit excited in that sort of position; it's not gladiatorial or anything but you do really want it to get started.

The snipers were lying on the tanks. It was hard to see these snipers because they might be hidden by all the stuff rolled up on top of the tanks – the sniper might look like an extra belt or an extra track. A lot of these snipers were getting away with it but nobody knew I was there and it was a disaster for them. I had everything my way. I had no worries about getting hit. I knew they didn't know I was there.[56]

After the attack by the Italian and German tanks it was time to take stock. It was mid-morning on 27 October 1942. At 1030 a call went from the X Corps headquarters to 1st Armoured Division. The news was not good. Word had come through that

Rommel was moving 21st Panzer Division from the south to the north with the intention of joining in with the counter-attack. 1st Armoured Division was going to have to make an important decision: continue to support 2nd Rifle Brigade at Snipe or let them fight it out on their own. Major-General Raymond Briggs, commander of 1st Armoured Division, made his decision – the riflemen would have to fight it out alone.

There now followed a period of relative calm at Snipe although relative was the key word, because Snipe was still under fire. Even the simple act of having a bite to eat was something which had to be done with one's mind on other things.

Lieutenant-Colonel Vic Turner VC

After this phase the position as regards anti-tank guns was serious, as we had only thirteen guns left in action, and the guns firing to the west and south-west were extremely short of ammunition. We had therefore to carry up ammunition under heavy fire in Jeeps from the guns which had not been so heavily engaged. Shell fire continued to be intense and six of C Company's carriers were hit and set alight.[57]

Captain F. W. 'Tim' Marten CMG, MC

The ammunition situation was already critical, all the more so as any movement brought down instantaneous machine-gun and shell fire from the enemy and made it difficult, at times impossible, to carry ammunition from guns that didn't need it to those that were 'dry'. But the colonel, Tom Bird, and Jack Toms were very gallant. We had lost all sense of time, and were firmly convinced that it was four o'clock in the afternoon when it was only ten in the morning, Signalman 'Busty' Francis who was in charge of my 9 [radio] set cooked me some beans and bully, which I ate with a slab of chocolate and some raisins which we had found in the dugout. This gave me indigestion; one never can stomach food in a battle, one's always too overwrought. At this time I should think our bag was 40–45 tanks and enemy trucks knocked out, amongst them at least twenty tanks burning away merrily.[58]

While the defenders of Snipe were busy with food and the redistribution of ammunition, the German and Italian forces were preparing for their main counter-attack. For Rommel the continuing presence of the riflemen could not be tolerated – he had to push them back and beat the 1st Armoured Division before it could advance and attack the Axis forces.[59]

At 1300 hours the Germans and Italians were ready and the risk that the riflemen had taken in shifting the ammunition around the position proved to have been well worthwhile. Nine M13s assisted by some self-propelled guns attacked the western flank – they must have realised it was a weak point because they could see the burning C Company carriers.

Lieutenant-Colonel Vic Turner VC

At 1300 hours nine M13s attacked the south-west flank. Only Sergeant Calistan's gun was able to bear. I happened to be with this gun and made Calistan hold his fire till the leading tank was 600 yards off. Then he did some wonderful shooting, brewing up six, one after the other. The remaining three tanks kept coming on, blazing away with their MGs. Calistan was now almost out of ammunition, so Lieutenant Jack Toms, his platoon commander, brought up some in a Jeep, but the Jeep was hit and set on fire about ten yards behind the gun. We managed, however, to manhandle the ammunition to the gun, and with his next three shots Calistan scored a hat trick, accounting for the remaining three tanks.

After this he coolly turned round and said, 'We haven't had a chance of brewing up this morning, and as the enemy has now kindly lighted a fire for us, it is a pity not to take advantage of it!' He thereupon poured some water from his water-bottle into an empty tin and placed it on the burning Jeep, and we then proceeded to have as good a cup of tea as I've ever tasted.[60]

Sergeant Charles Calistan DCM, MM, 2nd Rifle Brigade

Two of my gun crew crept out on their bellies, right into the open to get to some ammo. They were under enemy fire the whole time and their progress was terribly slow. Then our platoon officer decided to reach his Jeep, which had four boxes of ammo on board.

God knows how he got to it, they were machine-gunning the whole way. He started coming towards us and then they hit the Jeep and it caught fire, but he kept on coming. We got the ammo off and then I had an idea. We hadn't had a thing to drink and we naturally hadn't been able to light a fire but here was a perfectly good one. So I put a can of water on the Jeep and it brewed up well enough for three cups of tea! . . . When the next tank attack came in the colonel was acting as loader on my gun. He got wounded in the head, a nasty wound and we wanted to bind it up but he wouldn't hear of it. Keep firing, that's what he wanted and we didn't pause. When the gun ran short of ammo he got it from one of the others.

When the colonel was too weak to refuse attention we bound up his head and put him behind some scrub. He called out that he wanted to know what was happening and my officer kept up a running commentary. We hit three tanks with three successive shots, and the colonel yelled out, 'Good work, a hat trick!' Another gun got two tanks with one shell, they were one behind the other and it passed right through the nearest one into the other and knocked both of them out.[61]

Captain F. W. 'Tim' Marten CMG, MC

At about 1.00 nine M14/42s (Italian tanks, not, of course, so formidable as German Mark IIIs and IVs) attacked us from the west. Sergeant Calistan's gun was the only one able to fire on this flank at the time as two of the others were 300 yards away, [their loaders] crawling on their tummies to get ammunition, and couldn't get back. The third was quite badly shell shocked. Colonel Vic loaded and observed, while Calistan aimed and fired. They held their fire until the tanks were 600 yards from them and then hit and set six of them on fire. They then had only one round of ammunition left.

The three remaining tanks continued to advance, machine-gunning hard and the bullets were splashing on the shield of Calistan's gun. Jack Toms arrived at that moment and, realising that ammunition had almost run out, ran back to his Jeep which was a hundred yards away and on which he had a box of ammunition. He drove it up to the gun. Of course it was riddled with bullets and set on fire, but Jack got the box off and dragged it to the gun. Colonel Vic was hit at that moment and knocked out for a few moments, but he carried on. Sergeant Calistan took on the three remaining tanks at 300 yards, and scored a hat trick, setting all three on fire.

It was for this action, crowning all his other gallant and successful

154

acts, that Colonel Vic got his VC. We put Calistan in for a VC too, (I wrote what I thought was an irresistible citation) but it was changed to a DCM. They said they couldn't give more than one VC to a battalion but Calistan certainly deserved one as well as Vic Turner.[62]

> Calistan's coolness under fire marked him out and his action in brewing up a cup of tea under extreme duress has to be one of the defining moments of the Snipe action. Everyone who knew Calistan mentioned his disregard for personal danger and he received a richly deserved DCM for Snipe as well as a commission.
>
> With this attack beaten off, there was another lull in the fighting – although between tank attacks there were the infantry attacks to worry about and it was up to everyone who could fire a weapon to help repel these – everyone including Eddie Blacker, still in his lonely outpost outside the main position.

Captain F. W. 'Tim' Marten CMG, MC

After this there was a (comparative) lull until 4.00. Tom Bird (in the head), Jack Toms, Charles Liddell, Dick Flower, Jimmy Irwin and Martin Crowder (badly, as you know) were all hit by now. Later John Lightly went missing (nobody knows how, I saw him go forward and I thought he was going to check on the position but that was the last we saw or heard from him).[63]

Rifleman Eddie Blacker

There were at least forty machine-gun nests, at a guess. There were probably more. Tanks were harder to estimate because sometimes they'd be coming this way and sometimes they'd be going that way. But there were quite a lot of tanks there.

It wasn't only me at the machine guns because someone else was going round throwing grenades at them but I reckon I must have put out at least some of them because I had such a clean shot. They were sitting upright like with our Vickers. Sometimes there were two men, sometimes three. When I fired – there's no two ways about it, I was a good shot – I didn't miss very often.

I always knew if I had hit the snipers on the tanks because sometimes they rolled off, sometimes an arm would just go down. I always thought if the tank track got their arm, it would pull it off and mangle it up.

I was firing at whatever came along. The first part, it was all the machine guns. They never sent anyone up to take their places. The machine guns were about 600–800 yards away, even as far as a thousand yards. Some I just couldn't get to. 600–800 yards isn't too far away when you have a good rifle. Mine was number 151 and I'd had it ever since I joined the Army. The number was etched on just where the bayonet fixes on.

I had four grenades but I never used them. Much later on in the afternoon there was one of our guns left firing and three tanks approaching. I watched the first one hit. By then I had gone through over 200 rounds of ammunition. At times I had to lay the rifle down because it got hot. It wasn't hot like a machine gun got hot – you could still hold it and still keep on firing but I worried in case anything got stuck in the barrel and the bullet casing fired back on me and messed up the rifle.

I felt I wanted something to eat. I never really got hungry and a drop of water usually sufficed but we did have tins with chocolate in them which was like half a meal on its own.[64]

Sergeant Joe Swann DCM

During the afternoon I noticed over on my left the Italian infantry coming along. There were about four lorry loads, each lorry had about forty or fifty chaps on it. We couldn't move our guns round but we did get the Bren guns at them. I went down and saw the commanding officer and I told him that the infantry had arrived on that position.

When I came back I lay down with the Bren gun to repel the infantry and they asked the artillery to frighten them. They gave the position of the Italians. Our artillery opened up with shrapnel and the first shell cracked up in the air over the top of us. No casualties at all. The second one landed right smack and I was bowled over. When I picked myself up Eddie Cope was smothered in blood. My old friend Joe Flint (my No. 2) was dead.

I was walking around for about a quarter of an hour with my head ringing. After getting Cope back to first aid I went on to my other gun crew and they had sheared a bolt – they had fired a couple of rounds and the main gun nut had shot off so they couldn't fire. I ordered them up to the other gun. I went forward to the infantry trench and sat down with a couple of infantry blokes. The infantry were in a trench in front of us and just below us protecting the guns. I sat there recuperating with a cup of hot water given to me by one of the chaps (it was awful).[65]

Captain F. W. 'Tim' Marten CMG, MC

There were only nine guns left firing, and we were desperately short of ammunition. My dugout contained two wounded riflemen, a wounded sapper, two signalmen, the colonel (who was by this time quite delirious) Tom Bird (out, groaning quietly), Charles Liddell (very over excited) Jackie Wintour, our intelligence officer (in excellent and amusing form), and myself.

As it was a minute hole, and the flies were quite frightful, settling in hundreds on one's face, clothes and hands, the discomfort and smell were considerable. At 4.00 some more of our own tanks appeared about a mile and a half away, and some of our own 105-mm self-propelled guns (Priests) gave us quite the most unpleasant quarter of an hour of an unpleasant day, Simultaneously the Germans started forming up for a big attack in two groups each of 30–40 tanks. The front group headed straight for our own tanks, passing within 500 yards of our north flank as they advanced.

This was the moment when 239 Battery got their first good shoot at a reasonable range . . . So we gave them absolute hell, setting seven on fire. That stopped their attack and the second group detached about fifteen tanks to attack us. (I could well imagine the German commander, very angry, saying on the wireless 'Rub those bloody guns out, and then we can get on with the attack.') Anyhow they came slowly towards us, head on. Three unluckily got into position hull-down behind a low ridge which overlooked our whole position and from then on shelled and machine-gunned us intensively until after dark from 500 yards away without our being able to reply.

The situation was now very exciting. We had only three guns left firing on the threatened. flank, None of those had more than ten rounds per gun left. They held their fire until the leading tank was only 200 yards away. The enemy were well spread out, at ranges varying from 200–1,000 yards and they made brilliant use of ground. We hit and halted the first one. That caused them all to jink a bit. In the next ten minutes we set three more on fire.[66]

Sergeant Joe Swann DCM

Then suddenly we had a warning that the tanks were coming round the far side. We couldn't see them at that time. There were three or four tanks coming through and no gun could engage them. I stood up and shouted out to Sergeant Miles, 'Get on that gun!' but then I was told that Sergeant Miles had been hit. It was then that I decided that I'd better go across myself so I stood up and started to run, I had about fifty yards to run and as I did so the German tank opened up with a machine gun. I straight away went to ground and crawled thirty or forty yards on my stomach.

With a 6-pounder you had the legs coming out – the chap that was going to fire the gun was cuddled up to it and on top you had the sights and the firing mechanism was below. What you did was you twiddled around and you lined up your sights and you put your hand down. As you came on to the target you yanked the handle up. The gun jumped and there was a rubber eyepiece round the sights so you didn't get hit. If you wore a steel helmet it would have been clonked all the time so you either pushed your helmet back or you threw it away. We threw them away or we played with them – we put a hand grenade under it to see what would happen, to see how far it would jump in the air, it was interesting. The sights were cross sights. To test them you would put a piece of string across the muzzle of the gun and you could look through the breech and if that was pointing on to the target you could line up your sights.

The only trouble with the 6-pounders in the sand was of course the fact that after you'd fired one or two shots you had to reline the gun because the sand was all over the place and you just had to scurry around shifting the trails and everything else to get the gun back on target again. At Snipe we had to be accurate. When these tanks came along we had one chance of hitting them or they would have hit us.

When I got to the gun I found there was no available ammunition so I scouted around and found a box with three or four rounds in it. I then took one of these rounds out, put it up the gun, at the same time noticing that the German tank was searching for me, it had seen me go down somewhere. I thought to myself, 'I'd better move this gun quick before he can get one at me,' and I swivelled the gun round and let him have one over open sights. It hit the tank and jammed his turret.

I then put another round up the breech and put this one into him taking careful aim and this time I really hit him. The tank stopped. It didn't catch fire. Two chaps bailed out of the top and ran and they left one chap inside badly wounded who was screaming out for help. He screamed for hours on end.

Then another tank came around the side and I got one at him quick. I then got the rest of the gun crew up on to the gun at this stage [they had been taking cover in a trench] and I went back to my own platoon.[67]

Rifleman Horace Suckling

To the right of our position was an anti-tank gun of ours; it had not fired for some time. It was late in the day, the noise was subdued. I decided to put my head up to have a look round. To my surprise there was a Mark III tank. I shot down in my trench and told the lads of the tanks behind us. We got our heads together to decide what to do, there was this anti-tank gun on our right. Some of us had had training on the anti-tank gun, [so] one of us would attempt to crawl to this gun. I said hold on, we will do a John Wayne effort by putting a tin hat on the end of our sword bayonet and show it over our trench. It was seen – the tank fired a few machine gun bullets at it – it knew we were here. The next thing was a terrific explosion over our heads, we thought it was the enemy tank firing at us, the next we smelt burning rubber. We looked up at the tank . . . it seems this tank was knocked out by Sergeant Swann who dashed over from another gun and as luck had it, he was successful.[68]

For this action in saving the position, Sergeant Joe Swann was awarded the DCM. His use of the 6-pounder anti-tank gun was a testament to the quality of the weapon which had only been in British Army service since earlier in 1942. It went through several modifications but it remained a devastating anti-tank gun – its 6-pound armour-piercing round had a penetration of 65 mm at a thousand yards – almost a third more than the German 50-mm PAK 38 anti-tank gun.

For now Joe Swann had beaten off the tank attack. The remainder of the enemy tanks retreated to hull-down positions just behind cover some 800–1,000 yards away and proceeded to plaster the Snipe position with devastating machine-gun fire.

Captain F. W. 'Tim' Marten CMG, MC

We hadn't more than three rounds per gun left. We expected an infantry attack at any moment, and the position was grim. We couldn't raise our hands without attracting fire, and it was just like that day at Sidi Rezegh waiting for the dark. I decided that it was now essential I had to burn the codes just as we were receiving withdrawal orders in code. In various accounts of the Snipe action it says that Vic Turner ordered their destruction but he didn't – he was delirious by this time. I did it off my own bat.

Later the brigadier spoke to me on the air and said we should wait. We should be relieved at 'a fashionable dinner time', which I took to be nine o'clock. The Germans would have understood the English as they had what was called the Y Intercept, mainly English-speaking Poles who were very smart and who picked up everything that was being said and who was saying it.[69]

It was time for the riflemen to leave the Snipe position. The 'friends' mentioned by the brigadier were the men of the Royal Sussex Regiment who were sent in to relieve Snipe and to take Woodcock although, as outlined earlier, their advance was to be disastrous. They must have passed the riflemen leaving Snipe but neither saw the other.

Captain F. W. 'Tim' Marten CMG, MC

As it got dark, just before 8.00 the enemy tanks pulled away. They were nicely silhouetted against the pale patch in the sky, and we loosed off our remaining rounds at them, more as a gesture of relief than with any hope of hitting them. We were still expecting an infantry attack, and one company gave the alarm, and withdrew.

We got all the wounded away in the remaining Jeeps and carriers, though it was a long business. Two Jeeps (one carrying the wretched Martin Crowder, who was in fearful pain) ran over a minefield which our own troops had laid across our line of withdrawal without telling us. Of course it really would have been impossible for whoever laid the mines to tell us, they probably didn't know we were out in front. Both blew up. Although nobody received worse injuries than bruises or broken ear drums, it can't have done them any good.

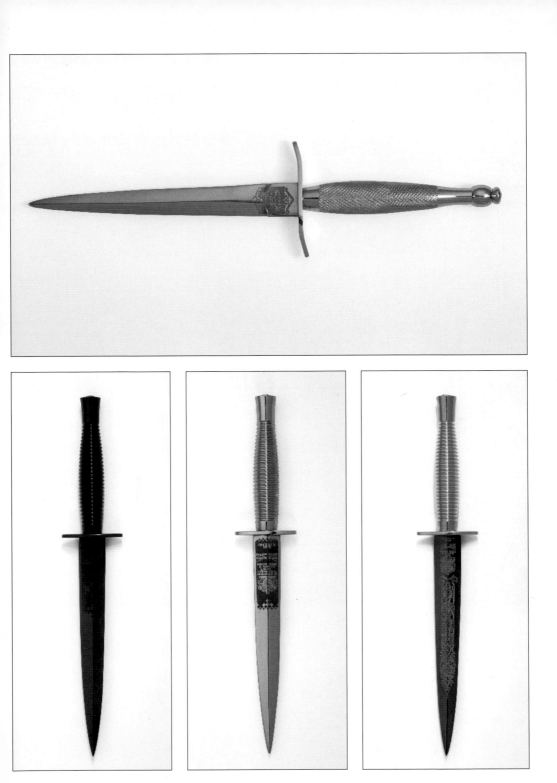

The Fairbairn Sykes Commando knife. The First Pattern knife (*top*) is the original design referred to in the text. The Black Knife, Silver Knife and Blue Knife (*above, left to right*) are the later and better-known mass-produced versions. *Reproduced with permission of Wilkinson Sword Ltd*

Above & right: Major W. E. Fairbairn demonstrating one of his favourite tricks at Camp X in Canada. He shakes hands with his unsuspecting victim and then pulls a knife and incapacitates him. *Reproduced with the permission of Lynn Philip Hodgson*

Left: The Shanghai Municipal Police Armoury where the Fairbairn Sykes Commando knife was first conceived and made. Sykes and Fairbairn are in the middle of the second row, both wearing glasses, Sykes on the left and Fairbairn on the right. *Peter Robins*

Above: Unarmed combat training of the Canadian Commandos, Ardentinny, Scotland, February 1944. *Gilbert Alexander Milne/National Archives of Canada/PA-183023*

Above left: Under the watchful eye of a Royal Navy instructor, Canadian Commandos learn how to disarm an opponent attacking with a knife, Ardentinny, Scotland 1944. *Gilbert Alexander Milne/National Archives of Canada/PA-183057*

Left: Able Seaman John Joyce of the Canadian Commandos (*right*) demonstrates the hold required against an opponent attacking with a knife. *Gilbert Alexander Milne/ National Archives of Canada/PA-183058*

British commandos disembarking in England after having participated in the raid on Dieppe, Operation Jubilee, 19 August 1942. In the foreground is Gunner Len Ruskin, B Troop, No. 4 Commando, who commented, 'We had gone a part way [to the battery] when we came across this barbed wire. I was getting across there when there was a big bang a bit further up. I tore myself away from the barbed wire and that's when my trouser leg was torn off.'
National Archives of Canada/PA-183776

The Lee Enfield Mark 3 rifle, the standard British and Commonwealth infantry weapon at the start of World War II.
National Archives of Canada/PA-63784

Oberstleutnant Willi Teege, Commander of Panzer Regiment 8, German commander on the ground at Snipe, killed in action, 2 November 1942. *Frau Dorritt Halverscheidt*

Above: A sniper in the town of Cupa, Italy, *ca.*1943. *Franklin D. Roosevelt Library*

Right: British Tommies move guardedly through the streets looking for snipers on the Italian front, *ca.* 1943. *Franklin D. Roosevelt Library*

Left: Corporal E. H. Pruner carrying a PIAT anti-tank weapon and a tommy gun, Motta, Italy, 2 October 1943. *Jack Smith/ National Archives of Canada/PA-167299*

Right: Demonstration of the Sten gun, 22 November 1943. *Barry Gilroy/ National Archives of Canada/PA-142630*

Below right: A 6-pounder anti-tank gun in action, Belgium, 9 September 1944. *Ken Bell/ National Archives of Canada/PA-137301*

Below: A German six-barrelled mortar – the Moaning Minnie – being examined by a happy crowd of newly-liberated Italians, 20 July 1944. *George Cooper/National Archives of Canada/ PA-132855*

Left: A Canadian Army chaplain gives absolution to a dying soldier, 15 July 1944. *Harold Aikman/National Archives of Canada/ PA-136042*

Below: A 2-inch mortar crew in action, 23 January 1945. *Michael Dean/ National Archives of Canada/PA-151019*

Above: This dead German soldier was one of the 'last stand' defenders of German-held Cherbourg. Captain Earl Topley, who led one of the first outfits into the fallen city, blamed him for killing three of his boys, France, 27 June 1944. *US National Archives, 111-SC-193970*

With German shells screaming overhead, American infantrymen seek shelter behind a tank. In the background can be seen the ruins of the town of Geich, Germany, which is still under heavy shelling, 11 December 1944. *US National Archives, 111-SC-197261*

A platoon surrounds a farmhouse in a town in France, as they prepare to eliminate a German sniper holding up an advance. Omaha Beachhead, near Vierville-sur-Mer, France, 10 June 1944. *US National Archives, 111-SC-190120*

The beachhead is secure, but the price was high. A Coast Guard combat photographer came upon this monument to a dead American soldier somewhere on the shell-blasted shore Normandy, June 1944. *US National Archives, 26-G-2441*

This Marine, a member of the 'Fighting Fourth Marine Division', threatens the enemy even in death. His bayonet fixed at the charge, he was killed by intense Japanese sniper fire as he advanced, 19 February 1945. *US National Archives, 109624*

The remainder of us waited for the relief. The Germans were active recovering tanks and collecting wounded. We didn't dare disturb them, even when they came quite close, as we were still getting wounded away, and they were in greater force than we. To start a fight wouldn't help the relief, which would anyhow be a tricky business.

By 2230 no relief troops had arrived, so the companies cleared off and I waited on with a few people, About 2300 a barrage by our guns started, which landed nicely into the German leaguer to our north. Being old hands the Germans moved towards us, reckoning that the barrage would move towards them. But it didn't, it thickened both backwards and forward and the German tanks were shifted right into the Snipe position.

We hastily rendered all the guns useless (of the original nineteen, ten were completely knocked to bits by enemy fire, and five others damaged) and cleared out. I was the last out together with Headquarters at about 2300. Three miles I walked. They were all asleep at brigade when I got there. Reported to the brigadier, who was surprised to see me, I was bloody tired.[70]

Major A. F. Flatow TD, *A Squadron, 45th Royal Tank Regiment*

About 2300 hours I heard the sentry's challenge and I walked forward . . . expecting to meet a volley of shots. Some weird swaying figures approached us. They were dressed in British uniforms but I was frightened of a trick. My mind itself was full of queer tricks and I asked the first wretched man for his AB-64. He nearly cried! 'Lord, Sir, we've been out there for twenty-four hours shot at by both sides and we're all in. Take my rifle!' They were, it transpired, the remnants of a battalion of the Rifle Brigade.[71]

It took a while for the achievements of Snipe to sink in. The riflemen had certainly frustrated Rommel's attempted destruction of 1st Armoured Division and they had inflicted grievous losses on the 15th and 21st Panzer Divisions as well as on the Italian *Littorio* Division. The official tally was twenty-one tanks, eleven M13s, five self-propelled guns and six other vehicles. But this was a minimum. During the action the riflemen had heard the clanking of vehicles being towed away and it seems certain that the actual tally was much higher. How high? Ask the men who fought there and they think a total of 100 not to be unreasonable.

As far as Snipe itself goes, there are a number of points about the battle which are worth highlighting. Firstly, the battle was made up of a number of individual phases and most guns participated in two of those phases. Interestingly two guns never fired at all and four guns claimed no hits. Secondly the forward observation officer could have been a huge help because most of the attacks started after the enemy formed up in dead ground or out of range of the anti-tank guns – they would have been ideal targets for artillery. Lastly, most of the casualties at Snipe came when the riflemen were moving around the position and not when they were firing their guns.[72]

However many tanks and guns were knocked out, they were losses that Rommel could ill afford. And Rommel knew it. He was forced to bring more men and machines north to replace those he had lost, leaving the south dangerously weak.[73] Snipe was a turning point at El Alamein and of course El Alamein was itself a turning point in World War II.

By the end of 1942 it had been shown that the main obstacle to the tank was the anti-tank gun, rather than other tanks, and this was a lesson which Rommel realised had to be learnt if the war was to be won. He called for more production of anti-tank guns which were cheaper and faster to build than tanks. But events overtook him. From Normandy onwards the smaller hand-held anti-tank weapons were what was needed in the confined spaces of the push into North-West Europe, not the bigger anti-tank guns which could be towed around the desert at will. And of course the Germans suffered from Allied air and armoured superiority.[74]

These same events which were to overtake the Germans also overtook 2nd Rifle Brigade. After the desert war the riflemen, minus many of the officers and men who had fought at Snipe, were sent to Italy where they would face the Germans on foot as ordinary infantry. The omens were not good.

Notes

1. Major H. G. Parkyn, *Rifle Brigade Chronicle for 1944*, The Rifle Brigade Club and Association, 1945, pp. 87–9
2. R. H. Haigh and P. W. Turner, *David and Goliath – The Great Stand at Snipe*, Sheffield Hallam University Press, 1998, p. 1
3. Grossman, *On Killing*, pp. 98, 120–2
4. Letter to the author
5. Lt Col Dave Grossman, *On Combat*, PPCT Research Publications, 2004
6. Grossman, *On Combat*, p. 197
7. Marshall, p. 150
8. Grossman, *On Combat*, p. 203
9. Lt-Col M. E. S Laws, *Campaigns in the Middle East*, National Archives, CAB 44/103, Part III, vol I, pp. 119–24, 186
10. Author interview
11. Letter to the author
12. Author interview
13. Imperial War Museum, Sound Archive, 13023
14. Letter to the author
15. *Sic*. He probably means company
15. Author interview
16. Lt-Col V. B. Turner vc, 'The 2nd Battalion at Snipe', *The Rifle Brigade Association Journal*, June 1949, p. 33
17. Turner, p. 34
18. Turner, p. 35
19. Author interview and subsequent correspondence
20. Author interview
21. Turner, pp. 35–6
22. Author interview and subsequent correspondence
23. Dick Flower interview *c.* 1982, provided to the author by Joe Swann
24. Author interview
25. National Archives, War Diary – TAC HQ Eighth Army, WO169/3911 sheet No. 33
26. Author interview
27. Author interview and subsequent correspondence
28. Author interview
29. Author interview
30. Letter to the author
31. Vic Gregg, unpublished memoir
32. Author interview
33. Author interview
34. Author interview and subsequent correspondence
35. C. E Lucas Phillips, *Alamein*, Heinemann, 1962
36. Imperial War Museum, AL 834/1
37. Author interview
38. Author interview

39. Royal Tank Regiment archive, Tank Museum, Bovington
40. Royal Tank Regiment archive, Tank Museum, Bovington
41. Author interview and subsequent correspondence
42. Turner, p. 38
43. Author interview and subsequent correspondence
44. War Diary 15th Panzer Division, Imperial War Museum, AL1657/1
45. Royal Tank Regiment archive, Tank Museum, Bovington
46. Royal Tank Regiment archive, Tank Museum, Bovington
47. Royal Tank Regiment archive, Tank Museum, Bovington
48. Author interview
49. Turner, p. 38
50. Author interview and subsequent correspondence
51. Author interview and subsequent correspondence
52. Dick Flower interview *c*. 1982, provided to the author by Joe Swann
53. Turner, p. 39
54. Appendix D to the official after-action report on Snipe provided to the author by Tim Marten. This after-action report was later heavily edited at Eighth Army HQ and the revised version placed in the National Archives.
55. Author interview and subsequent correspondence
56. Author interview
57. Turner, p. 39
58. Author interview and subsequent correspondence
59. Feldmarschall Erwin Rommel, *Krieg Ohne Hass*, Verlag Heidenheimer Zeitung, 1950, p. 243
60. Turner, p. 39
61. From the Eighth Army weekly newspaper *The Crusader* of 8 November 1942
62. Author interview and subsequent correspondence
63. Author interview and subsequent correspondence
64. Author interview
65. Author interview
66. Author interview and subsequent correspondence
67. Author interview
68. Letter to the author
69. Author interview and subsequent correspondence
70. Author interview and subsequent correspondence
71. Imperial War Museum, document archive 99/16/1, p. 34
72. Major N. O'Connor, 'Historical Analysis of Anti-Tank Battle – The Battle of "Snipe" (Alamein 1942)', Defence Operational Analysis Establishment, 1989 (670/201), p. 26
73. Rommel, p. 255
74. Major N. O'Connor, 'Historical Analysis of Anti-Tank Battles – Characteristics and Use of Anti-Tank Weapons, The Desert War 1941–1943', Defence Operational Analysis Establishment, 1989 (670/200), p. 37

CHAPTER 6

Italy – Failure at Tossignano

The period 27 October 1942–12 December 1944 was 778 days and in that time 2nd Rifle Brigade, went from a glorious victory at Snipe to inglorious defeat at Tossignano. Why?

Many of the clues for this drastic reversal of fortunes can be found in Alex Bowlby's famous memoir, *The Recollections of Rifleman Bowlby*.[1] Bowlby served with B Company, 2nd Rifle Brigade, after its arrival in Italy right through the campaign and he records how, a VC having been won at Snipe, the battalion expected to be sent home, but instead it finished up that only the 1937 regulars were returned; the rest had to go to Italy.

Between times the battalion was described by its commanding officer as 'restless'[2] and even had the audacity to boo the king when he came to inspect the riflemen, for which impertinence the battalion was sent off on route marches in Palestine.[3] None of this, of course, finds its way into the regimental history.[4]

Thus the battalion started the Italian campaign minus some of its most experienced and best soldiers. Colonel Turner, had gone, so had Major Bird, Captain Marten and Sergeant Swann, one of the old regulars. But others remained with the battalion. Eddie Blacker was still there, although he was badly wounded at Perugia and was out of action for Tossignano. Charles Calistan, now an officer with 7th Rifle Brigade, was also in Italy although he was killed on 30 July 1944 at Arezzo, a sad ending for a man who had been one of the heroes of Snipe.

181

Rifleman Joseph Belzar, 7th Rifle Brigade

We were still awaiting the return of Chas. Calistan's patrol. Sometime in the early morning I glanced up from our sheltered position to see a figure leaning against a lone tree, silhouetted on the brow of a hill to the right of the track. At the same time our platoon sergeant, Sergeant Brender called out, 'Don't shoot, it's Mr Calistan!' Even as he called there was the sound of a shot – enemy or friendly has never been satisfactorily determined – and Mr Calistan fell and rolled down the hillside into the long grass at its foot some sixty yards or so from where we were . . . I left the ditch and ran, crouching, across the track, behind the abandoned Jeep and into the exposed area beyond. I reached Mr Calistan and saw that a bullet had entered his neck. His head was covered in blood and it was obvious that he had been killed immediately.[5]

Although morale was certainly a factor in the downward spiral of 2nd Rifle Brigade, there were other factors too. In the desert 2nd Rifle Brigade had been a motor battalion, able to move fast and fight fast. This fighting was done at a distance. In Italy, however, the Bren carriers and anti-tank guns were taken away and riflemen who had prized their independence in the desert now found themselves in 3-ton trucks reduced to being ordinary infantrymen once again, expected to close in and fight the enemy close up. The groups who had served on the 6-pounders were broken up and the dynamic which had sustained their fighting was gone. Now it was each man fighting with a rifle.

It was not something they were trained for or were good at. If success in battle depends upon training and conditioning then the men of 2nd Rifle Brigade had neither for the type of fighting they were to undertake in Italy. 7th Rifle Brigade faced a similar problem as it too was stripped of its vehicles and reduced to ordinary infantry. Only 10th Rifle Brigade kept its motor battalion status. The three battalions were brigaded together as 61st Infantry Brigade.

Why were these battalions stripped of their status as motor battalions? Alex Bowlby concedes that the general who made the decision may have, 'had a case',[6] but that the messy action by 10th Rifle Brigade near Cassino caused the divisional general to decide that 2nd and 7th Rifle Brigade should lose their motor battalion status, while 10th Rifle Brigade should keep theirs. It was a decision all the more resented because the 10th Battalion was a Territorial unit.[7]

Of course there was a point to the change in status – the war in Italy was very different to that in the desert. But the problem for the riflemen was that they were thrown in at the deep end and had to learn as they went along. According to Alex Bowlby, 'We were never trained properly for hill fighting, we had to pick it up as we went along. The battalion was given the highest rating in the desert but it dropped to "unreliable" in Italy.'[8]

If anything the fighting in Italy was more reminiscent of the fighting in Portugal during the Peninsular War which the Rifle Brigade had taken part in as the old 95th Regiment. But thoughts of daring feats by riflemen of old were not going to help in Italy where the riflemen knew more about fighting at speed in the desert than about fighting in the Italian country-side on foot.

So what was this fighting in Italy which the riflemen had to adapt to? 7th Rifle Brigade made the change from motor battalion to infantry battalion just before the action at Perugia where, on 19 June 1944, the battalion was ordered to take a 652-metre mountain called Monte Malbe which, because of its position overlooking Perugia, was of critical importance. Perugia itself was a meeting of roads and was essential to secure the onward advance of the British Army.

In the following account note the attempted desertion by the British riflemen and the prompt action by Rifleman Taylor which stopped them, although they later did desert during the night. Once again in the course of the battle the willingness to fight by a number of key individuals was crucial.

Rifleman Henry Taylor, 7th Rifle Brigade

For the advance on Perugia all the battalion was dismounted,. The blokes in the scout platoon rejoined the infantry companies and our happy band sloped off to be with 3 Platoon in A Company. Our officer had been a sergeant in the carriers but had been made up to a one pipper [2nd lieutenant]. He told me and another carrier driver to form a section with another five blokes. I was to carry a Bren while the others were carrying, apart from their own weapons, extra ammo and picks and shovels.

There was no time for anything else but to check your weapons – some blokes spent ages oiling the .303 rounds before putting them in clips, this was so the ammo slipped easily into the breech of the weapon. Others filled Bren-gun pouches with magazines. The sections would go into action with more than the usual one Bren, to stand up to Ted [*Tedesco* – Italian for 'German'] you had to win the fire-fight with him; it was no use running out of ammo and having to withdraw. Our officers would carry rifles or Thompsons – you had to have this much firepower, there was not that many of us you see.

Night attacks had become an obsession with the British Army, especially when fighting Ted . . . but it left the attacking infantry tired and having to do a great many things before Ted's first counter-attacks came in . . . Our colonel made sure that the battalion had lots of wireless sets, lots of spares and that they worked. Having been trained as a motor battalion, we all knew the importance of the wireless . . . All pretence of surprise ended when C Company caught Ted trying to pull a 10-inch gun [*sic*] up to the summit. There were a couple of horses which the lead section shot, this stopped Ted moving the gun. If he had been able to position it, it would have blown Perugia down around the Guards' [Brigade] ears.

However, the shots woke up every Ted for miles around and once awake he responds to situations with breathtaking speed. A Company started taking mortar fire straight away. Ted was trying to drive us up the mountain so he could destroy us. He was always trying to inflict maximum damage by cutting off support and then doing you as you tried to withdraw. Even so, we had found the safest place to be around Ted was right up next to him, so the sections scrambled up the terraces reducing the range for his mortars . . . we did not see any of Ted's infantry as we scrambled up the terraces. Casualties did start to mount, a lad in the section in front of us was hit by a mortar, a fragment blew the top of his head off and he bounced back down amongst us.

He was a ginger haired kid – I had seen him around for a while, but I never did ask his name. Men hit in the head do not always die at once. The lad lay there in convulsions and this was enough to prompt five blokes in our section to try to bolt. I had the Bren so I put a burst over their heads and asked if they were leaving? This did the trick; desperate situations need desperate solutions. Officers were shouting that no one must stop before reaching the summit so were all swept along with the not so happy throng all heading for the top.

Our officers were very professional, not given to stirring speeches. All they would say was, 'You know what to do, let's get on with it!' So when we reached the top of Malbe we started to dig in. The summit was rock so we moved back down to some plough, which enabled us to dig scrapes just deep enough to kneel in. Ted's mortar was having trouble finding us. We were slightly off to a flank and on the reverse slope; any infantry attacks would be caught in cross-fire, from us and C Company's left-hand platoons.[9]

Rifleman Joseph Belzar

By now our arrival had been observed from the adjoining hills to our right and immediate front and we were being subjected to both mortar and machine-gun fire. The pause in fire before our arrival at the crest was probably due to the fact that we were so close on the heels of the previous occupants.

In a short time the incoming fire was becoming severe and the bare slopes of the hill were no place to be. As I crawled forwards a few yards I found a perfectly formed slit trench some four to five feet deep which would provide some reasonable protection. Fear of booby traps, S-mines and the like prevented me from using it and, as shells were beginning to rain down alongside it, I pressed myself close into the ground. In the brief intervals between the shelling I observed some 300 yards or so away, on the hill to the right, two or three figures hurling themselves into what was probably a machine-gun or mortar pit.

By now the Artillery OP officer had arrived and was crouching in a position nearby and I was able to provide him with the location of this possible target. Unfortunately the artillery had been unable to match our night time advance and little use could be made of my information. I saw Lieutenant Whitehead of D Company, who had instructed a class in German a few months previously, firing a PIAT mortar desperately in that direction, whether or not at the same target I never knew as he was killed minutes later.

As I lay alongside the inviting slit trench I could see forward down the slope beyond the farmhouse. [Belzar then recounts how he had a chance to shoot a German observer and did not do so; this passage is quoted above on p. 26] It may be that if the observer had been killed the enemy mortar would have ceased firing and there would have been fewer casualties in our ranks over the next few hours.

I am sure that in that situation it made no difference. We were so close that observation was not necessary – all the mortar crew needed to do was to pepper the crest of the hill at random, which is what they continued to do.[10]

Rifleman Henry Taylor

The first counter-attack came within a few minutes of me finishing my scrape. You could hear Ted as he started to come up over the top – his equipment banged and jangled. The mortars lifted to further back down the hill and then in came the infantry. The Rifle Brigade have an order, when an enemy is seen you are told to, 'fire to your front!' This means that you direct your fire immediately in front you, [so that] an enemy will receive one round and not a multitude with everyone firing at one bloke.

As Ted's infantry came up over the top of the summit they were met by rapid rifle fire and bursts from the Brens. Most must have died from head and chest wounds; they had expected us to still be on top of the ground and not under cover. The attack was stopped cold, as was the next, [but] the mortars still kept up their bombardment between attacks.[11]

Rifleman Joseph Belzar

I realised that, being on the forward slope of the hill, I was exposed to view and firing from such a position would not be to my advantage – to put it mildly – I realised that discretion was the better part of valour. By now mortar shells were raining down and some 88-mm guns had also found our range.

For the first time in Italy I was scared; it was time to make use of the slit trench. I dived in and huddled close to the bottom. After a while the shelling eased and I moved back to speak to the platoon commander or platoon sergeant. I found the platoon commander wounded in the leg, being assisted down the reverse slope. He gave me a half smile – his war was over. I never saw him again. Sergeant McCaffery sat in a small depression, head in hands, crying uncontrollably. The platoon was without an officer or senior NCO and Larry Fyffe, the company commander, came across to our position. Shelling was still severe but not as intense as before and a rifleman made a quick brew up for the half dozen or so of us around the small depression. I took a mug to each of Rifleman Reid and Rifleman Cole sitting together in a nearby slit trench. A minute or two later a shell landed at the side of their trench – I rushed over but they were both dead.[12]

Rifleman Henry Taylor

The first night came and went – we took it in turns to sleep. This is when the five blokes in our section 'tapped the sling' and bolted. This left two men holding a section front, not a very good situation, so with my comrade, the other carrier driver, we set the Bren up on fixed lines and fired at various intervals. Ted must have been able to infiltrate and I am sure he did.

The top of Malbe had ceased to look like an agricultural landscape. The impact of the mortars had blown away the thin topsoil and, along with our own shells, exposed the rock underneath. Each explosion showered the infantry with fragments of shell and rock. Most of the wounded were struck by this combination.

Empty cartridges lay piled around the riflemen; hand grenades were used by both sides. A 36 grenade, as used by the British Army, has a blast radius of about thirty yards. Cntrary to popular myth it does not break up into small bits but fractures in half or thirds . . . The cordite fumes from the weapons clouded the battlefield, this gave us some protection in our exposed position.

Ted's infantry attacks became more desperate. He had to take this position back; if it remained in our hands then large areas of his defences would be overlooked from the top of Malbe. Our own guns were breaking up his attacks, although our forward positions were only just holding on. Ted must have been losing dozens of blokes. We found out later that there were elements of several of his divisions involved . . .

Ted was able to infiltrate his snipers around our left flank, although we too had a couple of blokes up there from our sniper section. One in particular, an Irishman, was known to me. He took up a position where he had a good field of fire and claimed thirteen Teds while we were up there. He survived the rest of the year but was hit in the shoulder by a Ted while gathering water. The wound did not look that bad; he said he would be back but I did not see him again. When I returned to Italy several years ago I visited the British Commonwealth Cemetery north of Florence. Walking along the lines of graves I found this bloke; he had been dead for almost fifty years. Talk about a shock.

Everyone was involved in the defence of our positions: clerks, drivers, even the cooks. Officers would have a scratch around, form a reserve of a few blokes and use them when they were required. When Bombhead [Lieutenant-Colonel Douglas Darling, CO, 7th Rifle Brigade] was wounded in the shoulder his second-in-command took over. I was standing next to the wireless carrier half way up Malbe when he came past. My task had been to protect the wireless operator. This was better than sitting in my little scrape and having my arse shelled off.

I did not get too much time protecting him as a sniper put a bullet through his head. It was a good shot as the round must have passed over my shoulder. After running round to the other side of the carrier I poked my head over the top. Seeing Bombhead I moved smartly back but did not salute him. He glared at me, waiting for my usual grin. 'What are you doing?' he whispered. I thought, 'Keeping my bloody head down, and, by the looks of you, that's what you should have done!' Luckily for me, my reply came out as, 'Protecting the operator, sir!'[13]

The action to capture Monte Malbe was a typical one. The terrain was difficult and mountainous. Each hill or building which was the target of the fighting was one of many objectives which needed to be taken during the Italian campaign and the fire-fight was typically carried out at company level. The counter-attack always came back quick and hard and was often more difficult to repulse than the original fight to capture the objective.

However, 7th Rifle Brigade had succeeded at Monte Malbe, despite the inclination of some of the riflemen to desert the regiment, despite the fierce counter-attacks, despite the fact that they had just changed from being a motor battalion.

2nd Rifle Brigade was not to be so lucky at Tossignano.

The capture of Tossignano was crucial to success in Italy and the northwards drive to the Po before the winter set in. By now Allied troops were fighting from Normandy through to Germany and the end of the war seemed to be in sight. According to the regimental history,

The reason that the failure of the attack on Tossignano created such an impression was that it occurred at a time when success had become commonplace, when it seemed, even in Italy, that the process of advancing had become almost automatic.[14]

Tossignano and its neighbouring hamlet of Borgo Tossignano was on yet another hill and occupied a naturally strong defensive position, so before the attack could begin there was an initial period of reconnaissance and patrols.

Sergeant A. R. Minkoff MM, 7th Rifle Brigade

It was now November [1944] and it seemed certain that, with winter setting in, the advance would become completely bogged down. This was no terrain for tanks and their only route to Forli and the Po valley, considered ideal tank territory, was past a dominating feature way up on top of the mountain, a town called Borgo Tossignano, which was heavily fortified and completely dominated the roads beneath. Unless Tossignano could be captured by the infantry, there was no way that the tanks could advance and the campaign would be halted for the winter. The position was similar to the situation at Monte Cassino.

We accordingly made our way up the mountains on foot, carrying all our light equipment by hand. The heavier equipment went by mule train; no vehicle could cope with the steepness of this mountain and believe me, it was tough going. We were going to an area called Fontanelice which had been captured by another brigade, whom we were now relieving. This was now the absolute forward position.

Borgo Tossignano was only three-quarters of a mile ahead and you can consider the area in between as no man's land. Of course there were many farmhouses in this area, some occupied by Germans, some by us. And, of course there were many farmhouses, usually severely damaged, which would occasionally be occupied by either side. There were also slit trenches on either side, which had to be occupied at first light as defence against possible attacks. The whole area contained mines and booby traps. This type of warfare was as close to World War I trench warfare as one could get, because movement was so limited. The days were filled with the sound of machine-gun fire, mortar bombing and shell fire from both sides but all this stopped magically at 7.00 p.m. every night. The reason being that at 7.00 the mule trains that had carried our rations up the mountain arrived, together with the post and, as the German mule trains arrived at the same time at Borgo Tossignano, it was mutually accepted that war was bad enough with rations, but without them it would be bloomin' horrible!

The main activities were patrols, invariably at night. There were three types of patrols, known as standing patrols, recce patrols and fighting patrols. Most of the patrols we had to do were recce patrols which were always led by a sergeant who had to choose the men he would lead. Recce patrols were sent out to gain information – whether a certain farmhouse was occupied, in what strength, etc. etc. Fighting patrols were much larger and would be led by a commissioned officer and their objective was to gain information by fighting for it, if necessary.

There was going to be an attack on Tossignano in early December by our brigade so we had patrols out every night to get as much information as we could about Tossignano's defences.

On one occasion I led a patrol of five men to discover whether a certain farmhouse was occupied. We arrived at our destination and there was no sign of life. No sentry, so we moved even closer. There was a window open, so Gerdes-Hansen suggested that he crawl forward and lob a grenade through the window. I agreed, foolishly, because he lobbed his grenade, missed the open window, and the grenade bounced back towards him. He moved like lightning and the explosion caused only a minor wound to his leg, which I dressed before going back to make my report. The farmhouse was definitely unoccupied.[15]

The plan for the attack on Tossignano was simple. Reconnaissance patrols had established that there were two possible entrances to the town. One was called Point 222 and led into the bottom of the town at its south-east corner. The other was called Point 282 which led straight into the middle of the town. However, both were narrow with steep approaches which meant that only one platoon at a time could attack.

2nd Rifle Brigade led the attack on the night of 12/13 December 1944 with the start scheduled for 0200 hours. 7th Rifle Brigade staged a diversionary attack on Borgo Tossignano which went in three hours previously. This diversion went well but the German defenders started to cause casualties as the 7th started to move to their next objective, called Casa Frascoleto, on the way to Tossignano.

With the Germans awake and fighting, disaster loomed for 2nd Rifle Brigade, who were shelled by British 25-pounder guns on their way to the start line causing twenty casualties. The next problem was that the Germans knew from experience of the creeping barrage exactly where the British infantry were just from the fall of the shells. The stage was set for a monumental failure.

Extract from the diary of Rifleman R. L. Crimp, HQ Section, 2nd Rifle Brigade

14 December

Corporal Furze, with one or two others, was whacked in the opening assault . . . they say our creeping barrage got him. It wasn't creeping fast enough and when it was lifted 400 yards forward it was too far forward to give much help.

16 December

The attack has failed. Worse, the battalion has suffered a severe mauling. Cpl. Mac., who went forward as rear-link representative and spent most of his time helping battalion control wireless, gives us his version.

The first phase, he says, the assault on the town, was accomplished more easily than expected, despite the barrage balls-up. Our fellows, in fact, got well inside before meeting any serious opposition. But after a while resistance became more stubborn and dislodging Jerry from his houses and cubby holes, alive with every sort of booby trap, proved a slow job. All that night passed in house-to-house clashes . . . At dawn, however, ejecting operations had to be suspended; they would have proved too costly in daylight . . . Towards evening signals from B and C [Companies] were getting fainter and fainter . . . A Company and parts of S tried to get in after dark. But this time Jerry was ready . . . Having sealed off our supplies and reinforcements and no doubt strengthened his own, Jerry switched to the offensive within the town . . . Next morning the last message from B came through. They and C were still resisting with no thoughts of jagging in although all their officers had been killed or wounded. After this no more was heard . . . on the third night further attempts to relieve were made by 10th Battalion but they couldn't get in either. Tossignano had become a fortress . . . Getting out was as hard as getting in and only a handful of men cut loose after dark. By then the situation had become so bad they could throw no light on the final outcome.

<u>17th December</u>

Never has this battalion suffered such colossal losses in a single 'do' (in this war anyway). Previous casualties have been dribs and drabs in comparison.[16]

Rifleman Robert Beech, B Company, 2nd Rifle Brigade

Major Brown was second-in-command of B Company and he wanted to become a line soldier so he was delegated to plan the attack of Tossignano from the rear end of the village, with B Company hitting the front end, S Company was to follow Major Brown who became OC of C Company hoping that one of us should be able to break into the town.

To deal with B Company who lay up in a casa [house] till the stonk was over which went on for four hours, 4 Platoon went in first up a winding road with houses burning right, left and centre which gave the Teds a clear view and they took advantage and belted poor old 4 Platoon with Spandau fire.

Three survivors came back just as 5 Platoon had got outside ready to move off to make our attack. Was I glad to see them stragglers because it meant that our attack would be cancelled but to our dismay we were re-routed around the rear end of the village to assist C Company attack who, with the help of a 10th Battalion company, had penetrated to the village square.

On our way in we passed the dead rifleman who had got caught in a 25-pounder cock-up and we got to point 222. From here we were to do a sword [bayonet] charge down the hill and up the other side into the village.

I remember we got halfway down when Ted let us have it with his Spandaus, I toppled into a steam of icy cold water followed by our company commander, Major Reader Harris, who after giving me his opinion of the battle he decided to rally the company and get on with it. After a lot of whistle blowing and shouting we all got up and followed him; he was a great officer, that is why we went with him.

We got into the village and my best mate Johnny Street was cut down before we could really get it together. I dragged him into a house and fended off the first of many attacks. During a lull I attended to Johnny who told me he had stopped one in his bollocks. I pulled his trousers down but could find no wound or bruise but he insisted that he was hit thereabouts. At this time Corporal Francis came in to tell me to withdraw back to the church and he would send a stretcher party to bring back the wounded.

I carried Johnny back to the church and reported to the company commander who told me to man one of the windows. I had used up my last mag and was ready to kip down when I was told to report to the CO who told me to go and look after Major Brown, who was badly wounded in the leg.

The two officers had a chat and then asked me if I would lead a stretcher party out under a Red Cross flag with the hope of bringing back the MO. I asked if I could take Johnny Street out with me which was agreed. So the medical orderly and I carried out the stretcher with a walking wounded carrying the Red Cross flag. As soon as we hit the road we came up against a load of Teds all armed with Spandaus. They let us through and we made our way to point 222, then down the hill to the RAP. It was when we were ready to return that we spotted Corporal Dyer doing his bit.[17]

Citation for the Distinguished Conduct Medal[18] awarded to Lance-Corporal F. Dyer, 2nd Rifle Brigade

At 0600 hours on 14th December 1944 Lance-Corporal Dyer's platoon was ordered to seize a house on the southern side of Tossignano, to relieve pressure on C Company, 2nd Rifle Brigade, who were being counter-attacked in the western end of the village. The entry into the house was forced and the platoon established on the ground floor, which consisted of only one room. At first light the enemy counter-attacked and the Bren gunner covering the street was killed. Lance-Corporal Dyer immediately manned the Bren gun and was himself hit in the leg almost at once. He refused attention and continued to fire the Bren with such good effect that the attack was temporarily stopped. Later the house was attacked with bazookas, the ceiling blown down and the room set on fire with petrol, so that the platoon was forced to withdraw down the hill. Lance-Corporal Dyer, with his platoon commander and Rifleman Aldridge, covered this withdrawal, engaging the enemy at very short range.

Under cover of some rocks at the foot of the hill Lance-Corporal Dyer tended three wounded men and then, on his own initiative, crossed 200 yards of open ground under observed machine-gun and mortar fire, to get help from the Company HQ. Smoke was put down, but more men were hit near the Company HQ while crossing open ground. Seeing this Lance-Corporal Dyer improvised a Red Cross flag from a white handkerchief and the blood of a wounded man and repeatedly went forward in face of heavy machine-gun and mortar fire, each time helping back a wounded man. Finally as a result of Lance-Corporal Dyer's determined and courageous efforts, the enemy recognised the Red Cross flag and it was possible for stretcher bearers to collect the remaining wounded, who otherwise would have spent the day lying in the open exposed to enemy fire. Altogether twelve wounded were brought in and Lance-Corporal Dyer continued for three hours to bring in and help tend the wounded.[19]

Rifleman Robert Beech

I went back to 222 to help him [Dyer] and to see if any of our company was lying amongst the dying and dead. It was there I found another friend, Rifleman Bell, who was trapped in a little room but I could not help him only tell him it was all over because by this time I had spotted a Ted coming out of the church looking for his wounded.

By this time the RA had me spotted and started to drone smoke shells all over the shop and that is a no fun situation. Anyway after we had got all the wounded to point 222 and carried a few badly wounded back with us when I got back to the RAP, which was in full view of the enemy only 200 yards away, I found out that my mate was not evacuated. After a few well chosen words I got him slung on a mule and away he went smiling.

At this time quite a few of 10th Battalion had come from here there and everywhere. I remember a sergeant-major who had stopped one in the mouth lying on the floor, but at this time Ted decided to give us his attention with a round of mortar fire. I stayed with this CSM for quite a while because his nerves had gone and he was in a sorry state. Anyway during the night the RAP packed up and went home but somehow I did not want to return with them as I felt safer here in front of Ted.

So I stayed another night thinking that any stragglers from the company might turn up and one did, my old mate Lofty [who] had a wounded leg and a broken shoulder. He pulled himself in at dawn the next morning and told me that was it, they had all been taken prisoner. We waited till evening and started our return to our lines about 600 yards away in the dark.

On the way we met the CO on his own wandering about the track. His name was Orwain Foster and he asked us all about it and sent us on our way without giving us the password for the day, anyway we made our way to lucky A Company who always seemed to keep out of trouble led by a very good old friend Major Nauman who fed and bedded us down before returning us to company HQ.

Ever so sorry to say that Johnny Street died from a wound at the back of his balls made by a very fine sliver of shrapnel which tore his bowels open.

Let me tell you about the truces between us and Ted. The first was during a counter-attack Ted came out in, and I let off a mag at a steel gateway with the hope it would cool him off. It must have hit one of these Teds and he started with the '*hilfe*' and the '*bitte*', 'help' and 'please', situation and every time I let a few rounds go he would really plead, till all of a sudden a German voice shouted out 'cease fire' which we all did and when I took a butcher's two white coated medics was attending to him.

Anyway that cease fire stood us in good stead for later on the next cease fire was when we took the stretcher party out, and the other cease fire was when Cpl Dyer did his bit, and the last cease fire was when I tried to approach a wounded rifleman under the cliffs and was told to clear off with a hand grenade, only one, a kind of warning no further. That is why I stayed on hoping that rifleman would make it that night.

The final cease fire was when our own 25s opened up with smoke though at this point I did not need it as I was roaming around less than fifty yards from the nearest Spandau and they was watching me very carefully; they knew, so did I. That was Tossignano.[20]

2nd Rifle Brigade had failed to take Tossignano and had suffered losses amounting to 13 officers and 207 riflemen, including those taken prisoner. The losses were such that the battalion needed reforming, especially given the extra eighty men who were sent home because of their length of service abroad. To make up the numbers 10th Rifle Brigade was subsumed into 2nd Rifle Brigade.

So why did the 2nd Battalion fail? According to General Murray, the divisional commander, 'They put up a first class performance in extremely difficult circumstances and their failure was a magnificent failure.'[21] Hastings, the regimental historian, saw things more realistically, 'The chief cause of the failure was the intrinsic difficulty of the operation . . . there were also one or two strokes of misfortune . . . the past experience of the Brigade was a handicap rather than a benefit.'[22] Hastings here identified the key reasons for the failure of 2nd Rifle Brigade at Tossignano. At Snipe everything was in place for victory; at Tossignano nothing was in place for victory. The operation may have been difficult but too much was left to chance. The planning was clearly faulty – a plan for a renewal of the operation drawn up after the failure was very different to the old plan (in the event it was never acted on). Among other differences the new plan was based on very thorough reconnaissance.

But most of all, as Hastings acknowledges, the riflemen did not have the right experience, training or conditioning for the attack. They were skilled motorised troops for desert warfare, but the problem and the tragedy was that no one realised that they would not be as much use in the radically different conditions of the Italian campaign.

Notes

1. Alex Bowlby, *The Recollections of Rifleman Bowlby*, Cassell, 2002
2. Bowlby, pp. 7–8
3. Eddie Blacker, author interview
4. Hastings, ch. xvii
5. Joseph Belzar, unpublished memoir, p. 79
6. Bowlby, p. 14
7. Bowlby, p. 14
8. Author interview
9. Letter to the author
10. Joseph Belzar, pp. 70–1
11. Letter to the author
12. Joseph Belzar, p.71
13. Letter to the author
14. Hastings, p. 311
15. Imperial War Museum, Department of Documents, 99/77/1
16. Imperial War Museum, Documents Archive 96/50/1 and PP/NCR/245, quoted in Field Marshal Lord Carver, *The Imperial War Museum Book of The War in Italy*, Pan, 2001, pp. 264–6
17. Letter from Robert Beech to Jack Hodgson, ex 2nd Bn, The Rifle Brigade, reproduced here with permission of Mrs Beech. This action is also recorded by Bowlby, p. 199. Some of the names given above are the real names of those to whom Alex Bowlby gave fictitious identities.
18. Originally a recommendation for the Victoria Cross
19. Quoted in Committee of The Rifle Brigade Chronicle, *The Rifle Brigade 1939–1945*, Vol 2 pp. 89–90
20. Beech letter
21. Quoted in Hastings, p. 323
22. Hastings, p. 323

CHAPTER 7

The Far East – The Siege at Kohima

2nd Rifle Brigade had gone from glory at Snipe in the desert war to annihilation at Tossignano in the Italian campaign.

Like 2nd Rifle Brigade, the 4th Battalion, The Queen's Own Royal West Kent Regiment, had also been in the desert. However, 4th Royal West Kents were then sent to the Far East where they were to fight an epic and heroic action at Kohima, although first they had to adapt to the jungle. As Major John Winstanley MC put it,

We travelled to a camp not very far from Calcutta and there we began the metamorphosis from being a totally motorised desert battalion with everything on wheels and Jeeps to being totally animal borne infantry. All the drivers became mule leaders. I was issued with a horse and it was a rather interesting conversion.[1]

Also at Kohima and also fighting hard against the Japanese was 2nd Royal Norfolks. This battalion had been rebuilt after the massacre at Le Paradis and was then sent out to the Far East where it too was to distinguish itself in the capture of GPT Ridge as part of the battle of Kohima. Why did these two infantry regiments fight so hard and so well against the numerically superior Japanese? Why were the British soldiers able to fight so well in the later stages of the war in the Far East compared with other theatres? What made the difference?

For the war in the Far East a new and powerful emotion came into play on a mass scale: hate.

In *Men Against Fire* S. L. A. Marshall talks at some length about the Makin island fight in November 1943 when one battalion of the US 165th Regiment fought a defensive action against repeated Japanese charges. Marshall states that during the action only thirty-six men fired their weapons at the enemy and most of these were the heavy weapons men.[2]

Marshall's methods and the truth of his claims have been discussed at some length in Chapter 1 and if this account of the Makin battle be true then it goes against many of the facts of the British experience in the Far East. However, in Marshall's favour it does have to be said that the American experience of the Japanese was initially more remote than that of the British who had come up against the Japanese and their way of fighting and dealing with prisoners earlier in the war, in the Malayan campaign of 1941–2.

So what was it about hate which transformed ordinary British soldiers into highly effective killers with all the characteristics of soldiers who had been through full battle conditioning during training? The answer is that this hate was a reaction to Japanese atrocities which they visited on captured soldiers and airmen. These atrocities were so gut wrenchingly awful that the Allied soldiers ceased to think of Japanese soldiers as ordinary human beings and instead they became objects of hate to be killed at all costs.

Major John Winstanley MC, *4th Royal West Kents*

We had experienced Japanese behaviour in the Arakan when they captured a dressing station full of wounded and they had bayoneted the lot. They were known to have bayoneted prisoners. Their behaviour was undeniably savage. We had had a great respect for the Afrika Korps and for many of the Italians where it was a fair game. Not so with the Japs. We felt their behaviour meant they had renounced any right to be regarded as human and we thought of them as vermin to be exterminated if we could. That was important because it fired us. When we were aroused by that sort of feeling we fought well. It was certainly a factor and of course at Kohima our backs were to the wall and we were going to sell our lives as expensively as we could if we had to. But there was plenty to motivate us. They used to shout insults at us; they did everything in their power to make us dislike them. They got what they deserved. Our firepower and holding our ground enabled us to beat them.[3]

Lieutenant-Colonel Gerald Cree CBE, DSO, 2nd West Yorkshires, Arakan 1944

Nobody thought that this dressing station would be attacked. But it was. The Japs got into it and did the most appalling execution there amongst the wounded and the sick in this hospital. We could hear it going on, shouts and screams and shooting . . . Early the next morning A Company went in and counter-attacked the main dressing station and fought their way through it inch by inch. The Japs were still there in full force. They had made bunker positions in what had been the old wards. They'd also helped themselves liberally to all the food that there was going there and any drink ration that was lying about. They just had to be winkled out inch by inch. We lost fifteen men in that attack but we eventually got them all out of it inch by inch . . . [the atrocity] made everybody very furious and determined to get the better of them which we did. What happened was that the whole of the 9 Brigade B Echelon was in the position just a little way from us on both sides of a deep chaung [watercourse or gully]. This chaung ran up into the main dressing station area getting much narrower as it went up but it was a well defined channel. That night Japs started passing down this chaung on the way from the main dressing station – after we'd counter-attacked they pulled out. They started trickling down this chaung. Both sides of the chaung were held by our B Echelon personnel – muleteers, orderly room staff, sanitary men, quartermaster's storemen, chaps like that, nearly all old soldiers like the regimental sergeant-major. They twigged what was happening. They just let the Japs have it. They killed an enormous number of them in that place which became known as Blood Nullah afterwards.[4]

Sergeant Bert Fitt DCM, 2nd Royal Norfolks

We tore down GPT Ridge as fast as we could go. We were coming into the open. You'd got some places that were thick, other places were more open and then there was more of a track going down. I had a rifle slung over my shoulder and a Bren gun which had come from Grogan. I was firing from the hip and I used it for the remainder of the attack.

About half way down, leading my right-hand platoon, I saw what looked to me like a piece of flat ground and I thought perhaps that was a bunker, facing the opposite way. I jumped on to this parapet and when I looked down I was looking down the muzzle of a mountain field gun. I threw a grenade in because I knew there was people still there. Three got out and my runner came up on my shoulder with his rifle and he shot the first one that was running away from us over the valley. He twizzled him like a rabbit, a marvellous shot; he got him alright. We'd then got two prisoners.

I left these two prisoners with my runner, a soldier you could trust, and told him to bring them along. I said, 'Search them before you bring them,' and when he searched them he took two Britannia cap badges from them which were from our 4th, 5th or 6th Battalions. We had pushed forward and taken up position and Colonel Scott came up and spoke to me. I told him we had got these prisoners and he said, 'Where are they?' and I told him they were being brought along by one of the chaps.

Up came this chap, no prisoners. I asked him where they were. He said, 'Back there, up the track.'

I said, 'What do you mean? They're going to be gone.'

He said, 'Never, they won't go anywhere. Remember my brother got bayoneted on a hospital bed. When I searched them I took these badges off them. Well I bayoneted both of them, I killed them. That's it.'

So I had to go and tell the CO and when I told him that we hadn't got the prisoners he flew at me and he said, 'Bring the person who let them escape to me!'

I said, 'They didn't escape. We took these badges off them – they are officers' badges of the 4th, 5th and 6th Battalions.'

He said, 'So what?'

I said, 'Well his brother was bayoneted in bed in hospital and he bayoneted them and got his own back.'

Colonel Scott said, 'That's saved me cutting their bloody throats!'[5]

Why did the Japanese behave like this? This behaviour turned the normally civilised British soldiers into killers and the result was clearly to have a crucial effect on their fighting ability. This was arguably the decisive factor in winning the war in the Far East.

In his book *Defeat Into Victory* Field Marshal Viscount Slim argued against the use of special forces such as Commandos and commented that, 'Any well trained infantry battalion should be able to do what a commando can do; in the Fourteenth Army they could and did.'[6]

However, what Slim was unaware of was that his army in the Far East was able to match the fighting skill of the Commandos because his men were motivated to kill the enemy by their hatred. The Commandos, on the other hand, as explained in Chapter 3, killed because they were conditioned to do so.

Slim also pays tribute to the courage of the Japanese soldier, 'If 500 Japanese were ordered to hold a position, we had to kill 495 before it was ours – and then the last five killed themselves.'[7] This was certainly a common factor in fights which the British had with the Japanese and a product of the Japanese military mind-set.

It is very easy to be simplistic when discussing the Japanese Army of World War II. The view has grown up that the reason Japanese soldiers behaved so brutally was because their own officers and the Japanese system treated ordinary soldiers brutally, and therefore it is understandable that Japanese soldiers treated prisoners of war in the same way.

As always, the truth is more complex. Colonel Grossman, in his book *On Killing*, points to the use of conditioning in terms of what he calls 'killing empowerment' when atrocities are visited on the helpless and watched by others. He refers to the Japanese bayoneting of Chinese prisoners after the 'Rape of Nanking' in 1937 and the psychological pressures in play to condition those taking part and other Japanese soldiers watching so that any natural resistance to the killing was suppressed. Any who refuse will themselves be killed; those who go along with what is happening will be, 'strangely empowered'.[8]

It is also worth pointing out that the Japanese Army itself

was a more complex organisation than many give it credit for. John Morris, a professional soldier who fought in World War I and then on the North-West Frontier, taught English literature at a university in Tokyo from 1938 to 1942 and was in an ideal position to comment on the way the Japanese Army operated. He points out that, alongside the harsh discipline which was based on fear, there was also a democratic streak in the Japanese Army. He relates how he often observed private soldiers sitting down on buses and on the subway in Tokyo while generals stood due to lack of room. Of course the private soldier would get up to salute, but would then sit down again. This was due to the fact that Japanese officers were not drawn from the higher social classes.[9]

Apart from describing the system of discipline based on fear, with soldiers taught not to think but only to obey and never to surrender, Morris also describes the Japanese training system which sounds remarkably similar to the Commando training described in Chapter 3. The whole philosophy appears to have been based around conditioning and Morris draws attention to the fact that the Japanese had been practising jungle fighting in very difficult conditions for several years prior to the war and this constant practice together with rigid battle drills and plans made the Japanese virtually unbeatable by any but the best-prepared forces.[10] The Japanese tended to practise weapons training not on dummies but rather on live prisoners.

Other parts of their training seem familiar – route marches 30–40 miles long with no one allowed to fall out and finished at the double – and constant weapons' practice both day and night.[11] Morris concludes by saying,

Many people have asked me what it is that makes the Japanese Army so strong. Behind all more direct answers lies the basic fact that the Japanese are not afraid of death and hold that there is no greater honour than to die in battle.[12]

Of course this behaviour can be summed up in one word: *bushido*. This was the way of the warrior, the samurai code which has since been glamorised both in books and in film, although any prisoner of the Japanese during World War II will be quick to tell you there was nothing remotely glamorous in the way in which they were treated. *Bushido* was all about serving the cause or master; failure was so awful that surrender meant death and it was a disgrace to be taken alive. *Bushido*, then, ran straight into conflict with Western values when the Japanese Army started imposing its values, or its warped understanding of its values, on captured British and American servicemen. Consider this Japanese account of *bushido* in action and note the way the killing empowerment identified by Grossman kicks into play.

Blood Carnival

29 March 1943. All four of us (Technicians Kurokawa, Nishiguchi, Yawata and myself) assembled in front of the HQ at 1500 hours. One of the two members of the crew of the Douglas which was shot down by anti-aircraft fire on the 18th and who had been under cross-examination by the 7th Base Force, had been returned to the Salamaua garrison and it had been decided to kill him. Tai Commander Komai, when he came to the observation station today, told us personally that, in accordance with the compassionate sentiments of the Japanese *bushido*, he was going to kill the prisoner himself with his favourite sword. So we gathered to observe this. After we had waited a little more than ten minutes a truck came along.

The prisoner, who is at the side of the guardhouse, is given his last drink of water etc. The chief medical officer, Tai Commander Komai and the HQ platoon commander come out of the officer's mess wearing their military swords. The time has come so the prisoner, with his arms bound and his long hair now cropped very close, totters forward. He probably suspects what is afoot but he is more composed that I thought he would be. Without more ado he is put on the truck and we set out for our destination.

I have a seat next to the chief medical officer; about ten guards ride with us. To the pleasant rumble of the engine we run swiftly along the road in the twilight. The glowing sun has set behind the western hills, gigantic clouds rise before us and the dusk is falling all around. It will not be long now. As I picture the scene we are about to witness my heart beats faster.

I glance at the prisoner. He has probably resigned himself to his fate. As though saying farewell to the world, as he sits in the truck he looks about at the hills and seems deep in thought. I feel a surge of pity and turn my eyes away.

The truck runs along the sea shore. We have left the Navy Guard sector behind us and now come into the Army Guard sector. Here and there we see sentries in grassy fields and I thank them in my heart for their toil as we drive on. They must have got it in the bombing the night before last – there are great holes by the side of the road full of water from the rain. In a little over twenty minutes we arrive at our destination and all get off.

Tai Commander Komai stands up and says to the prisoner, 'We are now going to kill you.' When he tells the prisoner that, in accordance with Japanese *bushido*, he will be killed with a Japanese sword and that he will have two or three minutes' grace, he listens with bowed head. The flight lieutenant [the prisoner] says a few words in a low voice. Apparently he wants to be killed with one stroke of the sword. I hear him say the word 'one' in English. The tai commander becomes tense and his face stiffens as he replies, 'Yes' [in English].

Now the time has come and the prisoner is made to kneel on the bank of a bomb crater filled with water. He is apparently resigned. The precaution is taken of surrounding him with guards with fixed bayonets but he remains calm. He even stretches out his neck and he is very brave. When I put myself in the prisoner's place and think that in one more minute it will be good bye to this world, although the daily bombings have filled me with hate, ordinary human feelings make me pity him.

The tai commander has drawn his favourite sword. It is the famous Osamune sword which he showed us at the observation post. It glitters in the light and sends a cold shiver down my spine. He taps the prisoner's neck lightly with the back of the blade, then raises it above his head with both arms and brings it down with a sweep.

I had been standing with my muscles tensed, but in that moment I closed my eyes . . . All is over. The head is dead white, like a doll. The savageness which I felt only a little while ago is gone and now I feel nothing but the true compassion of Japanese *bushido*. A senior corporal laughs, 'Well, he will enter nirvana now!'

This will be something to remember all my life. If I ever get back alive it will make a good story to tell so I have written it down.

At Salamaua observation post, 30 March 1943, 0110 hours, to the sound of the midnight waves.[13]

The Japanese were therefore a formidable enemy for the British forces in the Far East and neither the West Kents nor the Norfolks were well trained for this fighting. Therefore after the desert the West Kents were sent to a camp near Calcutta where they embarked on jungle training and the Norfolks were sent to a camp near Bombay.

New tactics were considered which were a long way from those used at the beginning of the war – Sergeant-Major Herbert Harwood of 4th Royal West Kents recalled that, 'In France in 1940 they were still doing the old style advancing over open country just like in World War I. Later in the jungle we came round the back of the Japanese which made the difference.'[14] This tactic was found to be an important one because the Japanese did not like being outflanked and usually withdrew. For their training the Norfolks concentrated on acclimatisation which consisted of a lot of route marches in the heat of the day. After a spell in the Arakan for 4th Royal West Kents and a spell in India showing the flag during some civil unrest for 2nd Norfolks, both battalions were sent to Kohima.

On 6 February 1944 the Japanese Army started its campaign to break out of Burma and to capture the important British base at Imphal, in eastern India. Key to this was the hill station at Kohima which commanded the all-important supply route from Dimapur to Imphal which the Japanese 31st Division was ordered to cut.

General Slim was caught out by the Japanese movements and when the Japanese Army arrived in force at Kohima on 4 April 1944 there was only a garrison of non-fighting personnel in residence. The British 161st Brigade was hurriedly sent to assist the garrison but from this only the 4th Royal West Kents made it into the enclave to help before the encirclement was complete. From then the Japanese remorselessly closed in on the defenders from positions on GPT Ridge which they had taken early on. The stage was set of a siege of epic proportions.

Major John Winstanley MC

Kohima was a delightful hill station with a hospital, transit camps, stores. The existing garrison were all scrap troops, people in transit, Service Corps and other non-combatant troops. There was one wonderful Indian regiment, the Assam Regiment, who were the only fighting troops of the garrison.

Our guns and the rest of the brigade were outside the perimeter because the perimeter had closed behind us and this was a blessing in disguise because they formed a box and we could call down their fire and this was crucial in the whole battle. They had these 3.4-inch mule-borne howitzers which could lob shells over the hills which was ideal for us.

A Company was down on the tennis court by the DC's [district commissioner's] bungalow, B Company was on Kuki Picquet which was in a reserve position. A and C Companies were up on Jail Hill and the eastern fringe of the perimeter. Garrison headquarters and battalion headquarters were all placed on Garrison Hill which was the main feature of Kohima.

The village of Kohima was separated from this area by about half a mile along a narrow ridge along which the road ran, called Treasury Ridge. The Japs were in occupation of the village and Treasury Hill and they had moved up from Imphal to confront the south-eastern face of the garrison. Of course it turned out that it wasn't just a battalion or a brigade, it was an entire Japanese infantry division which had taken the route north to Kohima.

The 4th Royal West Kents, the Assam Regiment and other odds and sods settled down to defend the perimeter against the repeated assaults of an entire Japanese division and this was a fourteen-day siege. Bit by bit in the face of these attacks the perimeter shrank and shrank until just before relief it only included Garrison Hill and the tennis court which was the [site of the] final stand.[15]

Sergeant-Major Herbert Harwood, 4th Royal West Kents

We dug these trenches on DIS Ridge [*sic*]. The sappers set light to some bashas [huts] where the Japanese were and they all ran out and Sergeant

Tatham had a Bren gun and when these chaps ran down the hill to the road he had his Bren trained there and as they hit the road he got them. By the time it was finished there was a big mound of bodies there. We were attacked two or three nights running.[16]

Major John Winstanley MC

B Company started life on Kuki Picquet where we were just observers. After five days we were ordered to relieve A Company on the tennis court. My second-in-command, Tom Coath, had been taken to command C Company as their commanding officer had been wounded. So it was just myself and two platoon commanders. The third platoon was commanded by a sergeant.

We held that tennis court against many desperate attacks for five days. We were able to hold the attacks by two means. I had instant contact by radio with the guns and the Japs never seemed to learn the ability of how to surprise us. Whenever they formed up for one of these banzai charges they used to shout in English as they formed up. 'Give up!' so we always knew when a major assault was about to come in.[17]

Private John Crouch, Pioneer Platoon, 4th Royal West Kents

We couldn't see a lot because of the trees and the jungle. The main troops were further round to our right. The ground there was not quite as steep as where we were. We were defending HQ although we were sent out to relieve the rifle companies several times during our stay there.

The Japanese always attacked our position at night. They would come up shouting after they got quite close, as close as fifty feet away, you wouldn't hear them until they came close. They would fire and we would just fire back with rifles and grenades. They didn't seem to be afraid of death so they made for easy targets.[18]

Major John Winstanley MC

One would judge just the moment to call down the guns and the mortars to catch them as they were launching the attack (they were only a matter of fifty yards away) and this was a most effective way to break them up and so by the time they reached the hand-to-hand part of the battle they were decimated. This was repeated again and again. The right-hand platoon was particularly effective, they used untold boxes of grenades in the same way. As soon as they formed up they just showered them with grenades. One thing we didn't lack was grenades because Kohima was a store.

We had a steady toll of casualties. These were to a considerable extent from snipers; the Japs were very active in getting into places where they could dominate our positions and it was jolly difficult to spot them. It came to the point in daylight that, unless you were very careful in how you moved and the cover you used, you would certainly be shot by a sniper.

The other punishment that they doled out to us was direct gunfire. They could fire from the Naga village and the hills beyond over open sights straight into our positions and that was another very unpleasant business. They always used to have morning and evening 'hates' and we always knew when this intense artillery fire was coming. We were well dug in so it was lot of noise but it did cause mayhem amongst the wounded. They were all collected on Garrison Hill and they lay in the open or in slit trenches. Many were wounded again or killed. They suffered more than anybody.

The Japs had gone round us and were now being confronted by the advancing 2nd Division and we could hear the gunfire. But they were new troops and they found the going tough. They did reach us and the situation was one of desperation when we were relieved. We were relieved by the Assam Regiment and I took over a position in the hospital sector which was under less fire.

We marched out in a pretty filthy state. They had tried to supply us from the air but because the position was so small many of the drops landed among the Japanese who had a lot of 3-inch mortar shells which we then got the benefit of. Water and medical supplies did reach us – they were both in desperately short supply. The first to be evacuated were the wounded. A few nights before there had been a very daring evacuation of the walking wounded.[19]

Corporal H. F. Norman, 4th Royal West Kents

Wednesday 5 April 1944

We packed up all our kit and left this camp at 0645 hours in trucks . . . when we arrived at the 43 milestone we got out of the trucks. The village of Kohima is on the 47 milestone. We then started climbing up past the hospital for about one mile . . . we carried on for another mile and then we marched past A Company and took up positions . . .

Thursday 6 April 1944

Stand to (0545–0615 hours). For breakfast we had hard biscuits and one tin of blackcurrant jam which we scrounged from a 'basha'. We were mortared all day today and had many narrow escapes . . . At 2100 hours we heard the clanging of picks and shovels and saw that the Japs were digging in at the bottom of our feature. We opened fire on them and Sergeant Tacon ran down and grenaded them. Butch afterwards told me that he counted forty Japs with picks and shovels and fifty Japs behind them. When we fired on them they scattered and Corporal Webber's section shot ten of them, Butch killing three of them. One had reached his pit and had his arm poised back ready to throw a grenade when Butch killed him . . .

Friday 7 April 1944

Good Friday. The worst Good Friday I've ever spent . . . by 1500 hours the game was on. There was plenty of firing and we set fire to the bashas which the Japs and Jiffs [Indian troops fighting on the Japanese side] were in, then the sideshow started. They started running from the bashas and our lads fired everything they had at them. I saw Jap bodies falling everywhere and piling up all over the area. I was firing Ernie Thrussel's rifle and killed two Japs. This lasted for about two hours and when the bashas had burnt themselves out we found approximately seventy Jap bodies (twelve Japs got away but they were all wounded) . . .

Saturday 8 April 1944

It gets dark at 1900 hours and at 1920 'Japie' started mortaring and then he lifted the barrage and attacked. There were about 200 Japs trying to capture our feature but the four pits about ten yards from the road and up to our feature stopped them and after three hours' fighting in which they tried to put ladders on to the side of our feature and climb from the road (we were throwing grenades on to them) the Japs still hadn't captured any part of our feature. Altogether they made three assaults each with 200 Japs. The firing was terrible and the Bren-gun barrels were getting red hot and these were being changed very often and we had to keep supplying the forward pits with fresh ammunition where they were using so much and running short . . .

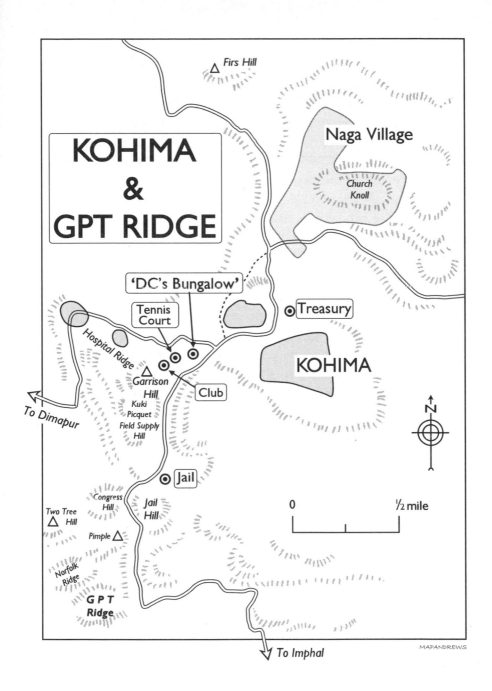

KOHIMA
&
GPT RIDGE

Firs Hill

Naga Village

Church
Knoll

'DC's Bungalow'

Tennis
Court

Treasury

Hospital Ridge

KOHIMA

Garrison
Hill

Club

Kuki
Picquet

To Dimapur

Field Supply
Hill

N

Jail

Congress
Hill

Two Tree
Hill

Jail
Hill

Pimple

0   ½ mile

Norfolk
Ridge

GPT
Ridge

To Imphal

MAPANDREWS

<u>Sunday 9 April 1944</u>

There was again 200 Japs attacking and again they were mown down like flies . . . the attack finished at 0400 hours, the Japs having gained a foothold on the bottom of our feature and they commenced digging in. 15 Platoon's Bren group halfway up the feature, level with us, had suffered no casualties and had a Bren gun covering the entrance to our pit so that, if the Japs attacked, it could have been costly for them but this was necessary because we were pinned in our pit unable to move or put out our heads in the daylight because we were now surrounded by thousands of Japs who were occupying the big feature in front of us which overlooked us and their snipers could see our every movement. I had no breakfast or tiffin today . . . We heard that Lance-Corporal Harman . . . had volunteered to go on a one-man bayonet attack past our pit to clear the Japs off our feature. He went down past our pit and killed some Japs. He was covered by Sergeant Tacon who was in a pit well behind us and could move about. He killed a Jap who was just going to throw a grenade at Harman. Harman killed the rest of the Japs but instead of running back as we were shouting for him to do he walked back calmly and the inevitable happened. He was shot in the spine by a Jap machine gun and was killed (later we heard he had been awarded the VC for this action).[20]

Captain Donald Easten MC, 4th Royal West Kents

I awoke to find that some Japs had occupied a disused bunker between us (D Coy) and C Company. They had a light machine gun and were covering the ground between C and D Companies. While Haynes (my CSM) and I were surveying the scene and discussing how we might dislodge them, Harman ran past, got beneath the angle of fire of the Jap machine gun and reached the base of the bunker. He then took a four-second grenade from his belt, let the lever go, counted three and lobbed it into the bunker through a firing slit. After the almost immediate explosion he went into the bunker and came out with the machine gun. We dragged out the bodies of two Japs afterwards.

Later that day John Wright (Sapper officer) and I blew up the bakery which had also been occupied in the night. This allowed us to join up with C Company.

As described in Norman's account, some Japs had got into one of C Company's forward trenches during that night. Harman didn't 'volunteer'; he just dashed down the slope calling for covering fire as he went and went for the enemy with bayonet and fire. So far as anyone could see he bayoneted one and shot at least two while the remainder fled. As he came back towards me up the slope he was hit by enemy machine-gun fire. I managed to drag him into my trench and shout for the stretcher bearers, but before they could get to us he died in my arms.

When I told the above to my CO (Lieutenant-Colonel Laverty) I explained that Harman was a strange man who had a feeling he was almost immortal. However, the colonel said, 'Donald, you judge bravery against how ordinary men would act and this was outstanding by any measure.' So I wrote my citation [he was awarded the Victoria Cross], CSM Haynes added his eye-witness account and we obtained an account from another soldier.[21]

Corporal H. F. Norman

Tuesday 18 April 1944

At 1100 hours the Japs started shelling us, killing Corporal Judges and a large number of the walking wounded and also seriously injuring Captain Topham. The shells started exploding among us and it was terrible to hear the screams of the injured (I saw trunks without legs and arms and bodies with heads blown off) . . .

Thursday 20 April 1944

For breakfast (0800 hours) we had hard biscuits, baked beans, bacon, tea. At 0900 hours we packed all out kit and at 1200 hours we were relieved by the Royal Berks Regiment and the Royal Welsh [*sic* – Welch] Battalion. Were we glad to get off the hill.[22]

With the siege lifted, attention now turned to the recapture of GPT Ridge. This was an action to be carried out by 2nd Royal Norfolks, which had been rebuilt after the massacre at Le Paradis and which was now trained in jungle warfare.

This training had a different emphasis and resulted in a different fire philosophy to that which had been adopted in France in 1940. There the British Army had placed its trust in the quantity of fire rather than the quality of fire. In the jungle the rule was reversed – you fired only when you could see something to fire at. Of course this then provided an ideal excuse for anyone not wanting to fire their weapon although, as we have seen, most British soldiers seemed to want to punish the Japanese.

Whatever the arguments over the number of soldiers prepared to fire, the policy caused practical problems for the Royal Norfolks on their way up to the start line on 4 May for the attack on GPT Ridge the following day.

Sergeant Fred Hazell, 2nd Royal Norfolks

The Intelligence squad had marked the path through the trees with tape. We started advancing slowly through the trees at 6.00 a.m. We hadn't gone fifty yards before we came under fire. The Japs had moved towards us and positioned themselves up in the trees. They had strapped themselves up in the trees so that when you fired they didn't fall out when they got hit. We advanced through them so that we were being shot at from both the front and the back. A shot whistled past my head and I thought, 'Jesus!' I ran forward to a tree and lay down beside it, poked my rifle forward and poked my head round the tree. Obviously whoever it was was waiting for me to do just that and another shot rang out and it hit the tree. The bark opened up and stuck in my cheeks. I thought I'd been hit and I sort of rolled back and I put my hand to it which of course only pushed the splinter into my face all the more. There was no blood, I thought, 'That's funny!' and I picked all these little pieces out. I thought I was off back to Calcutta at that stage.

The Japanese were well camouflaged, I never saw a Jap until we got almost to the top of the ridge. All you knew was that you suddenly had this sharp crack every time a bullet passed your head.

Our instructions were always, 'Don't fire until you can see the whites of their eyes!' but this was one of the reasons we lost as many men as we did. If we had gone forward spraying we would probably have done better. You have to bear in mind that we had carried our ammunition for nine days and we didn't want to go just spraying it about. By and large this discipline was maintained.

The trees suddenly opened up and we went through an area of tall grass, four or five feet high. By then the whole momentum was beginning to slow down and Major Hatch was telling everyone to zig-zag about to avoid the snipers. We were having a little conference when a grenade came over and hit the wireless set, bounced off the wireless set, sailed over my head and went off down the slope.

When we got out of the long grass I said to the lads, 'Get down on your hands and knees and crawl!' We came out into the open and there was this slope going up and a grenade landed, believe it or not, between my hands and it rolled out between my knees and my feet and under the chap behind me. I yelled out and flattened myself as everyone else did and the grenade went off.

I thought to myself, 'Oh my godfathers!' I turned round expecting to see this chap in shreds instead of which he was sitting back on his haunches. He looked at me and he blinked. I said, 'Are you alright?' He said, 'Yeah,' and he opened his shirt and the grenade had disintegrated into a powder. It looked like hundreds of blackheads on his chest and apart from a bit of blood he spat out here and there he seemed to be perfectly alright and he carried on. I believe quite a lot of the Jap grenades were like that. They were very inferior and instead of breaking up into nasty pieces of metal they just completely disintegrated.

When we got to the top of the ridge it was almost like World War I. There were four, five or six Japs, I imagine they must have run out of ammunition but suddenly they leapt out of their holes and raced at us with their bayonets. They held them up in the air. Of course they didn't get very far because the lads' machine guns just went bzzztt. They got to about twelve yards from us and threw their rifles at us as they dropped but it was fairly easy to side-step them.[23]

That night the commanding officer of the Norfolks, Colonel Robert Scott, disobeyed a direct order from brigade that fires must not be lit. His motive was simple – he wanted the men to have hot tea before they went into battle against the Japanese. Unfortunately Brigadier Goschen arrived just at the wrong time and Scott was lucky to escape arrest by explaining he needed water for the men's wounds.

Like Vic Turner at Snipe, Scott was an extraordinary commanding officer in other ways. The next day he insisted on leading from the front on the advance through the jungle, 'behaving as a platoon commander,' as one of his officers later recalled.[24] He also quickly realised that the policy of firing only at clear targets was not working in this case and yelled, 'Start blasting them and advance. Shoot up in the trees, get shooting!'[25]

The problem for the Norfolks was that their way lay through dense jungle and they were in single file. As they attacked the hill the ground opened up and the Norfolks could really get to grips with the Japanese. It was a fight which was to end in the award of the Victoria Cross for Captain Jack Randle and the Distinguished Conduct Medal for Sergeant Bert Fitt.

Sergeant Bert Fitt DCM, 2nd Royal Norfolks

The plan was to attack Norfolk bunker from the front at first light. I had had a rough ride up until then and I thought I would be going in reserve but no, I was to lead the attack with my platoon and B Company with Captain Randle.

We moved forward to the start line. My platoon was the spearhead, 12 Platoon was to the right – there was just the two patoons to go forward. The reserve platoon was 10 Platoon and a Support [Company] platoon under Captain Davies. We were going in at dawn and we thought that was the most obvious way we were going to take it because we had to climb up a hill to get to the bunker, about 600 to 800 yards. It was open ground [and] the trees had been shelled so there was very little cover.

We laid up on the start line and Captain Randle came up and he said, 'I've seen all the horrible things that have happened to me in my past.' I think he had an idea he wasn't going to come out of that attack. I said, 'So have I.'

We moved forward and got about half-way to the base of the hill. When we got to the bottom Captain Randle had already been hit and he was hit again on the upper half of his body. I shouted at him to go down and leave it to me because he had lost blood. He said, 'No, you take that left-hand bunker, I'm going to take this right-hand one.'

There were two light machine-gun posts and they were carving up the company terribly. They called it the Norfolk bunker but in fact it consisted of seven or eight different bunkers on the hill. I lost Corporal Sparrett – he was killed about four yards from me. I went straight in and got this bunker. I came up from underneath. It had a protection cover over it and I pushed a grenade in through the slit. I immediately spun right because I thought I could have got to where Captain Randle was and got on top of that bunker before anything happened.

Unfortunately as I turned right I saw Captain Randle at the bunker entrance. He had a grenade he was going to release into the bunker and he had his protective weapon with him. I just stood there, I couldn't do a thing to save him. If he could have held out for about three minutes I would have got on top of the bunker and knocked it out without getting hurt. But unfortunately he had been hit again at point-blank range.

As he was going down he threw his grenade into the bunker and he sealed the bunker entrance with his own body so that nobody could shoot from it. But in actual fact he had got the occupants and killed them. I was then on top of the bunker.

Then we had the decision to take, we had to go still further and take the position itself. I took the platoon in and knocked out two more bunkers with grenades and hand-to-hand fighting. The first bunker was about fifteen yards further on and it had a bloke in just going to have his breakfast, he had a tin of curry opened. I threw my grenade (that bunker was open) and I shot him at the same time and that was where I used my last round of ammunition.

At the next bunker one soldier came out to meet me from the back door of his bunker who shot me in the side of the face. He took my top teeth out and fractured my maxilla and I just spat out a handful of teeth and I spun round and he was only a matter of a few paces away from me. It felt as if someone had hit me with a clenched fist on the jaw. I was a boxer and it didn't bother me.

He had a rifle and bayonet and I had my Bren. I pressed the trigger and I'd got no ammunition. As he came towards me I had that feeling it was either me or him. When you get to hand-to-hand fighting you realise either you're going to be killed or he's going to be killed. What do you do? You close in and you hope for the best. At the time I was good instructor on unarmed combat. I could go hand-to-hand or meet anyone with a rifle and bayonet, I knew how to deal with them.

I let him come (he was an average-sized man) and I crashed the Bren into his face, I threw it straight into his face. Before he hit the ground I had my hand on his windpipe and I literally tried to tear it out. It wouldn't come out and we got fighting on the ground. If I could have got his windpipe out I would have twisted that round his neck. I managed to get his bayonet from his rifle and I finished him with that – he was the one that died, not me.

I then stood up and I had a call from 12 Platoon telling me that they were pinned down by another bunker which I couldn't see. I asked them where they were and I threw a grenade, it went over the top and a chap who was there yelled out a correction and told me that the grenade had gone over and I threw a second one and that was short. The grenade bounced and it hit the ground and went straight into the bunker. The occupants in there were obviously killed as well.

That was the last bunker we took but there were still more bunkers on the other side of the hill (by now we were on the crest of the hill). One of my corporals, Corporal Sculthorpe, spotted another bunker which was slightly over the crest to the left. He started going towards it, I yelled to him and tried to stop him but I couldn't. He continued on, went about four or five paces and he was shot down.

Then Captain Davies came up and I'd been hit about two hours previously and I had been bleeding heavily and my front was pretty red with blood which I had lost. I said, 'Well you'd better take over now Sir.' I was getting weak. Davies said, 'No, you consolidate the position, you know what's going on more than me, I'll do anything you ask me to do.' It was the right thing to do as I knew where all the positions were. He was [commanding] our support platoon. I told him I'd have to sit down and I sat inside an old bunker. They put a field bandage round my head to make it look respectable.

Then we had orders to withdraw because the Royal Scots were going to take over. I never had any kind of nervous reaction at all. But some of the men did. One chap lost his nerve and wanted to run forward after the Japanese; he wanted to go after them on his own. I hit him to quieten him down. That was the only thing I could do to stop him, otherwise he would have run out and got killed. I punched him, told him to be quiet pull himself together, and he did. This was after we had withdrawn. He'd come through it, done an excellent job right the way through, but he lost his nerve at the finish. That's a horrible thing to happen and if you're near them the only thing you can do is to hit them to stop them.

We pulled back to the battalion position and we were met there by the colonel and the medical officer. The first words the colonel said to me was, 'They got you then Fitt!' I said, 'That's right Sir!' He said, 'Let's have a look.' The medical officer removed the field dressing and Colonel Scott went in front of me and said, 'You never was any bloody oil painting!'

I didn't know whether to laugh or what to do. He and the brigadier had watched the whole action through field glasses. He said, 'Well done, you've done an excellent job!'[26]

Sergeant Fred Hazell, 2nd Royal Norfolks

May 5th was probably my luckiest day. After dealing with Major Hatch I dropped into the first hole I came across and when it got first light a crowd of Japs had got into our perimeter up in the trees and I think I was the best target they could see. My hole was about four feet six inches deep and was half full of water and it was on the line of a track.

Fortunately when they first shot, the shots came over my shoulder and landed in front of me, bang, bang, bang. I ducked straight away and I thought, 'Where'd they come from?' So I put my hat on my rifle and poked it up. Another volley of shots came over which I thought was rather amusing.

I was sitting there in my hole doing this, up and down, and every time I did it over came four shots. I'd taken my pouches off and put them on the ground behind me. Suddenly there was a most deafening bang and I got covered in dirt that came down my ears and all down my tunic. I thought, 'Crikey, they've put the mortar on me now.' I carried on popping my hat up and down and then suddenly I felt cramp developing in my left leg. I knew then that I'd got a couple of minutes to do something pretty drastic.

So I popped my hat up, over came the shots, I stuck my head up, quick look around, I could see some bushes. I waited for a few moments, popped the hat up again, over came the shots and I rolled over into these bushes. They didn't afford me an awful lot of cover but they couldn't see me because nobody shot at me from then onwards. I lay out flat there for half an hour and never moved.

While I was laying there A Company which had been back in reserve spotted the problem and sent four Bren gunners who just sprayed the trees and that was that. I then went back to pick up my pouches but of course the bang that I had heard was one of the shots had hit my pouches and blown all the grenades up. My water bottle had gone, everything had gone, so the only thing I was in possession of was a rifle. I had nothing else. But there were plenty of wounded and dead so you could make good any deficiencies.[27]

If the British were empowered to kill because of their hatred of the Japanese what of the Americans? As mentioned at the start of this chapter, S. L. A. Marshall referred to the Makin battle as justification for his views on the low ratios of fire when American soldiers were in action.

Certainly the United States, like Britain, used the traditional types of training of its soldiers which we have already identified as not being up to the job of conditioning men to kill. George Green, a former US Marine, recalled how it was poor preparation for battle:

Rifle fire was done at a rifle range at various ranges but mostly at 300 and 500 yards. We were required to fire at the prone, sitting, kneeling and off hand [standing]. The same goes for the pistol except it was at 25 yards and in the off-hand position only. It was not good training for combat as you seldom had the opportunity to have the time to aim and most action was at a much closer range and was more of a reaction than an aim.[28]

Despite the fact that the US Marine training was not as good at conditioning for battle as modern training is, the fact remains that when the Marines came up against the Japanese at Iwo Jima, for example, they distinguished themselves in a similar way to the British at Kohima – they fought well at a distance and they fought well close up. By the time of Iwo Jima the Marines, like their British counterparts, knew about the Japanese atrocities although for many this was through propaganda films, if by no other way. As George Green recalled about the Japanese, 'They were going to die for their emperor and our attitude was – help 'em along.'

When the battle began on 19 February 1945 American commanders estimated that Iwo Jima, an island 650 miles south of Tokyo, would take fourteen days to capture. In the event it took thirty-six days and over a third of the Marines became casualties in the fight to dislodge the Japanese from their bunkers and foxholes. It was the sort of fighting the British had encountered at Kohima and was no less blood-thirsty and brutal.

Warrant Officer George J. Green, Artillery Forward Observer, 3rd Battalion, 21st US Marine Regiment

One day in the battle for Iwo Jima

23 February D + 5

Good night's sleep – only woke up once during the air raid. The company area was hit by mortars last night but none of my FO Team was hit – several casualties in K Company.

It was still dark, but dawn was beginning to break when we crawled into the Jap pillbox that Lieutenant Colonel. W. Duplantis, CO, 3rd Battalion, was using as his battalion command post. I know we reviewed the situation and what we were supposed to do – but the only specific thing I remember is him saying, 'We have got to get the airfield today.'

We started the attack this morning with about 220 men, and before we were back in reserve, K Company had around 90 men left.

We were to pass through the lines of the 1st Battalion, continue the attack, and get Airfield No. 2. We moved into position and took off behind a rolling barrage. The first thing I noticed was a group of Japs in a low trench, someone {had} got them with a flamethrower, and they were still burning. Next, on this bright morning, saw a wounded Marine walking calmly back to the rear, the white bandages and crimson red of his blood standing out over his dirty dungarees. We were with Captain R. L. Heinz and his headquarters section moving up by bounds, It seemed as if everybody was moving up. Over to the right I could see I Company keeping up with us. After seeing only dead Japs, I finally spotted one live one. He was off to my right front in a shell hole beyond reach of my carbine effect range. He was a typical poster Jap . . . the kind you see in all the cartoons, wearing thick, round-rimmed glasses. He kept putting his head up and down. I tried to interest an infantryman to fire on him, but he says 'He's {in} the I Company sector – let them get him.' When I looked back later, there was no sign of him.

It's funny how word travels in combat; here we were fighting away and we got the news that Captain C. S. Rockmore of I Company had been killed – shot through the neck.

We moved up to the runway and I kept the team spread out and in the foxholes. We were doing pretty well on communications, as we were in touch with Lieutenant Pottinger at battalion. He wanted to know why we were not doing any firing – I told him I could not see anything to shoot at, and troops were moving up fast. He said to pick out some prominent landmark and fire away. I set up a fire mission on the high ground where the runways crossed and fired one round of smoke. Just as it hit, Captain Heinz yelled that they were going across the runway and heading for the high ground, I called off the fire mission, having fired only one shell. Captain Heinz, sitting on the edge of the runway about ten feet up from where I was, asked for my compass, as he [had] lost his. As I got ready to toss it up to him, he yelled for me to look out. And as I turned around, there was a Nip grenade sputtering about three feet in front of me. I [was] sat in a small shell hole about two feet deep, looking at the grenade [as] it exploded. Instinctively I ducked my head then looked back up and started to aim my carbine in the direction the grenade came from. As I aimed, I saw another one come flying toward me from some bushes, It landed just about the same place as the other one did. This time I got to duck my head before it went off. I felt my face expecting a handful of blood, I got only a little bit. I had some fine particles of the grenade in my face, but fortunately none hit my eyes. Captain Heinz came sliding down the slope of the runway with his pistol out, holding his right leg – he got a good size piece of one of those grenades in his right thigh on the inside. We helped him back to a deep shell hole. I tried to get a BAR [Browning Automatic Rifle] man to spray the bushes, but he walked up to them and toppled over – the Nip shot him in the stomach. Now I could see the Nip in a foxhole with a top that he moved up and down like a spider trap. We got a fire team directed at him, and they dropped a few grenades into his hole. The next time I looked at him, we were moving up again, and he was plastered to one side of the hole – quite a mess. Looking back to our rear, I saw all these 4.5-inch rockets coming down at us. They were easy to see, as there were so many of them and they were making such a loud racket. From a good, deep shell hole, we sat helpless watching those rockets creeping up on us and exploding on our rear troops of the machine-gun section. Finally they stopped – the last one about ten feet behind us. I heard later this barrage by our own rocket trucks just about wiped out the company machine-gun section. Lieutenant R. Archambault, K Company executive officer, came up to take Captain Heinz's place.

Lieutenant D. J. Grossi's platoon was on the high ground across the runway. We moved up along the slope of the runway and one by one we rushed across that flat strip of land. I noticed the amount of steel fragments from shells lying on the runway. I couldn't get over it. As we were moving up along the runway, I saw two Marines helping a third, who was a victim of combat fatigue. He got loose of their grip and fell down on his knees, beating the ground with his fists and crying.

Our team all got across the runway safely, and we dug in next to Lieutenant Archambault's CP [command post]. A few yards to our rear there was a Sherman tank that had been knocked out by the Japs. One Marine was lying underneath it. A corpsman was working him over and giving him something out of a bottle. I saw him change in color from very pale to a more natural look; I never did see what finally happened to him. We were all pinned down there by a heavy mortar barrage and could do practically nothing except dig a little deeper.

Early in the evening, elements of the 2nd Battalion came up to fill in the gap on our left. It seemed that K and I Companies were the only ones to get across the runway. Along with them came Warrant Officer Cormier and his FO Team from D Battery. We never did make contact with the 5th Division on our left that night, and I'm positive they tried to cover this gap with artillery and that some of it landed on us. We were having a lot of luck without telephone communications. I fired in some barrages and got set up for the night. Still not much success with radio, though.

How they did it I don't know. After dark we heard a tractor coming, and sure enough, there was a guy driving that thing in the pitch black night, pulling a tracked trailer with food, water and ammo. To this day, I don't know how he knew where he was going. It looked as if he aimed his Cat toward the front lines and kept going until he found someone. This guy had guts. With the good tidings of food, ammo and water also came the loss of our telephone communications; since radio was so undependable we decided to get the wire fixed. I sent Corporal McClosky and one man out to see if they could find and repair it by following the wire from the telephone back. It was really dark now – you couldn't see too far. They took off without hesitation but were back before too long with no luck. They didn't know how far they had gone out. Then

Sergeant Chest and myself started out along the wire, and after going what we guessed was about 100 yards, we found the break. George repaired it and we got back to our position without difficulty. How and why that wire didn't break more than that one time, I'll never know as we were mortared all night long. It was a simple matter to locate ourselves because we were on the hill where the two runways of Airfield No. 2 crossed. We were sure of our location and realised that as long as we fired, the Japs let up on their mortars that were falling all over us. So, Chest and I got under our poncho and started firing using the target squares on the map for targets. We kept moving the shells around in front of our lines. Before long, in scampered a rifleman asking us to move the shells out a little farther, as they seemed only to be fifty feet in front of the outpost Marines. Lieutenant Archambault and I decided not to come in any closer, but not to change what we had now. I often wondered if that infantryman ever knew that we didn't move the firing out farther. About 3:00 a.m. I got a call from a Captain Karch, who was S-3 of the battalion of the 4th Division Artillery, we were directing the fire of and he complained about my using up all their ammo. Since all of my firing was unobserved, he asked if I knew what I was shooting at. I told him all I knew was that when I fired they didn't, and I knew where I was there was nothing in front of us but Japs and they, battalion, could get more ammo. After the discussion we decided to reduce the number of rounds per gun fired at one time.

We occasionally got heavy artillery exploding in our lines. I was convinced that it was coming from our positions in the rear. Reported this to the 14th Marines. I think the 5th Division was trying to fill the gap between the 2nd Battalion on our left and their right flank unit and were not aware that we were as far left as we were.

Sometime during the early evening, the scout sergeant from Lieutenant Stevens' naval gunfire section, who I served with in Iceland, came into our position and he was pretty shaken up as the entire team got hit with an air-burst from a large caliber shell. These gave a big black blast, just above the ground. He said Stevens was hit real bad in the chest and wanted to know what to do. We sent him to the company CP, and that was the last we saw of him. I never found out if Stevens died or was saved.

I was glad I'm not a smoker, as the fellows who were had to get under their ponchos to smoke their cigarettes.

Ever since we started the attack, and got close to the runway of Airfield No. 2, there had been a high velocity gun firing, and it seemed as if it was firing its projectile at about head level – we could feel the pressure from the gun blast – but no matter how hard we tried to find it, we just couldn't.

When daylight finally came, the Japs let up on their mortaring, George Chest and I looked around for a more satisfactory spotting position to try to determine where all this stuff was coming from. The Japs had a rocket large enough to see as it took off. Evidently, it was difficult for them to control the range of these rockets, as earlier in the battle we could see them arch up and fly over Mount Suribachi. Almost everybody saw them because of the noise they made. In our new position we could see these rockets taking off and reported the compass angle from our position. I could not reach them with my artillery, as they were in the 4th Division's zone of action.

This was our best day for spotting live Japs. They could be seen running from hole to hole and manning trenches and machine-gun positions. Off to our right rear there was a sharp conical hill that had a lot of holes in it like cave entrances and we could see Japs running in and out, again too far to shoot at. We finally found a Jap trench and machine-gun position to our left front, and we watched them for a while to determine what they were doing. Every time someone opened up, they ducked back into the covered position. Chest hadn't fired a mission yet, so I told him to fire this one and we would fire a battalion for effect (all guns firing at one time) on call with air-burst. He adjusted by using air-burst, and darned if the first or second shell wasn't right on. We got the battalion set and waited until the Japs filtered out of the concealed cover before giving the word to fire. I have never seen such a perfect shot. The first shells were aimed just above each of the trench positions, and those Japs were caught out in the open, the rest were about 50/50, half air- and half ground-burst. After the firing had ceased, we could not see any more live Japs.[29]

Lieutenant Colonel Wendell Duplantis, commanding officer,
3rd Battalion, 21st US Marine Regiment

That night I was ordered to relieve the 1st Battalion at daylight and screen a tank attack as the corps' main effort. All available tanks were to be organised under a central command and hurled at the seemingly impregnable positions guarding Airfield No. 2. Our job was to keep the Jap infantry from swarming over our tanks and to consolidate gains made by them.

Historical accounts differ widely as to what happened that day. The truth is that the 100 to 150 tanks we were to screen never arrived. I had no other alternative but to order the attack without them, so that the advantage of the tremendous artillery barrage put down in front of us would not be wasted. Without time to redispose themselves from the screening formation, or to re-equip with extra flamethrowers and bazookas, the men 'jumped off' relying primarily on their bayonets and grenades.

With blood-curdling screams they surged up and over the camouflaged bunkers, darting from one shell crater to the next, pausing briefly to hurl a grenade in a fire port or through the back door, bayoneting those who dared to emerge. They smashed through the belt of defensive positions, for a gain of about 700 yards.

In the first few minutes, Captain Clayton S. Rockmore, CO of I Company, was killed and Captain Rodney L. Heinz, CO of K Company, was wounded and had to be evacuated, Captain Daniel A. Marshall . . . took over I Company and 1st Lieutenant Raoul Archambault Jr. took over K Company and the attack continued unabated . . .

The companies had been attacking to the north-east, paralleling the airfield and had momentarily paused to regroup opposite the center of the airstrip. Continuing the attack, Archambault now led his K Company across the airstrip in a savage charge to seize Hill 199, which dominated the leveled surfaces of the airfield.

The fight for that hill has been described as one of the most dramatic series of events of the campaign. K Company, in hand-to-hand fighting, seized the hill, occupying the trenches from which they had driven the Japanese. Though I was constantly reporting my changing front-line positions, through some error they were not being correctly shown in the fire direction center. 'Friendly' artillery fire came down on the beleaguered K Company and drove them off the hill, which was immediately reoccupied by the Japanese. Once again K Company attacked and seized the hill and this time they were driven off by the Japanese. Once more the valiant and determined company smashed into the position and regained the hill.

This struggle is described in the 3rd Marine Division's history as follows: 'That fight in the ankle-deep sand, which clutched at men, tripped them and clogged their weapons, will be recalled as one of the most freakish nightmares of the Iwo battle. Led by Archambault, K Company battled with bayonets, knives, clubbed rifles and entrenching shovels in a savage, hacking, screaming melee that was over in a few minutes with nearly fifty Japanese killed in hand-to-hand combat.'

The grim determination of those heroic men was beyond anything I had ever seen or anticipated. One sergeant was attacking a light machine-gun position above ground, protecting the approach to a bunker. A burst of fire struck him in the leg, knocking him down. He struggled to his feet and hobbled forward. A hand grenade exploded just in front of him, knocking him down again. Once more he got up and stumbled forward and I could see that his right foot was blown off yet he continued on, his shattered shin bone sinking deep into the soft sand.

Again the machine gun spat out a burst, striking him in the chest, ripping through his back. Somehow he made the two or three last steps and drove his bayonet up to the hilt into the machine-gunner as he fell forward across the gun and died.

At another bunker, a large one, a Marine was methodically tossing grenades through a fire port. His buddy was standing by the back door, swinging a steel barbed wire post he had pulled out of the ground, smashing the heads of the escaping Japs as they crawled out on their hands and knees. As he struck each one, he would drag the body behind him and stand poised, his post in the air, waiting for the next one. When no more emerged he and his buddy stripped several grenade carriers from the dead Japs and started on to the next bunker. Suddenly a fire port appeared in a hummock of sand where none had been visible before, then the muzzle of a Nambu jutted out and a staccato burst of fire cut them down. No quarter was asked and none was given, and scenes similar to those described were being repeated all up and down the line.

The midday administrative report by my staff staggered me. In the first hour and forty-five minutes I had lost over 500 men, almost half my command. Other front-line battalions were in even worse shape and we still had a long way to go.

The battalion was in a most precarious situation. Our wedge-shaped salient deep into the enemy's position offered him an opportunity to envelop or enfilade both flanks, and we were in grave danger of being cut off and wiped out. Many bunkers, that had been over-run or by-passed behind the front lines, still contained numerous live and angry Japs waiting in darkness to attack from the rear.

K Company, across the airfield, was very low on ammunition, especially hand grenades. A trailer-load of ammunition was hurriedly collected and the trailer hooked onto the rear of a tank. As darkness fell, a nameless hero volunteered to lead the tank through the minefield at the end of Airfield No. 2, and down the airstrip to the isolated company. Carrying a shielded flashlight, he walked slowly ahead of the tank through a hail of bullets and so guided it to the weary company, reaching it just in the nick of time, for the enemy had just launched the first of a series of counter-attacks that were to continue throughout the night. Seventeen times the determined Japs hurled themselves at that critical hill and each time were thrown back by K Company's stubborn defense. Archambault's reports grew fainter and fainter as his radio battery grew weaker. I sent two men with spare batteries but they were cut down before they had gone a hundred yards. I sent two more and one of them finally got through and our only communication link was restored.

War has its grim humor, It was reported to me that when field rations were being issued the next morning in the growing light, four Japs had been discovered patiently waiting in line with one of the platoons. They did not get breakfast that morning or ever again.[30]

Notes

1. Imperial War Museum, Sound Archive, 17955
2. Marshall, pp. 55–7
3. Imperial War Museum, Sound Archive, 17955
4. Imperial War Museum, Sound Archive, 104695/5/2, transcript pp. 13–14
5. Imperial War Museum, Sound Archive, 16970
6. Field Marshal Viscount Slim, *Defeat Into Victory*, Pan, 1999, p. 547
7. Slim, p. 538
8. Grossman, *On Killing*, p. 209
9. John Morris, *Traveller From Tokyo*, Penguin, 1946, p. 246
10. Morris, p. 213
11. Morris, pp. 212–16
12. Morris, p. 217
13. Imperial War Museum, Misc 79/1210

14. Author interview
15. Imperial War Museum, Sound Archive, 17955
16. Imperial War Museum, Sound Archive, 20769
17. Imperial War Museum, Sound Archive, 17955
18. Imperial War Museum, Sound Archive, 21102
19. Imperial War Museum, Sound Archive, 17955
20. Imperial War Museum, Department of Documents, 81/16/1
21. Letter to the author
22. Imperial War Museum, Department of Documents, 81/16/1
23. Imperial War Museum, Sound Archive, 17229
24. Captain John Howard, Imperial War Museum, Department of Documents, 99/21/1, quoted in Hart, *At the Sharp End*, p. 178
25. Imperial War Museum, Sound Archive, 17230/18, quoted in Hart, p. 174
26. Imperial War Museum, Sound Archive, 16970
27. Imperial War Museum, Sound Archive, 17229
28. Letter to the author
29. Imperial War Museum, Department of Documents, 02/52/1
30. Imperial War Museum, Department of Documents, 02/52/1. Extract from an article by Brig Gen Wendell Duplantis 21 February 1965 in the *Battle Creek Enquirer and News*, reproduced here with the kind permission of the *Battle Creek Enquirer*

CHAPTER 8

Northern Europe – D-Day at Omaha

The M-1 Garand rifle is 43.5 inches long, weighs 9.5 pounds and holds eight 0.3-inch calibre rounds in a box magazine. It is semi-automatic and gas-powered which means that it can be fired at a rate of 30 rounds per minute and is accurate to 600 yards. However, there are a few drawbacks with this weapon. Once a clip is started it cannot be topped up until all the rounds have been fired and when the last round is fired the clip ejects with a distinctive ping. Added to this is the problem that if a soldier messes up the loading of the clip then the bolt can shoot forward causing the injury known as 'M-1 thumb'.

This was the principal personal weapon which the American infantry soldier took into battle in World War II and, despite its drawbacks, which were fairly minor compared to its advantages, it was probably the best mass issue rifle used by any army in World War II. According to General Patton it was 'the best battle implement ever devised'. Its fan club increased dramatically after D-Day where it was found in some cases to function perfectly well even after taking a soaking on the way in to the beaches.

The was only one question mark over this weapon as the Americans prepared for the invasion of Europe – would the soldiers who carried it actually fire it at the enemy?

In *Men Against Fire* Marshall states the case for the no camp: 'The thing is simply this, that out of an average one hundred men along the line of fire during the period of an encounter, only fifteen men on the average would take part with their weapons.'[1]

Was he right? Earlier chapters of this book have considered the British experience and suggested that the situation was probably more complex than Marshall suggested. And of course Marshall was basing his findings on his work with the US Army – so was he right when he came to the US Army? In the previous chapter we have seen how US Marines fought the Japanese. But what about the US Army in Europe against a more amenable enemy? We have already seen how the British Army operated and how the type of training or conditioning was the key factor in how well units fought. We have also seen how the British policy of laying down a lot of fire meant that Marshall's fire ratios might have been too low – after all there were soldiers firing but not necessarily wanting to kill anyone.

US military ethos in World War II was similar to that of the British in terms of fire – in other words do not wait to see the enemy but fire at where the enemy is likely to be. Or, as General Patton put it in a letter of instruction to the US Third Army in April 1944, 'If you cannot see the enemy, you can at least shoot the place where he is apt to be . . . infantry must move in order to close with the enemy. It must shoot in order to move.'[2] So there might have been some soldiers who felt able to fire because they were not going to be hitting anyone.

But when it came to tactics the US Army did not follow the British example. Whereas the British deployed in order to bring the maximum fire to bear, the Americans preferred the approach adopted by the Germans and moved in rough files rather than spread out in an arrowhead like the British. Of course there were times when the file was no good and then the Americans deployed a wedge formation, although this was then more vulnerable to enemy fire. Attack was by fire and movement, keeping the momentum going by keeping up fire and if necessary splitting the attack up so some of a unit covered the advance with fire and then caught up while the forward portion covered for them.

Apart from the M-1 rifles carried by the GIs, each squad in

the US Army had one (or two) Browning Automatic Rifles (BAR) which provided the same firepower function as the British Bren. This weighed just over 20 pounds and used the same 0.3-inch ammunition as the M-1 but its magazine held only 20 rounds. This, plus the fact that it did not have a quick-change barrel, meant that in practice it was used for short bursts in support from the flanks, but when the BAR and M-1 were taken together the US Army had very good, evenly distributed, firepower throughout its units.

In order to see what happened when the US Army went into action this chapter is devoted to the experiences of the 16th Infantry Regiment of the 1st Division on D-Day when the US Army had the hardest job of the day – perhaps even the war – the landing in Assault Area Omaha. This unit gets no mentions from Marshall in *Men Against Fire*; he only talks about M Company, 116th Infantry Regiment, as an example of what a single company can achieve.[3]

The accounts which follow mostly come from Marshall's own combat history section of the US Army so would have been familiar to Marshall as he was involved in their collection and, more than likely, would have been involved in the interviews reproduced below. The combat historians worked in teams and would interview soldiers either alone or in groups. Despite the fact that these interviews took place immediately after the battle when possible (or later in the war if they wanted to catch up with particular individuals [such as Lieutenant Spalding from E Company]), inconsistencies still appeared, an indication that events were sometimes confused, even at the time.

It is interesting to note that the fighting is always dependent on one or perhaps a couple of exceptional individual soldiers taking charge and getting the assault moving while the majority follow or do nothing. Marshall may indeed have had a valid point about the face of battle.

Assault Area Omaha was always going to be difficult to take. It consisted of a good sandy beach with cliffs on either side and as such represented an obvious place for the Allies to attack. The fact that the Allies knew it would be a good place for a landing also meant that the Germans knew it would be a place they might well have to defend, and defend well.

Unfortunately Allied planning proceeded on the basis of intelligence which suggested that Omaha was defended only by one battalion of low-grade troops from Poland and Russia. This was wrong. There were three German battalions waiting for the Americans and they had every intention of fighting and fighting hard.

However, the Allied planners did not rely on intelligence alone. They reckoned that a naval and air bombardment, followed by 40,000 assault troops, would do the trick. Unfortunately the air bombardment never happened as the aircraft were late and could not see their targets through the cloud so that their bombs were released inland. The naval bombardment did take place but it was all too brief.

This left the men of the US Army who would have to save the day. The 16th Infantry Regiment was scheduled to land on the beaches in the two eastern sectors in Assault Area Omaha, Easy Red and Fox Green with the 116th Regiment landing on the beaches in the western sectors Dog Green, Dog White, Dog Red and Easy Green. There were also twelve companies of the 2nd and 5th Ranger Battalions who landed on Dog Green and Charlie beaches. Unlike other units going in to Assault Area Omaha on D-Day the 16th had seen action before. The regiment had taken part in the landings in North Africa and Sicily. But none of this was to prepare them for what awaited on the Omaha beaches on 6 June 1944.

If you have seen the film *Saving Private Ryan* you will be familiar with the opening sequence which is set in Assault Area Omaha on D-Day. It bears a remarkable similarity to the eyewitness accounts of the men who were there.

Rear Admiral John L. Hall Jr, Naval Commander, Task Force O

The first landings on Easy Red and Dog Green were made at 0635 and it is believed that the leading waves landed on the other beaches at approximately the same time. Due to the state of the sea, the loss of the

DD [Duplex Drive – amphibious] tanks, the absence of five LCTs [Landing Craft Tank] and damage to others by enemy gunfire the order of landing was somewhat mixed. Simultaneously with the landing and the cessation of the naval gunfire bombardment, the enemy commenced firing. This fire, from artillery mortars, machine guns and small arms, was heavy and accurate and casualties were numerous. Many of the tanks which had reached the shoreline were knocked out and losses to the infantry advancing shoreward through the obstacles, and to the demolition parties trying to clear lanes through them, were severe . . .

Due to the failure of the demolition parties to clear and mark gaps through the underwater obstacles, and to the heavy enemy fire, great difficulty was experienced in getting anyone or anything ashore. Some craft carrying infantry and elements of the shore party managed to land their personnel but the bulk of the craft proceeding shoreward was stopped between the seaward row of obstacles and the line of departure. With the strong tide, fresh wind and choppy sea this soon resulted in a mass of craft in which all semblance of wave organisation was lost until the Deputy Assault Group Commanders arrived on the scene, took charge of the situation, moved the craft to seaward to give them more room and reformed the waves as best they could . . . few, if any, troops actually crossed the beach during the early hours of the forenoon. The supporting destroyers and gunfire support craft stood in as close to the beach as the depth of the water would allow and engaged all the defensive installations which they could locate. Despite this, however, little progress had been made prior to 1100 when there was still considerable machine-gun fire, sniping, artillery and mortar fire on the beaches between the exits and opposite the exits the situation was critical. A number of enemy strongpoints on the beach were still holding out and our troops were not able to move inland. The first encouraging news came at 1100 from a message to Commander, Transport Division 3, intercepted by the Force Commander, to the effect that German troops were leaving their posts and surrendering to US troops . . . By 1340 the beaches of Sectors Easy and Dog were clear of opposition except for artillery and mortar fire . . . which, while neither heavy nor sustained, was deadly accurate. The fire was obviously observed because enemy batteries would be silent until craft beached when there would be a few quick salvos, usually right on target . . . By 1530 advance elements of the 1st

Division and 29th Division staffs were setting up command posts ashore near the beach exits from Sectors Easy and Dog . . . By 1730, except for sniping and the recurring artillery and mortar fire, hostile action against the beach area had ceased.[4]

Combat Interview, HQ Company, 16th Infantry Regiment

Landing at extreme low water the men had but a short distance to cover before they came to the first obstacles. They were in some depth of water when they met their first enemy fire. They immediately hit the sand but the rushing tide made cover impossible. Many of the wounded that were unable to walk were swamped; heroic efforts were made by other personnel to escort them to the safety of the beach. Considerable confusion resulted. The officer in charge, Lieutenant Colonel Matthews, was among the first to be hit and died immediately. Thirty-five men in all were wounded and killed from the time the ramp went down till they reached the beach. The beach was crowded, no exits had been made in the wire and the beach was under continual cross fire from small arms and artillery.[5]

Private Steve Kellman, L Company, 16th Infantry Regiment

Looking towards the beach we couldn't believe that anybody was left alive after the tremendous bombardment that they received both from the battleships, the rocket launching ships, and the air force pounding. Once we hit the beach we found out how wrong we were. The British coxswain of our boat got us right up onto the beach and we only got off into water perhaps knee high. Our training stood us in a good stead because we did not run straight up the beach but zig-zagged back and forth trying to make ourselves more difficult targets to hit. As I moved up the beach I got behind the bluff perhaps ten feet high and sought shelter there. We were moving laterally on the beach looking for an area that could afford us cover so that we could move off the beach. At that time, shells landed about ten yards away and the concussion just flipped me over on my back. A man immediately to my right was killed and I had a numb feeling in my right leg. I thought that it was just from the concussion but when I tried to stand I kept falling down. We had been issued uniforms that had a chemical added to the material that was supposed to repel gas in case the Germans had used it. We had also treated our canvas leggings and shoes. After falling down twice, I looked at my leg and saw that there was blood coming through the legging. I pulled the legging off and pulled up my trousers to see that I had been hit halfway between the knee and the ankle. I crawled against the bluff and tried to put a bandage on to cover the wound. Our lieutenant came along and said we were moving off the beach and he was upset that I had been laying back. When I stood up and fell down he realised I was wounded and said to stay where I was and that they would try to get me some help.

Succeeding waves of ships came in and a great many of the men were cut down coming across the beach. The fire from the 88s and machine guns took their toll. I later found out that of 180 men in our assault group only seventy-nine of us came across the beach alive. Those that could, moved off the beach because it was better going inland getting away from the terrible artillery fire we were exposed to. I handed over my rifle and my grenades to some of the men who struggled across the beach. Some of the coxswains of the LCVPs approached the beach and let the ramps down so that the men got off into the water waist deep and in some cases higher. They struggled ashore and many lost their packs, their helmets, and their rifles. As a result when they got up to the beach they had nothing to use and that is why I gave them my weapons. A fellow that was laying next to me on the beach had been wounded in the leg. I was talking to him when a very concentrated bombardment came very close to where we were located. We hid our heads and when the shelling stopped I looked up to talk to him and found out that he had been hit again and he was dead. I laid on the beach for about twelve hours, and once during that period of time a medic came by to see how I was doing. He just gave a cursory examination of my leg and told me to keep my bandage covering the wound. At approximately 6.00 p.m., that evening, a team of medics came along and started evacuating the wounded from my area.[6]

Combat Interview, L Company, 16th Infantry Regiment

The aid men were treating right at the edge of the water. They worked back and forth from the water dragging those back to the cliff who could not move under their own power. First Army troops, both engineers and medics, went to the rescue of the wounded. Some were shot while so

D-DAY— ASSAULT AREA OMAHA

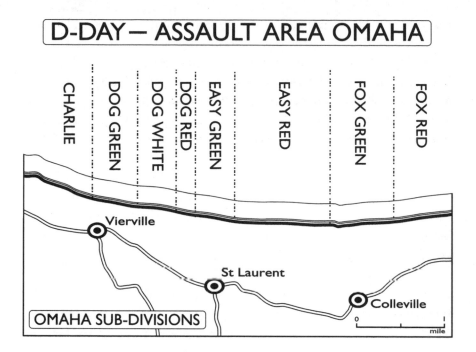

CHARLIE | DOG GREEN | DOG WHITE | DOG RED | EASY GREEN | EASY RED | FOX GREEN | FOX RED

Vierville

St Laurent

Colleville

0 ____ 1
mile

OMAHA SUB-DIVISIONS

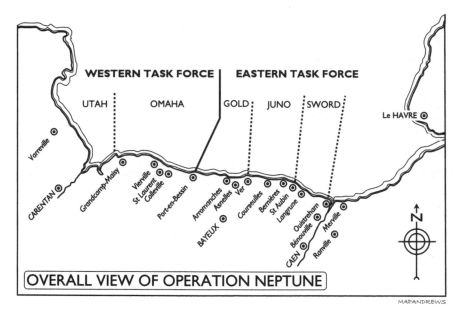

WESTERN TASK FORCE   EASTERN TASK FORCE

UTAH   OMAHA   GOLD : JUNO : SWORD :

Le HAVRE

Varreville

CARENTAN

Grandcamp-Maisy

Vierville
St Laurent
Colleville

Port-en-Bessin

Arromanches
Asnelles Ver
BAYEUX

Courseulles
Bernières
St Aubin
Langrune

Ouistreham
Bénouville
CAEN   Ranville
Merville

N

OVERALL VIEW OF OPERATION NEPTUNE

MAPANDREWS

doing. The Germans fired at all that moved and made no exceptions of sick men . . . The first Section under Lieutenant Kenneth E. Klenk struck out immediately to the right to feel out the strongpoint confronting the beach and between the two draws. However, upon finding that the approach to this strongpoint exposed his men unduly he moved his men back . . . in retracing its steps, however, the first section had closed in behind the second, third and fifth sections who were already fighting their way up the slope with the second in the lead. The second section swung in toward the strongpoint and got behind it. The third and fifth moved oblique right and continued up the draw. By this time naval fire was holding up the movement and preventing the second and first sections from closing in on the strongpoint.

The sections attacking the strongpoint had come up the hill under bullet and rifle-grenade fire. The men had moved along in squad column and were taking advantage of the shrubbery within the draw so that the enemy fire did little hurt. They could see the Germans moving around in position on the top of the hill and the BAR men not only in the sections closing on the strongpoint, but in the two sections which had gone on rightward, were spraying the ground steadily. The BAR fire was extremely effective and they saw some of the enemy fall . . . First section moved in to the outlying trenches of the strongpoint and began mopping up with grenades and satchel charges. About four or five of the enemy were knocked out during the close fighting before the remainder surrendered. The Americans lost only one.[7]

Combat Interview, G Company, 16th Infantry Regiment

There were no casualties coming in. 'Bullets were dropping around us like rain but the Good Lord seemed to be with us (Captain Joseph T. Dawson. Note: This man is an unusually accurate witness) . . . G lost most of its men – 63 men all told – in getting from the boats to the shingle . . . Except for the wounded and perhaps a few stragglers, the men streamed on up the shingle. The light MGs and the mortars were all with Dawson, he put the MGs on top of the shingle and the mortars at the base of it. Five minutes after hitting the shingle, these weapons were ready to fire. At first the men could see no targets so they put down a general 'zone' fire. At least ten minutes passed in this way. Then new boat waves came in to the beach. At that, enemy fire shifted from the beach and shingle to the oncoming boats. 'They caught all of the unshirted hell that G Company had been catching. When that happened the men at the mortars and MGs had their first chance to see the targets clearly. They spotted eight or ten emplacements – some of them looking like Tobruk pits – and we directed all our fire towards these points. The BARs and rifles added to the volume. We tried to put rocket fire on the emplacements but the rockets were ineffective. So was the mortar fire.' (Lieutenant E. A. Day).

The wire – two double aprons and a concertina, about ten feet broad – was about five yards beyond the shingle. While the offensive fire was being built up, four or five men from each section blew the wire ahead with bangalores, having to use four bangalores to cut one lane. (Dawson). Private First Class [Pfc] Henry J. Pezzek wiggled through with Lieutenant John D. Burbridge. They got part way through and Burbridge got his pack hung up. He shook himself loose, Pezzek yelled to him, 'Keep going! I'm going back for the bangalores!' He exploded two of them, both men were lying within six feet of the torpedoes when they exploded. Pezzek got creased on the arm by a bullet while laying the second torpedo but kept working. This was the best placed and cut a lane along the beach. Through it most of the men of G passed and the battalions which came after them took the same route.

A minefield lay beyond the wire. There were two dead Americans lying in the mine area, they had been blown up. The men of G went through the field over the bodies of two dead men, figuring that this was their safest route. They then continued through the Roman ruins and proceeded up the draw. Dawson was out ahead of them. He had crawled through the wire and gone on up the hill with Pfc Frank Baldridge to see if he could clear the way for his men. They got half-way up the draw. Dawson then found himself caught between the fire of his own men and fire from an enemy MG at the head of the draw. Having walked up to that point, they flopped next to a fallen log for cover. Dawson told Bainbridge, 'Leave your equipment here. Go back and get the rest of the company.'

Bainbridge crawled on back and Dawson crawled another seventy-five yards. He moved to any cover he could find. The draw was V-shaped, the ruins being right at the bottom of the V. There was a promontory at the top near the left-hand angle of the V. He crawled on behind this and around, which move put the enemy emplacement a little behind him and to his right. He was within ten yards when the Germans saw him, swung the MG round and fired wildly. He heaved a fragmentation grenade; it exploded between them and killed both men . . .

The men of G continued on for about 100 yards. They then saw Germans 'milling around' 150 yards or so to their leftward. Staff Sergeant [S/Sgt] Joseph Barr moved out along the hedge with an M-1 and took eight prisoners, routing them from out of a dugout. They were a mixture of Germans and Poles (the company had seen mortar fire coming from this position) . . .

Save for his dead and wounded, Dawson had brought every man off the beach. He did not have one malinger. To the eye of [S/Sgt Vincent J.].Kachnik it seemed that the new men came along quite as well as the old men and in some cases with more dash . . .

The plan was for 3rd and 4th Sections to attack the German bivouac area on the right . . . about twelve men were lost in cleaning the enemy from the bivouac area in a close-up house-to-house action fought through with rifles and grenades.[8]

Sergeant William Funkhouser, F Company, 16th Infantry Regiment

On 6 June 1944, Company F of the 16th Infantry Regiment stepped out of the landing barge at Omaha Beach into water waist-deep. And it was cold! My thoughts were that I might not get wet all over. It wasn't too long until my nose was the only thing sticking out of the water. When I tried to inflate my life preserver, I forgot to unflap it first and I thought it would squeeze me to death. Finally when I was partially out of the water, I tried to get the life preserver off by puncturing it with my knife. I dropped my knife and was searching for it when machine-gun fire burst across my legs. The strangest thing was the gunfire didn't faze me. At that point I did stop searching for my knife. I started crawling because you didn't dare stand up. I ditched my 60-mm mortar. To the left front there was an explosion and a white flash. It was a man carrying TNT and something had set it off. In front of me were small pieces of his body scattered all over the sand. I kept staring at a piece the size of my fist that was as white as snow. (In December I was called back to CP [the unit command post] and asked to sign a form that I had viewed his body and knew he was dead. I told them I couldn't sign because there was no body.

They told me to sign anyway so they could get the insurance started.) I knew I couldn't crawl through the body parts so I tried to walk, but my knees were so weak they wouldn't hold me. I thought I had been shot. And again the idea of being shot did not faze me. I guess all I could think about was surviving. The tide was still coming in and I didn't know whether to wait for the tide to wash the body parts away, but I knew I couldn't lay there that long. I just closed my eyes and crawled. It was 6:25 or 6:35 a.m. when we landed.[9]

Combat Interview, F Company, 16th Infantry Regiment

By the time that each section had reached the beach and the cover of the high water mark, only two of the officers were capable of command. All units were badly scattered . . . The fifth section received a lot of machine-gun fire on the beach area. Technical Sergeant [T/Sgt] Raymond F. Strojny found a better position and he called his men to it. There he built a line of fire. Soon he saw two enemy machine-gun positions and directed all the fire to these. Both guns ceased to fire. Then Strojny saw a pillbox about a hundred yards away which was firing a 75-mm gun towards the tanks on the beach. He fired his rifle at the pillbox then called for a bazooka. None of his men had one but a sergeant from the 116th appeared with one. Strojny told the sergeant to fire at the gun. The sergeant said he couldn't see it. Strojny pointed it out to him but the sergeant said he did not have anyone to load. Strojny loaded the first round which went way wide. A second was loaded but it was too short. At this time a mortar round landed in the five yards between the two men, severely wounding the sergeant. Strojny was not wounded so he took up the bazooka but it was [damaged] up the tube by shell fragments. The enemy gun continued firing which made Strojny mad. He decided to try the bazooka anyway so loaded again and fired. The first two rounds missed, the next two were direct hits. Nevertheless the gun continued to fire. Strojny yelled for more ammunition but there was none. He then went down the beach and returned with six rounds he found. He fired all six from the ammunition, all rounds hitting the target – the last one causing the ammunition to explode. A number of dead were observed and only one German was seen to escape. Strojny fired at the German with an M-1 but was wounded by a sniper. The bullet entered his helmet over his left eye, going through the helmet and leaving a large hole in the rear of it. Despite this Strojny was only superficially wounded. For this action Strojny was awarded the DSC.

Seeing the pillbox in flames Strojny urged his men forward . . . his men followed him but the men from the 116th Infantry, who were nearby, would not. Sergeant Strojny had his men pick up the two BARs the 116th had abandoned. He worked to the left of the point where his unit was to cross, but as there was wire he could not get through. Strojny got a man from the 116th to blow a hole through the wire. The BAR men were placed on the right to fire into a wooded area. Private Charles Rocheford had his hand blown off by a mine as he came into position. Strojny ran through the gap and cleared the minefield. He motioned for the others to follow. Five men from Strojny's section and an officer and a squad from the 116th followed. They received machine-gun fire from their right flank. The entire group headed for this fire and seven Germans were killed. One American was killed, one wounded. Both of these were from the 116th. Another machine-gun emplacement was found and silenced with a demolition charge.[10]

Private Warren Rulien, 16th Infantry Regiment

I felt so rotten from the seasickness, that I was half enthusiastic about hitting the shore just to get off that landing craft. As we got nearer to the shore, bullets began hitting the sides of the landing craft, but could not penetrate as we ducked down low. It wasn't long after we stopped when the front of the landing craft was lowered. For a few seconds, everything seemed quiet, and nobody moved. The images that flashed through my mind was, 'They can shoot us through the front of the craft.' Someone shouted, 'Let's go!' Instantly, we began pouring out of the craft. As I stepped off of the ramp, I dropped into water up to my chest. This threw me off balance, and I lost my rifle. I floated around for a few seconds, trying to find my rifle then gave up and began wading into shore. On both sides of me were many soldiers coming from other landing craft all wading into shore. In front of me were steel rails driven into the bottom of the sea which extended about six feet out of the water. On top of them were mines. They were wide enough apart so troops could easily walk between them. By the time I got to the steel rails, the water was about up to my waist. There was a sandbar which was perpendicular with the shore. About fifteen or twenty feet of it extended above the water. There were many dead soldiers floating around in the water. Bullets began hitting the water only a few feet in front of me, so I stepped behind one of the steel rails and squatted down. The rail was only about six or eight inches wide. A young replacement about nineteen years old that was from my platoon shouted at me 'Hey, Rulien, here I go!' and began running toward shore. He stepped onto the sandbar and machine-gun fire opened up and he dropped into the water on the other side. I took one of the bodies that was floating in the water and pushed it in front of me toward the shore. I had only gone a short distance when three or four soldiers began lining up behind me. Seeing this, I stood up and shouted, 'Don't bunch up!' and walked off leaving them with the body. I got down as low as I could in the water until I reached the sandbar and then I crossed the sandbar on my belly.

When I got across the sandbar, I noticed that the water was deep again, about up to my chest. I kept moving forward, until I reached the beach. In about two yards in the beach was a sand bank which was about four feet high and ran the whole length of the shore. Behind this, soldiers from each direction began bunching up. About 100 feet further inshore were two rolls of barbed wire. There, the terrain began getting steeper. The terrain continued to rise until it crested at about 150 feet. Halfway up the hill was a pillbox, but there was no gunfire coming from it. In the back of the pillbox was a path leading up to the top of the hill. A German soldier who came out of the back of the pillbox began running up the path in back of the hill. Small arms fire from the American soldiers began pouring onto him. He turned back around immediately and ran back into the pillbox.

Between the barbed wire and the pillbox were many land mines planted. Lying beside me, on his back, was an American soldier who had been shot in the stomach. He held his hand over his stomach, moaning, but only for a short time. Then he died. Seeing his rifle lying beside him, I picked it up, threw back the bolt, and looked down the barrel to make sure that sand hadn't been jammed into the barrel. I put a clip of ammunition into the gun, looked up the hill and saw German soldiers running along the crest of the hill. At the distance that I was from them, they looked about two inches high. I began firing at them. On the shore, there were officers sitting there, stunned. Nobody was taking command. Landing craft were continuing to bring waves of soldiers in and they were bunching up on the beach. Finally, out on the water, coming towards the shore, walking straight up with a staff of officers with him, I recognised Colonel Taylor, regimental commander. He stepped across the sandbar and bullets began hitting the water around him. He laid down on his stomach and started crawling towards shore, his staff officers doing the same. I kind of chuckled to myself, thinking, 'Crawl on your stomach, like I did.' When he got to shore, he sized up the situation immediately. I heard him say to the officers, 'If we're going to die, let's die up there.' It seemed to take effect, because the officers began moving their men along that two yards of beach to reach their objective.[11]

Captain Edward F. Wozenski, commanding officer, E Company, 16th Infantry Regiment

With H-Hour at 0630 hours apprehension increased as we continued to rendezvous after 0600 hours. At approximately 0600 hours heavy naval support weapons opened up with their fire display followed by flashes from the distant low shore where the shells were landing.

A few enemy planes floated over the massed invasion forces dropping their long burning flares. Anxious eyes scanned the dawn, lightened skies, searching for the hundreds of promised bombers – especially any heading for Easy Red – our beach. Damn few were seen . . .

About a mile offshore we began to pass a few and then more and more men passing about in the water in life belts and small rubber craft – at first we thought these were shot down airmen but soon realised that they must be tank men from tanks that had sunk.[12]

Combat Interview, E Company, 16th Infantry Regiment

The roughness of the sea, the dense smoke along the beach and some mist at sea all contributed to E coming in at the wrong place and becoming dispersed over a wide area. (1/Sgt Lawrence J. Fitzgerald, T/Sgt Joseph A. Toth and T/Sgt Calvin L. Ellis). The men noted that the Navy crew seemed green and that when fired upon, they would not get to their guns. When at last ordered to get to the guns they fired wildly and would not expose themselves. In Ellis's boat the coxswain didn't know where to go and asked Ellis, 'What is the objective?' Ellis pointed it out to him and then noted he was moving too far right. He said, 'Bear left!' He then told the coxswain he was bearing too far left but the man kept on the same course.

The company boats began stringing out and finally lost one another. All were supposed to [be guided by] the CP boat but that boat was bearing far left and the others realised it. (Fitzsimmons). The men kept yelling at the coxswain, 'You're going left!' but he ignored them and kept on the same course . . .

In all of the boats the in-passage was not too costly but when the ramps were dropped, automatic fire caught the open ends dead on. Some of them were caught in crossing bands of fire. The CP boat took its heaviest losses at that moment and only twelve out of thirty-six men got to the beach. The rest got it in the water, as they waded in from a sandbar, or were shot as they returned to drag in the wounded. Section 1, however, didn't lose a man in the water, the fire against the section was small in volume and erratic. (T/Sgt Phillip Streczyk).[13]

Lieutenant John Spalding,[14] leader 1st Section, E Company, 16th Infantry Regiment

Because we were carrying so much equipment and, because I was afraid that we were being landed in deep water, I told the men not to jump out until after I had tested the water. I jumped out of the boat slightly to the left of the ramp into water about waist deep. Then the men began to follow me. We headed ashore and the small arms fire became noticeable. We saw other boats to our left but nothing to our right. We were the right front of the 1st Division. There was soon a noticeable decline of sand beneath our feet and we were soon over our heads, so we tried to swim. Fortunately when I pulled the valve on my life belt it inflated and saved me. I lost my carbine. We lost none of our men but only because they helped each other or because they got rid of their equipment . . . in addition to the flamethrower and many personal weapons we lost our mortar, most of [our] mortar ammunition, one or two bazookas and much of the bazooka ammunition. However, the men who kept their weapons were able to fire them as soon as they came ashore. It shows that the M-1 is an excellent weapon . . .

Our first casualty came at the water's edge. Private William C. Roper, rifleman, was hit in the foot by small arms fire . . . Just after we got ashore one of my two BAR men was hit. Pfc Virgil Tilly was hit in the right shoulder by a shell fragment which drove a hunk of the shoulder out through the back but did not come all the way through.

By this time I noticed a number of my men on the beach, all standing up and moving across the sand. They were too waterlogged to run but they went as fast as they could. It looked as if they were walking in the face of a real strong wind. We moved across the shale to a house which was straight inland.[15]

Captain Edward F. Wozenski

MG fire was rattling against the ramp as the boat grounded. For some reason the ramp was not latched during any part of our trip, but the ramp would not go down. Four or five men battered at the ramp until it fell and the men with it.

The boats were hurriedly emptied – the men jumping into water shoulder high under intense MG and AT [anti-tank] fire. No sooner was the last man out than the boat received two direct hits from an AT gun and was believed to have burned and blown up.

Now, all the men in the company could be seen wading ashore into the field of intense fire from the MGs, rifles, AT guns and mortars. Due to heavy sea, the strong cross-current and the loads the men were carrying, no one could run. It was just a slow, methodical march with absolutely no cover up to the enemy's commanding positions. Many fell left and right and the water reddened with their blood. A few men hit underwater mines of some sort and were blown out of the sea. The others staggered on to the obstacle-covered, yet completely exposed beach. Here men, in sheer exhaustion, hit the beach only to rise and move forward through a tide inlet that threatened to sweep them off their feet. Men were falling on all sides but the survivors still moved forward . . . to a pile of shells at the high-water mark. This offered some protection against the murderous fire of close-in enemy guns but his mortars were still raising hell.

A firing line was built up along this pile of shells and the enemy was brought under small arms fire but unfortunately most of our guns were jammed with sand but every arm was brought to bear on the enemy . . . Finally in an effort to reorganise in some strength a lateral movement along the exposed beach was started. Men were picked up at scattered intervals and were being led to our originally scheduled landing. Approaching this point it was seen that the first platoon of Company E had broken through just east of Exit E-1. There Lieutenant Spalding with his platoon made the initial break-through from the beach and the entire beach Easy Red was attempting to clear inland by this route despite the fact it was being swept by machine-gun, artillery, mortar and AT fire.[16]

Staff Sergeant John Souch, E Company, 16th Infantry Regiment

Finally the ramp went down in the water. The landing craft didn't even come close to the beach. We went off the ramp and into the cold water, holding our rifles above our heads so as not to get the water in the barrel. We finally seen the beach. Shells were exploding in the surf and machine-gun bullets were whipping up sprints of water and mortar shells exploding all around us. We could hear the naval gunfire over our heads. As we moved inward, there was jagged barrels of steel rails and rows and rolls of barbed wire which were pretty high, concrete blocks and what not, planted by the Germans.

It seemed like a long time before we finally hit the beach. There were bodies laying all over the beach. Some were wounded and some were dead and they told us to dig in. You couldn't dig in on the beach as it was nothing but rocks, the size of potatoes. You couldn't even use your shovel. As you stood around you hardly knew anyone. We were brought in at the wrong part of beach. Then I had diarrhoea, and no place to go. So I crawled under between the barbed wire until I found a small opened place and it was pretty hard, because you had to take all the equipment off your back, the toilet paper was wet, along with everything else. We had gas impregnated uniforms on. I was lucky I didn't step on a mine as the place was fully mined all over.

There was an amphibious tank on the beach but it wasn't operable and many of us were huddled in back of it so as not to be hit by machine-gun fire or mortar fire.[17]

Combat Interview, E Company, 16th Infantry Regiment

Toth's 2nd section was dropped in water over its head, the coxswain having started shying off as he drew into the beach. More than half of the men came in swimming, some it was believed, were carried down by the weight of their equipment (Toth).

All told E lost 105 men during the day and only one of these was lost during the movement inland. Most of the others were lost in the water. Many of the wounded crawled to the edge of the sand, fell exhausted and were there caught by the tide. In trying to pull these men in the able-bodied were caught by enemy fire and some of these wounded also died from drowning. The medical detachment, coming in on the fourth wave, took enough casualties that its own wounded monopolised its attention (Lieutenant Thad A. Shaw, Ellis). On the beach the men of E noted only other infantrymen. The wire and obstacles had not been touched. A few minutes later the men of E saw the first engineers arrive and set to work.

Stretching ahead of the company were 300 yards of sand and then a steep hill. The seasoned men among them knew that they had to move but even they felt their strength and will fading. The fire was hot, their loads were heavy. Their natural inclination was to stay there (Fitzsimmons and Ellis). They went on a few feet and then flopped again. The tide came racing in behind them and pushed them on. Fitzsimmons saw two of his men – Pvts Spencer and Walsh – take a few strides, flop down and then be blown bodily into the air by mines buried on the beach. Both were killed.

It took one hour to get the survivors across the beach and to the foot of the hill. They went forward one at a time, figuring that they would be less of a target this way. German riflemen were firing at them from the brow of the hill and they were getting automatic fire from both flanks along the beach. Ellis saw four enemy riflemen fire at his men from atop the hill and then move along it in silhouette. He tried to get some fire on them but discovered that every weapon in his section was out of action. The riflemen disappeared suddenly as if the ground had swallowed them and he figured that they had dropped into an emplacement.

Some of the men froze on the beach, wretched with seasickness and fear. Most of the survivors toiled painfully to the foot of the hill where the enemy might well have found and destroyed them, since they had no firepower (Fitzsimmons).

Streczyk's section – which was to contribute one of the most intrepid actions of the entire day – came in exactly where F was supposed to land. Streczyk got thirty-two men on to the sands, took twelve casualties, mostly from bullet fire, in getting across the beach and continued onward immediately with twenty men. The German SP [strongpoint] – covering Exit 3 on the eastern side – when the debouchement took place was to the party's immediate right, and from this they were drawing most of the fire. Dead ahead of them was a small ravine and their approach was direct toward it. This put them a little to the left of the first line of emplacements serving as an outwork for the SP. A communications trench led back from the emplacements. The party moved rapidly up the draw, then went right and slightly uphill in such a way that they emerged on the rear of the outwork before the enemy had noted the movement (Streczyk). The fourteen Germans inside the work were caught flat-footed. The party attacked them with grenades and bazookas and they made a futile attempt to reply with grenades. Several were killed, two were captured and the others got away from the SP.

The party then attacked the SP from the rear and had its rearward exit covered before a shot was fired. From the cover of an outer trench they engaged it with grenades. The enemy fire gradually fell off as the occupants went to cover but there was no sign of a surrender. For 4½ hours Streczyk's men stayed there, keeping this point neutralised and thereby greatly assisting the movements of G and of other units across the beach. Yet they did not feel strong enough to assault it directly and under the conditions in which the men were employed, the Streczyk party was wholly scattered with each man fighting his own battle and doing what he could to harass the enemy. In this time they took twenty-one prisoners and left an equal number of German dead behind without themselves losing one man. They had kept under cover in the outworks, worked in small groups through the trenches and gradually reduced the enemy strength so that the SP was not capable of an strong action. It had become 'contained.'

Streczyk's men had blown the wire confronting the ravine just after landing. There was thus a convenient avenue for the advance of other troops.[18]

Lieutenant John Spalding

My assistant section leader was T/Sgt Philip Streczyk. The sergeant, who was [later] wounded in the Hürtgen forest action, was the best soldier I have ever seen. He came into the Army as a selectee and worked his way up to platoon sergeant. He was on the landing at Oran and in Sicily. If we had more like him the war would soon be over . . .

Down near the water's edge we ran into wire. S/Sgt Curtis Colwell blew a hole in the wire with a bangalore. We picked our way through . . . on our left we had bypassed a pillbox from which MG fire was mowing down F Company people a few hundred yards to our left. There was nothing we could do to help them. We could still see no one to the right and there was no one up to us on the left. We didn't know what had become of the rest of E Company. Back in the water boats were in flames. I saw a tank ashore about 0730–0745. After a couple of looks back we decided we wouldn't look back any more.

About this time Gallagher said to follow up the defilade which was about 400 yards to the right of the pillbox. We were getting terrific small arms fire but few were hit. About this time we were nearly at the top of the hill (Lieutenant Spalding was unable to be specific on the 'about this time' statements). We returned fire bit couldn't hit them. We were also getting rifle fire.[19]

Staff Sergeant John Souch

Then we moved out, behind this wall where we huddled and then the officer in charge had us push a bangalore torpedo on the barbed wire. It is a long pipe, and you push it under the obstacle and then you screw the next one on to it, and then the next one, and then you pull the charge and it goes off and blows the barbed wire and mines with it in order to make a hole for us to be able to go through it.

I remember how we were shaking from being afraid of getting killed or wounded. We could hardly screw the pipe together. We really didn't know if we were going to be dead or alive. It was one big mess and confusion.

Finally, we started getting organised to move up the hill. The bulldozer made a hole through the tank trap and mines were cleared. There was a man-made canal to trap the tanks. We had to wade through the water, which was up to my chest. We had [chemical] impregnated gas masks in front of our chest which helped to hold me up as we were going across it. It was about 50–75 feet wide. We started up the hill going zig-zag very slowly. If we seen a mine we were supposed to put a marker on it with anything you had.

A GI in front of me whose name is Merolla, said, 'Souch I think my foot is on a mine.' It was his right foot. It was an anti-personnel mine. We were sweating it out. I told him to take his weight off slowly and shift his body to the left. If the mine goes off he would only lose his foot or the heel on his foot. I told him if the mine goes off, it would go between his legs and kill him. So, then I told him to slide his foot off real fast which he did, and the mine didn't go off. We placed a white cloth on it as the ones in back of us would not step on it. It was a slow process walking up the hill. I remember to the right of us there was a GI. He must have been in shock and wounded. I didn't know how, but he was cutting off his leg with his bayonet. We finally reached the top of the hill and reorganised, and went to our objective and everyone was cold and damp. A lot of the guys were missing. Our uniforms were still soaked and weren't drying and it was getting dark and you couldn't sleep.[20]

Lieutenant John Spalding

When we found the way up I sent word back for my men to come up on the right. Sergeants Hubert W. Blades, Grant Phelps and Joseph W. Slaydon and Pfc Raymond R. Curley went first. I went next, Sergeant Biscoe followed me and the rest of the section came along. I couldn't take my eye off the machine gun above us so Sergeant Bisco kept saying, 'Lieutenant, watch out for them damn mines.' They were little box type mines and it seems that the place was infested by them but I didn't see them. We lost no men coming through them although H Company coming along the same trail several hours later lost several men. The Lord was with us and we had an angel on each shoulder on that trip.

Trying to get the machine [gun] above us Sergeant Blades fired his bazooka and missed. He was shot in the left arm almost immediately. Pfc Curley – rifleman – was shot next. Sergeant Phelps, who had picked up Tilley's BAR on the beach, moved into position to fire and was hit in both legs. By this time practically all my section had moved up. We decided to rush the machine gun about fifteen yards away. You may say – why hadn't we hit it? I don't know. As we rushed it the lone German operating the gun threw up his hands and yelled, 'Kamerad!' We would have killed him but we needed prisoners for interrogation so I ordered the men not to shoot him. He was Polish. He said that there were sixteen Germans in the area, that they had been alerted that morning and told they had to hold the beach. They had taken a vote on whether to fight and preferred not to but the German non-coms made them. He said there were sixteen Germans in the trench to the rear of his machine gun. He also said that he had not shot at Americans although I had seen him hit three. I turned the PW over to Sergeant Blades who was wounded. Blades gave his bazooka to Sergeant Peterson and guarded the prisoner with a trench knife. We moved Curley, Blades and other wounded into a defile and the medic – Private George Bowen – gave them first aid. He covered the whole beach that day, no man waited more than five minutes for first aid. He got the DSC for his work.

Coming up along the crest of the hill Sergeant Clarence Colson, who had picked up a BAR on the beach, began to give assault fire as he walked along, firing the weapon from his hip. He opened up on the machine gun to our right, firing so rapidly that his ammunition carrier had difficulty getting ammo to him fast enough.

At this point Lieutenant Blue of G Company came up and contacted me. He had come up our trail. His company had landed in the second wave behind us. Just a few minutes later Captain Dawson of G Company came along. We still saw no one on the right. Captain Dawson asked if I knew where E Company was and I told him that I didn't know. He said that E Company was 500 yards to my right, but he was thinking in terms of where they were supposed to land, they were actually 500–800 yards to our left. I later found out that they had lost 121 men. Dawson said that he was going into Colleville and told us to go in to the right. He had about two sections. Said he had just seen the battalion commander. This was about 0800.

I went over and talked to Lieutenant Blue about the information we had gotten from the prisoner. I asked him to give us some support where the sixteen Germans were supposed to be. As we went up in this direction we hit a wooded area. We found a beautifully camouflaged trench which ran along in zig-zag fashion, but we were afraid to go in. We went along the top of the trench spraying it with lead. We used bullets instead of grenades since we had very few grenades, and thought that the bullets would be more effective. We did not fix bayonets at any time during the attack. We turned to the right and hit a wooded area, got no fire from there, so we yelled to Lieutenant Blue to shove off and he started for Colleville. There I stood like a damn fool waving him a fond farewell. We were headed for St Laurent; G Company went on to Colleville-sur-Mer. H Company came up next under Lieutenant Shelley.

We were on top of the hill by 0900. Advanced cautiously. We were the first platoon of the 16th to hit the top. Now had 21–22 men in section. Had spent more time at the rubble than anywhere else. Had taken up some time with prisoner.[21]

252

As we went inland we heard rifle and machine-gun fire to our right. Streczyk and Gallagher volunteered to check on the situation. Our men were spread out over an area of 200–300 yards. They located a machine gunner with a rifleman on either side of him. Streczyk shot the gunner in the back and the riflemen surrendered. The two prisoners were German and refused to give us any information. With them in tow we continued to the west. We still saw no one to the west. We were now in hedgerow and orchard country. We were watching our flanks and to the front and scouring the wooded area. We tended to send a sergeant with three or four men to check up on suspicious areas. We usually sent up someone with an automatic weapon to cover them (we did not have any MGs at this time, however). We crossed through two minefields – one had a path through it, which looked like it had been made for a long time. When we got through it we saw the Achtung Minen sign. No one was lost, we still had an angel on each shoulder.

We now found a construction shack near the strongpoint overlooking the E-1 draw . . . Sergeant Kenneth Peterson fired his bazooka into the tool shed, but no one came out. We were about to go on when I spied a piece of stove pipe about seventy yards away sticking out of the ground. I formed my section into a semi-circular defensive position. We were now getting small arms fire again. Sergeant Streczyk and I went forward to investigate. We discovered an underground dugout. There was an 81-mm mortar, a position for a 75[-mm gun] and construction for a pillbox. All this overlooked the E-1 draw. The dugout was of cement had radios, excellent sleeping facilities, dogs. We started to drop a grenade in the ventilator, but Streczyk said, 'Hold on a minute,' and fired three shots down the steps into the dugout. He then yelled in Polish and German (he had interrogated the prisoners earlier) for them to come out. Four men, disarmed, came up. They brought two or three wounded. I yelled for Colson to bring five or six men. We began to get small arms fire from the right (west). I yelled for Piasecki and Sakowski to move forward to the edge of the draw. A fire-fight took place. The Navy now began to place timed fire in the draw; this was about 1000. Piasecki deployed six or seven men, shot several Germans and chased a number down into the draw where they were taken care of by Navy fire. (The 81-mm was not manned, had beautiful range cards, lots of ammunition.)

When Colson came over I started down the line of communication trenches. The trenches led to the cliff over the beach. We were now behind the Germans so we routed four out of a hole and got thirteen in the trenches. The trenches had teller mines, hundreds of grenades, numerous machine guns. They were firing when we came up. We turned the prisoners over to Streczyk. We had a short fight with the thirteen men; they threw three grenades at us, but they didn't hit anyone. We found one dead man in the trenches, but don't know if we killed him. If we did, he was the only German we killed. Several of us went to check the trenches. I did a fool thing. After losing my carbine in the water I had picked up a German rifle, but found I didn't know how to use it too well. When I started to check on the trenches I traded the German rifle to a soldier for a carbine and failed to check it. In a minute I ran into a Kraut and pulled the trigger, but the safety was on. I reached for the safety catch and hit the clip release, so my clip hit the ground. I ran about fifty yards in nothing flat. Fortunately Sergeant Peterson had me covered and the German put up his hands. That business of not checking guns is certainly not habit forming.

We next took out an AT gun near the edge of the draw. There was little resistance. We now had the prisoners back near the dugout. We had split the section into three units. We got a little ineffective machine-gun fire from the draw to the right at this time. We tried to use the 81-mm mortar, but no one could operate the German weapon. For the first time I saw people across the draw to the west. I supposed that they were from the 116th. They seemed to be pinned down.

About this time two stragglers from the 116th came up. I didn't ask what company they were from but just took them along. We went back and checked trenches since we were afraid of infiltration by the Germans. In the meantime I sent the 17–19 German prisoners back with two men the way we had come. I told them to turn them over to anyone who would take them and to ask about our company.

At this point I saw Lieutenant Hutch of Company E (second section which had been directly to my left in the boats) coming up. I pointed out a minefield to him and he told me that there was a sniper near me. We had sniper fire every few feet; now we were getting pretty jittery. We set off our last yellow smoke grenade to let the Navy know that we were Americans, since their fire was getting very close.

About 1045 Captain Wozenski of Company E came up from the left.

He had come along practically the same route we had used. I was very happy to see him. We had orders to contact Major Washington, 2nd Battalion executive officer, just outside Colleville. Our objective was changed; there were to be no patrols into Trevières that afternoon as we had been told originally we would. We never crossed the E-1 draw. Instead we went along the trail towards Colleville. We were to swing in the fields to the right of Colleville. Lieutenant Hutch and I had about thirty men; he was in charge (I was a 2nd lieutenant and he was a 1st lieutenant). Lieutenant James McGourty had also come with Captain Wozenski. Three of our section leaders had been killed on the beach, Hutch, McGourty, and I were here together. Wozenski is now commander of 3rd Battalion, 16th Infantry.

We ran into Major Washington, executive officer of the 2nd Battalion, near Colleville; he was in a ditch outside town. Captain Dawson had come up to Colleville, his original objective, earlier. G Company was already in and around the town. We got some small arms fire in this area, but no one was hurt. Lieutenant Hutch and I contacted Major Washington about 1300. He told us we were to go to the right of Colleville and guard the right flank of the town. We went out and were surrounded in about forty minutes. Lieutenant Knuckus of G Company, with about fourteen men, came up and said he had the right flank, so we reinforced him (altogether Lieutenant Hutch, Lieutenant Knuckus and I had about forty-five).

In the position to the west of Colleville we had set up our defensive position. We selected a position where no digging was necessary; used drainage ditches; were now in orchards and hedgerows. We moved cautiously; didn't know where anybody was. About 1500 got German fire. Di Gaetano was hit in the butt by shrapnel fire, we told him that he was too big to be missed. Sergeant Bisco was killed, rifle fire hit him in the face and throat. Only one round of artillery came in; we thought it was from one of our ships – exploded about 300 yards from us; had orange and yellow flame.

As we looked back towards the beach we saw several squads of Germans coming towards us. We had no contract with the battalion. Just as a G Company runner started over to us and got to the edge of our defenses they opened fire on him. After he fell they fired at least 100 rounds of machine-gun fire into him. It was terrible but we do the same thing when we want to stop a runner from taking information. Of course, we didn't find out what he was coming to tell us. We fired until we were low on ammunition that afternoon. I had six rounds of carbine ammunition left. Some of the fellows were down to their last clip. We were still surrounded. We called a meeting of Lieutenants Knuckus, Hutch, T/Sgt Ellis, T/Sgt Streczyk and myself. About 1700 we decided to fight our way back to the battalion. We sent word for the men to come to us in the ditch where we were; we were several hundred yards south and west of Colleville.

At about 1900 or 2000 we set up automatic weapons to cover us as we crawled down the ditch back towards Colleville. Lieutenant Hutch went in front. We got back to battalion and ran into C Company of the 16th on the way to reinforce us. We didn't know where we were. We found Major Washington in a little gully at the west of town. He said we were to go back to about the same point with C Company in support. We took up defensive position about 500–700 [yards] from our original positions – this was closer to Colleville. We were still in hedgerows; we guarded roads and avenues of approach. I think that part of the company area bordered on the roads into Colleville. We now had machine guns (I believe from Company H). This was about 2100, nearly dark. Was quiet except for some aerial activity. We had heard American machine guns earlier in the afternoon; it is possible that they drove Germans towards us.

We spent the night of the first day in the positions near Colleville.[22]

Combat Interview, G Company, 16th Infantry Regiment,

At about 0800 on D + 1, Dawson put his first patrol through the town – Burbridge, Kruckas, Gaetano, Pezzek and four others. They worked down the main road, moved carefully from house to house, shot a few enemy riflemen and captured eight prisoners. As they reached the edge of the town the 20th Engineers and some MPs came along behind them. The patrol was followed by exactly one block by an MP carrying 'Off Limits' signs. Gaetano cleaned out one house, went on a short distance, went back and tried to re-enter the same house as he wasn't sure whether he had completed the job. An MP said, 'You can't go in there!'

Gaettano replied, 'The hell I can't. Just try to stop me!' and went on in (Burbridge).[23]

256

Notes

1. Marshall, pp. 50–4.
2. Quoted in Bull, *World War II Infantry Tactics – Squad and Platoon*, p. 41
3. Marshall, pp. 120–1
4. ANCXF Report Vol. 3, Report by N.C, Force 'O', pp. 6, 7, quoted in *Battle Summary No. 39, Landings in Normandy June 1944, HMSO*, 1994, pp. 95–6
5. US Army Historical Section combat interviews, NARA, microfilm records held in Liddell Hart Centre for Military Archives, King's College, London, ref GB99 KCLMA MFF 7
6. Courtesy of The National D-Day Museum Foundation, Peter Kalikow World War II Oral History Collection
7. US Army Historical Section combat interviews
8. *Ibid*.
9. Story courtesy of The National D-Day Museum, Share Your Story online WWII accounts
10. US Army Historical Section combat interviews
11. Courtesy of The National D-Day Museum Foundation, Peter Kalikow World War II Oral History Collection
12. *Ibid*.
13. *Ibid*.
14. The combat interview spells his name (incorrectly) as Spaulding
15. Courtesy of The National D-Day Museum Foundation, Peter Kalikow World War II Oral History Collection
16. *Ibid*.
17. *Ibid*.
18. US Army Historical Section combat interviews
19. *Ibid*.
20. Courtesy of The National D-Day Museum Foundation, Peter Kalikow World War II Oral History Collection
21. At this point the interviewer seems simply to have reproduced his notes of the interview rather than continuing the earlier narrative
22. US Army Historical Section combat interviews
23. *Ibid*.

CHAPTER 9

Conclusions

S. L. A. Marshall

A commander of infantry will be well advised to believe that when he engages the enemy not more than one quarter of his men will ever strike a real blow unless they are compelled by almost overpowering circumstances or unless all junior leaders constantly 'ride herd' on troops.[1]

Was Marshall right? The short answer is – in part, yes. The long answer is that the war is too complex for sweeping statements like this to apply to all soldiers in all battles. Whether it was just a headline-grabbing statement or not, Marshall certainly focused the minds of the military on the question of how to increase fire ratios so that 100 per cent of soldiers became active firers in battle.

Of all the British armies in the field in World War II Marshall's ratio of fire most likely applied best of all to the British Expeditionary Force in 1940 whose preparation for modern war was utterly abysmal and which was still ready to fight World War I rather than World War II. Having said that, British fire doctrine might have worked against Marshall, even here. This worked on the basis of quantity rather than quality of fire and might have meant that Marshall's figures were too low.

It was almost certainly the case that the World War II battlefield had three elements in it. Firstly, there were the active firers – soldiers actually trying to kill as many enemy soldiers as possible. Secondly, there were the firers contributing to the amount of fire but not aiming at specific targets and rather hoping not to have anyone's death on their conscience. Thirdly,

258

there were the non-firers, any soldiers not firing either due to not moving out from cover or else assisting the firers, the wounded or performing other necessary duties.

What were the percentages for each of these groups? We will never know and they might well have varied according to the battle and the soldiers fighting that battle. And the situation is complicated by the arrival of the Commandos and other Special Forces who changed the way soldiers were trained. For the Commandos their intensive training, based on conditioning soldiers to kill through realistic battle scenarios using life-like and life-size enemies, changed these ratios and it is likely that they achieved somewhere close to the magical 100 per cent of active firers.

The make-up of individual units was also a complicating factor. The 4th Dorsets included men who were trained the old traditional way as well as men who were trained by Major Henry Hall, who had been through the Lochailort advanced assault course and then taken this training back to the men in his own platoon and company. This made for an interesting mix of fighting abilities within the one battalion and it is interesting to note that when a mixed battalion like this went into action the traditionally trained soldiers suffered higher casualties than the soldiers who had been exposed to the Commando type training.

Major R. F. 'Henry' Hall MC

There is a small hill called Hill 112 which overlooked Caen. Both the Germans and ourselves reckoned that, 'He who holds Hill 112 holds Normandy.' Unfortunately the Germans had got there before us. So it was our job to push them off 112 in order that the attack on Caen could commence.

On 10 July [1944] 4th Dorsets attacked a little village called Etterville on the slopes of Hill 112. The regimental bugler sounded the charge, my platoon shouted our *haka* and off we went. Typhoons were supposed to drop anti-personnel bombs on the village just before we entered but they were late!

We took our objective at 0630 hours as planned and planted our totem. Before we had a chance to dig in the Typhoons arrived. My only casualty was Sergeant Fowler, my new platoon sergeant, who was killed. The reason why was because he made the mistake of not watching the bombs coming down and [not] dodging them and staying standing up (thus exposing only the legs to splinters – also a good defence against Nebelwerfers which you can hear coming if you are caught in the open) but he lay flat on the ground and therefore was killed.

We dug in and we were relieved by the Cameronians at midday and then we attacked another village called Maltot at 1600 hours. The Cameronians took over from us at midday before we attacked Maltot. We took our objective by 1645 and planted our totem.

The other companies suffered heavily. Then we were surrounded by Tiger tanks and one silly one came to about fifty yards of our totem and blew it to pieces. I gave no order but my chaps rushed in and the tank and its crew were dead in about three minutes.

We hung on there, under considerable fire, surrounded by tanks and our battalion (or what remained of it) was ordered to withdraw at 2030 because we had suffered severe casualties so, just for fun, we killed two more Tigers on the way out and fortunately only suffered three or four casualties. But at the end of the day there were only five officers and about eighty other ranks (mostly mine) remaining of 4th Dorsets.

We managed to kill the first of the Tigers by stuffing a very heavy angle iron into the tracks and stopping it and then smothering it, the other silly one stopped of its own accord and so we just smothered that one as well.

You can't kill a Tiger tank when it is moving unless you are extraordinarily lucky. First you have to stop it and the easiest way to do that is to interfere with the tracks being the least armoured part of the vehicle. The only weapon we had was a PIAT anti-tank weapon which was quite effective but which certainly would not pierce a Tiger tank's armour but if you aimed it at the tracks, nine times out of ten it would break the track and thus stop the tank. Or you could stuff something into the track, something like angle iron or a piece of metal or tree trunks, something pretty hefty which would break the track and stop the tank.

You have to get fairly close to the tank but tank guns are always designed to fire almost horizontally with very little depression so you are completely safe as any shots will simply go over your head.

Conclusions

The conditions inside the tank also have to be considered. There were probably four or five people inside, it was very hot, sweaty and stank of hot oil, cordite, urine and of course they could only see out through visors and that is why ninety-nine times out of a hundred the lid of the tank would be open and very often the tank commander would be looking out.

So the crew are not in a very happy state of mind. Having stopped the tank you then leapt on to it, covered up any visors with mud, cloth or anything else which did the job. If you were lucky enough to find the top open you could throw a couple of grenades inside and then shut the top and that was the end of that or you could place a charge on the lid (we used to carry charges similar to Lewes bombs for use on tanks) or on the engine cover (where the armour was thin) or on the back of the tank and it would set the tank on fire. It was easier than it sounds, providing you had the guts and the courage and the training to do it.

My general impression of the day was of horrendous noise, a lot of dirt and muck flying about, terrible sights of bodies here and there, German and our own, some of them whole (but dead of course) others in bits, bits of bodies lying around. There wasn't much smell except of high explosives, but a lot of dirt and muck and horrendous noise all the time from enemy fire and from our own fire going over. It was quite a sobering experience but my lads stood up very well and having come back from Maltot we dug in and held a position at the bottom of the hill for the night.

When we were out one night we discovered a Tiger tank which had broken down but the gun was still firing and we discovered that the German engineers were trying to repair the tank. We waited two or three nights – we could hear them and see them doing their best to get the tank going again and then early one morning we suddenly heard the tank's engines start up. That was the sign for me to fire the 4.5-inch gun which scored a direct hit on the tank and destroyed it. That was a way of wasting enemy manpower!

We also used our *haka* by day, but more effectively by night, to keep the enemy on their toes, the same as we had done in the UK, to deprive them of sleep and wear them down. The Germans always feed at midday (we fed at night) so that was a good time to shell or mortar them when they were gathered together – depriving them of food.

We looked for targets by day and then went out at night, mostly singly, to kill lone men or throw grenades at our target. We never had a chance to have a go at dumps or HQs as we could only get at the front line and these targets were well back.

We looked out during the daylight to see if we could pinpoint any weak area in the enemy line or any place or thing that was worth attacking the following night and then we would go out and destroy or kill that objective when it was dark.

The Germans, stupidly, used a lot of tracer, various coloured tracer which made it very easy to avoid their fire. You could either go to the left or right of it or even, if it was high, duck underneath. They also used Very lights, or flares, of various colours. If you could get hold of one of their bags full of flares you could set them off and add a little confusion to whatever they were setting them off for.

The whole object was to disorientate the enemy, confuse him, deprive him of sleep, deprive him of food and generally wear him down as well as the simple point of killing him.

The reason why I brought more men out of it than others was because my men were better battle trained than the rest of the battalion, just that simple fact. The motto of the SAS is, 'Who Dares Wins,' but Jock Lapraik who trained the SAS in the Far East and John Woodhouse who trained them in England and the Near East changed the motto from, 'Who Dares Wins,' to 'Who Trains Wins.' Who trains does win. The more you are trained, particularly under live battle conditions, the more chance you have of staying alive.[2]

Unfortunately men like Major Hall were spread thinly throughout the Army which instead had to rely on its conventional soldiers to fight the battles of World War II.

The question of relative casualty rates is an interesting one. Chapter 4 described the No. 4 Commando action at Dieppe. Here the highly trained and conditioned British Commandos attacked the Hess battery at Varengeville and carried off the only success of the day. Despite the fact that the Commandos were attacking a well defended position their casualties, compared to other Dieppe units, were much fewer with sixteen killed and twenty wounded against the German losses which were fifty-eight dead (including losses in the fighting outside the battery estimated by Lord Lovat) plus thirty-three wounded and four prisoners.[3]

Other Commando actions in the war had similar success against the odds and it was all due to the type of training which the Commandos went through at Achnacarry. This training turned ordinary soldiers into Army Commandos and the ordinary Royal Marines into Royal Marine Commandos.

The following account shows the effect of this training on the Marines (including some range work before they arrived at Achnacarry which provides an interesting contrast to how they were trained at Achnacarry) and how it kicked into action at Comacchio during the Italian campaign when the Marine Commandos had to fight their way across flat open ground to close in with the Germans and their allies from the eastern part of the Reich.

Sergeant Bill Ash, C Troop, No. 43 (RM) Commando

C Troop was a general fighting troop. As a sergeant I had a section of twelve including one Bren group.

We did our range work at Galashiels before we went to Achnacarry. We did a mixture of fixed bullseye targets and pop-up targets where you fired and they went down. We did six weeks on the range, it was a 600-yard range and you fired five rounds in the line position at 600 yards' range then you dashed to the 500-yard mark, got down, fired ten rounds and then to 400 yards and so on. When you got to 200 yards about five pop-up targets appeared in different positions – you had to get them and once you hit them down they went.

We didn't do much range work at Achnacarry, this was because we were always doing exercises there. These exercises incorporated the pop-up human-shaped targets. When you moved, the target would appear, you would fire and down the target would go.

For Comacchio we started very early in the morning. As we went up the spit past Joshua we had the sea on our right and Lake Comacchio on our left. C Troop was the lead troop and as we went along we came across these dugouts which were full of the Turkoman soldiers [fighting for the Germans]. The dugouts were on our left facing the sea and as we advanced we ran over these dugouts. Each one had to be cleared out, we would give them a burst of fire and this would tell them they were surrounded. Some of them had the habit of pretending to surrender and then lobbing a grenade at us which made us a bit twitchy – the result was that we came to one dugout and one of my chaps thought they were going to sling a grenade even though they were surrendering so he shot the first one or two and the others scuttled back into their dugout where we left them to the follow-up troops.

After that we crossed the canal in boats and made our way up towards Saglioca. Beyond the Valetta canal which was on the far side of Saglioca the Germans had a lot of troops and snipers in the houses.

The enemy rearguard in Saglioca was a nuisance but it was the fire from across the canal which was causing us the most problems. Once past Saglioca the land was bare and absolutely flat and we had to go to ground. Corporal Hunter was in the next section to mine and I saw him grab a couple of Bren magazines from the chaps around him. Then he was up and he was racing and firing his Bren gun from the hip as he ran and as he was running he was changing magazines, which took some doing. All the time he was running the Germans were directing intense fire towards him. He ran about 150 yards towards this demolished house and set his Bren gun on a pile of rubble and carried on firing but it was at that moment that a sniper got him. The whole thing lasted about ten minutes. He got the VC.

During the time that Tom Hunter was doing this we had the opportunity to shift to better positions and to return the fire. I myself had a Tommy gun which was good at close range but no good at longer range.

We were withdrawn during the night and our positions taken by others.[4]

One of the effects of conditioning soldiers and Commandos to kill is that they then do go and kill the enemy. The human mind then has to cope with the effects of this in later life. Eddie Blacker received an ordinary infantry training but was an outstanding sniper during the Snipe action. Looking back he said,

I didn't know then what an easy job I had, dug in in the sand under that burnt-out German tank – looking back I feel sorry for the killing of so many German soldiers who were trying to kill us through the odious personality of Adolf Hitler.[5]

One of the distinguishing factors of the Desert War was the chivalry shown by both sides. Unfortunately the chivalry of the Desert War was not carried over into the war in the Far East where hatred ruled supreme and the British, in particular, fought hard because they hated the Japanese for what they had done and what they did to innocent prisoners and civilians.

In the Far East Marshall's ratio of fire was almost certainly too low for the British and perhaps for the Americans as well as the war progressed.

On D-Day through the eyes of Marshall's own combat historians the ratio of fire identified by Marshall has a valid feel to it. Despite the fact that here was a desperate fight to get off the beaches, the US soldiers were waterlogged and they had witnessed their friends being mown down and blown to bits so the battle was still down to a number of exceptional individuals taking charge and getting the advance moving. Of course it might be the case that more than twenty-five per cent were firing – after all US Army doctrine was similar to the British one – fire at the enemy or where you think the enemy is. But as we saw in Chapter 1 the twenty-five per cent was never Marshall's accurate calculation.

In suggesting that Marshall's fire ratios might have been too low it is not to overstate the case by claiming that most soldiers were firing. No doubt there were many who were not. Some too, might simply have fired with no knowledge or wish for a kill. It is possible that in some battles these soldiers firing without wishing to kill anyone might be part of Marshall's twenty-five per cent of active firers. We will never know for sure.

What there is no evidence for is the opposite view to Marshall – that soldiers were killing the enemy because of some blood lust which they all had. Probably a tiny, tiny percentage of soldiers killed because they enjoyed it, I have never come across any and I would be suspicious of any who said they did. Peter Hart, the distinguished oral historian at the Imperial War Museum, told me he had come across only one during his career of interviewing hundreds of World War II veterans.[6]

After World War II the British and US Armies changed the way they trained their soldiers. From then on the training given during World War II to the British Commandos and US Rangers at Achnacarry would be extended to all fighting soldiers. As a consequence the nature of battle would change forever.

Notes

1. Marshall, p. 50
2. Major R. F. Hall, correspondence with the author, autumn 2004
3. Fowler, pp. 229–30
4. Author interview
5. Letter to the author, 19 September 2003
6. Author interview

Bibliography

Stephen E. Ambrose, *D-Day*, Simon & Schuster, 1994

Anon., *Battle Summary No. 39, Landings in Normandy June 1944*, HMSO, 1994

Anon. (Martin Lindsay), Notes from Theatres of War No. 11, *Destruction of a German Battery by No. 4 Commando during the Dieppe Raid*, HMSO, 1943

Anon., *SOE Syllabus*, Public Record Office, 2001

Anon., *The Rifle Brigade, 1939–1945*, Committee of the *Rifle Brigade Chronicle*

Colonel Rex Applegate & Major Chuck Melson, *The Close Combat Files of Colonel Rex Applegate*, Paladin Press, 1998

Michael Asher, *Shoot to Kill*, Cassell, 2004

John Bierman & Colin Smith, *Alamein – War without Hate*, Viking, 2002

Joanna Bourke, *An Intimate History of Killing*, Granta 1999

Alex Bowlby, *The Recollections of Rifleman Bowlby*, Cassell, 2002

Herbert Brunnegger, *Saat in den Sturm: Ein Soldat der Waffen SS Berichtet*, Leopold Stocker Verlag, 2000

Dr Stephen Bull, *World War II Infantry Tactics – Squad and Platoon*, Osprey, 2004

Dr Stephen Bull, *World War II Infantry Tactics – Company and Battalion*, Osprey, 2005

David M. Buss, *The Murderer Next Door*, Penguin Press, 2005

Paolo Caccia-Dominioni, *Alamein 1933–1962: An Italian Story*, George Allen & Unwin, 1966

Field Marshal Lord Carver, *The Imperial War Museum Book of the War in Italy*, Pan, 2001

William L. Cassidy, 'Fairbairn in Shanghai', *Soldier of Fortune*, September 1979

Bibliography

John Whiteclay Chambers III, 'S. L. A. Marshall's *Men Against Fire*: New Evidence Regarding Fire Ratios', *Parameters*, US Army War College Quarterly, Autumn 2003

Robert M. Citino, *The Path to Blitzkrieg – Doctrine and Training in the German Army 1920–1939*, Lynne Rienner, 1999

Carl von Clausewitz, *On War*, 1832

John Colvin, *Not Ordinary Men – The Story of the Battle of Kohima*, Pen & Sword, 1994

R. L. Crimp, *Diary of a Desert Rat*, Leo Cooper, 1971

James Dunning, *It Had To Be Tough*, Pentland Press, 2000

James Dunning, *The Fighting Fourth*, Sutton, 2003

Captain W. E. Fairbairn, *Get Tough*, Paladin Press, 1979

Capt W. E. Fairbairn and Capt E. A. Sykes, *Shooting to Live*, Paladin, 1987

Niall Ferguson, *The Pity of War*, Penguin, 1998

Roger Ford and Tim Ripley, *The Whites of Their Eyes*, Pan Books, 1998

Will Fowler, *The Commandos at Dieppe*, Harper Collins, 2002

Lt Col Dave Grossman, *On Killing*, Little Brown, 1996

Lt Col Dave Grossman, *On Combat*, PPCT Research Publications, 2004

R. H. Haigh and P. W. Turner, *David and Goliath – The Great Stand at Snipe*, Sheffield Hallam University Press, 1998

Peter Hart, *At The Sharp End*, Pen & Sword, 1998

Donna Hart and Robert W. Sussman, *Man The Hunted*, Westview Press, 2005

Major R. H. W. Hastings, *The Rifle Brigade in the Second World War 1939–1945*, Gale & Polden, 1950

Cyril Jolly, *The Vengeance of Private Pooley*, Heinemann, 1956

Günther K. Koschorrek, *Blood Red Snow*, Greenhill Books, 2002

James Ladd, *Commandos and Rangers of World War II*, BCA, 1979

George Langelaan, *Knights of The Floating Silk*, Quality Book Club, 1959

Lieutenant-Colonel M. E. S. Laws, *Campaigns in The Middle East*, National Archives, CAB 44/103

David Lee, *Beachhead Assault*, Greenhill Books, 2004

B. H. Liddell-Hart (ed.), *The Rommel Papers*, Harcourt Brace, 1953

Bibliography

James Lucas, *Das Reich – The Military Role of the 2nd SS Division*, Cassell, 1991

C. E. Lucas Phillips, *Alamein*, Heinemann, 1962

John Morris, *Traveller From Tokyo*, Penguin, 1946

Williamson Murray and Allan R. Millett (eds.), *Military Innovation in the Interwar Period*, Cambridge University Press, 1996

S. L. A. Marshall, *Men Against Fire*, University of Oklahoma Press, 2000

John Parker, *Commandos*, Headline, 2000

Major H. G. Parkyn OBE (ed.), *Rifle Brigade Chronicle for 1944*, The Rifle Brigade Club and Association, 1945

Timothy Harrison Place, *Military Training in the British Army 1940-1944*, Frank Cass, 2000

Erwin Rommel, *Krieg Ohne Hass*, Verlag Heidenheimer Zeitung, 1950

John K. Singlaub, *Hazardous Duty*, Summit Books, 1991

Field Marshal Viscount Slim, *Defeat Into Victory*, Pan, 1999

Lieutenant-Colonel V. B. Turner VC, 'The 2nd Battalion at Snipe', *The Rifle Brigade Association Journal*, June 1949

Peter Young, *Commando*, Ballantine Books, 1969

Index

270

Index